# BALLROOM DANCING

ALEX MOORE

# BALLROOM DANCING

## ALEX MOORE

*Chairman of the Imperial Society of Teachers of Dancing,
Technical Instructor to the leading Teachers' Societies in
England and Abroad, Judge—"Star," World's, and
national Championships and Contests in South Africa,
Australia, Japan, U.S.A., Canada, and most European
countries*

WITH 100 DIAGRAMS AND PHOTOGRAPHS
OF THE QUICKSTEP, WALTZ,
FOXTROT, TANGO, Etc.

FOREWORD BY

## PHILIP J. S. RICHARDSON

*EIGHTH EDITION*

PITMAN PUBLISHING

*Eighth edition,* 1974
*Reprinted* 1975

PITMAN PUBLISHING LTD
Pitman House, 39 Parker Street, London WC2B 5PB, UK

PITMAN MEDICAL PUBLISHING CO LTD
42 Camden Road, Tunbridge Wells, Kent TN1 2QD, UK

FOCAL PRESS LTD
31 Fitzroy Square, London W1P 6BH, UK

PITMAN PUBLISHING CORPORATION
6 East 43 Street, New York, NY 10017, USA

FEARON PUBLISHERS INC
6 Davis Drive, Belmont, California 94002, USA

PITMAN PUBLISHING PTY LTD
Pitman House, 158 Bouverie Street, Carlton, Victoria 3053,
Australia

PITMAN PUBLISHING
COPP CLARK PUBLISHING
517 Wellington Street West, Toronto M5V 1G1, Canada

SIR ISAAC PITMAN AND SONS LTD
Banda Street, PO Box 46038, Nairobi, Kenya

PITMAN PUBLISHING CO SA (PTY) LTD
Craighall Mews, Jan Smuts Avenue, Craighall Park,
Johannesburg 2001, South Africa

ISBN 0 273 00381 X

Reproduced and printed by photolithography and bound in
Great Britain at The Pitman Press, Bath
G.186:14

# FOREWORD

BY

## PHILIP J. S. RICHARDSON

Mr. Alex Moore's name is so well known in the dancing world to-day, not only in this country but also abroad, that any introduction from me is really superfluous, but, having been invited to write a few words, I may say that I do so with great pleasure.

I have known him for a number of years and one of my first recollections of him is his success, with his sister, in the big "Blues" competition at Princes Galleries in 1923, and when for three years the World's Championships were held in London, I seem to remember that he was generally "close up" in the professional section.

From this it will be gathered that he was a first-class dancer even in those days, and his present-day demonstrations with Miss Pat Kilpatrick are always an attraction. Nevertheless, I think that it is as a teacher that he excels. He has a keen analytical mind and, though a staunch believer in the modern technique as laid down by the leading authorities, does not hesitate, as will be seen in several instances in the following pages, to point out cases in which he considers this to be at fault.

Mr. Moore has had considerable teaching and lecturing experience both at home and in Norway, Denmark, Holland, and South Africa, and is well able to realize and appreciate the difficulties which confront the beginner.

I am sure that the following pages will prove of great assistance not only to the absolute beginner, but also to the more advanced dancer who wishes to reach the "competition" standard, and to the student preparing for examinations.

## AFTERTHOUGHT—1950

IT is nearly fourteen years since I wrote the above Foreword to the first edition of Mr. Alex Moore's book and, except for one word, I see no need to alter what I then penned. The word "considerable" as applied to Mr. Moore's teaching and lecturing experience seems to me to-day to be totally inadequate. He has now had very great experience indeed, and as the results of his experience are embodied in the following pages, this volume should be of very great value to the dancer.

P. J. S. R.

# PREFACE TO THE EIGHTH EDITION

In earlier editions it was necessary for me to suggest many deviations from the standard technique but the majority of these suggestions have now been incorporated in the technique accepted by the leading societies of teachers of dancing. It can be stated quite confidently that the dancing of all first-class dancers is based on the present technique, and although personal expression will account for some slight deviations among our leading dancers, the keen amateur and student cannot go wrong in following the technical descriptions and diagrams given in this book.

In this eighth edition a number of the recently standardized figures have been added, together with additional diagrams.

ALEX MOORE

*June,* 1973

# PREFACE TO THE FIRST EDITION

When I was invited to undertake this work two difficulties became apparent to me: one, the feasibility of presenting to both amateurs and students something sufficiently comprehensive within the limits of a book of restricted length; and the other, the possibility of ensuring that the work was prepared in such a form and in such a sufficiently interesting manner to satisfy oneself that it could be assimilated by all classes of dancers. The introduction of a new form of Dance Chart may prove of assistance to amateurs in learning the various figures more speedily, but it is sincerely hoped that the keen amateur will regard the book as something more than a means of acquiring a knowledge of steps and variations. It is also to be hoped that no student will be foolish enough to be gulled into the belief that a parrot's knowledge of its contents will be sufficient to satisfy an astute examiner.

If I have succeeded in producing something which will aid the pupil in the study of Ballroom Dancing and create a desire to strive to appreciate the art, I am amply repaid.

It may be that some of my views may not meet with universal approval, but they are given in the conscientious belief that they will assist towards a truer interpretation of the Dance, and its recognition as the finest of indoor recreations.

In suggesting slight deviations from the recognized standard technique of Ballroom Dancing, I in no way wish to dissent markedly from the views of my fellow members of the Ballroom Committee of the Imperial Society of Teachers of Dancing, who have done so much to raise the standard of dancing in this country.

My grateful thanks are extended to my partner, Miss Kilpatrick, for the assistance which she has so freely given to me during the course of the preparation of this book, and to my friend and pupil Mr. Edward Youel for his generous help with the Charts.

ALEX MOORE

KINGSTON-ON-THAMES
*September,* 1936

# CONTENTS

# SECTION VII

# INTRODUCTORY SECTION

PERHAPS the most significant point regarding the progress of Modern Ballroom Dancing can be found in the way in which it was able to achieve international prominence in a fairly short space of time. It is now, however, some years since the English dancing public made the great change from the sequence and set dances, and engaged themselves in the turmoil of what was then known as "Jazz." Naturally enough, chaos existed for a number of years, but the standardization of a few basic steps and the gradual clarification of the technique that governs them, have resulted in tremendous progress being made, until, to-day, the English style of Ballroom Dancing stands pre-eminent throughout the world.

This international interest, achieved without very much publicity, is the natural result of the recognition of English Ballroom Dancing as the greatest indoor sport *and* recreation the world has ever known. As a competitive sport it has already aroused the interest of practically every country in the world. Australia, New Zealand, South Africa, India, Ceylon and Japan, to mention but six countries, have long been holding their national championships, and the standard of dancing is sufficiently high to challenge our best English dancers. Of the European countries, perhaps Denmark, Holland, Austria and Germany are the most advanced, and Russia is improving rapidly.

During the past few years Canada and the United States of America have shown an increasing interest in the English style and both countries have sent teams to compete in the World Championship, now held annually in a different country each year.

Primarily, Ballroom Dancing is a mental and physical recreation and as such it can scarcely be said to have an equal. Taken seriously, it can give the young person as much physical exercise as is desired; to the middle-aged dancer, it can give exercise that is effective without being too strenuous; to the busy man or woman it will provide that mental relaxation which is so necessary to physical health.

To reach a reasonable standard of efficiency is neither difficult nor laborious, and the added pleasure of executing a few simple steps correctly, and with a good poise and balance, will give full compensation for the time spent in learning them.

## SUGGESTED METHOD OF APPROACH

### (1) **The Novice**

The novice whose initial desire is to learn sufficient about dancing to be able to move both comfortably and unobtrusively in the ballroom will only need to assimilate a very little of the information in this book. To many people dancing is a hobby, a recreation, or a pleasant means of obtaining healthy physical exercise. Others approach it from different aspects, one of the most important being the mental relaxation that an evening's dancing can give. Obviously, the method of approach must vary in each case. The unambitious beginner need not be alarmed by the (to him) intricate details which follow the simple descriptions of the various figures. They are as unnecessary to him as the intricacies of motor racing are to the ordinary car driver.

After reading the general instructions at the beginning of this book, paying especial attention to the Hold, and the Poise and Balance of the Walk, the beginner should turn to the Quickstep Section, and learn the Walk, Quarter Turns and the Natural Turn. Full use should be made of the charts. They are quite easy to follow, especially if the squares are marked out on the floor. The various steps should be danced with the feet kept flat at first, afterwards a little attention being paid to the Footwork, as the turns will be much easier with some little use of the ball of the foot.

The fundamentals of the Waltz should be learned next, and the best method of approaching this dance is given at the beginning of the section dealing with it.

The beginner who enters the ballroom with just a knowledge of the Walk, Quarter Turns and Natural Turn in the Quickstep, and the Closed Change, Natural Turn, and Reverse Turn in the Waltz, will be able to take part in about three-quarters of the average dance programme.

It must be remembered that a good carriage and the ability to move easily and rhythmically are of utmost importance. There is much more pleasure to be obtained from dancing a few simple figures well than from dancing a dozen indifferently. When an easy and *comfortable* interpretation of the basic figures has been achieved, the desire to learn further variations will soon follow.

## (2) The Competition Dancer and Keen Amateur

The reader who aspires to competition dancing should remember that a judge's first impression comes from the general appearance of the couple. A good poise and a hold that is stylish and unaffected are most essential, for however well a couple may dance they will never command attention if such important details are lacking. Much useful information on these points is given in the early part of this book, and it should be studied with great care. Footwork, so important because it is so noticeable, should be neat and correct, whilst the subtle difference between "Body Swing" and the rather hackneyed "Contrary Body Movement" is well worth investigating. Finally, the controlled use of Body Sways and the new Rise and Fall which should be felt in the body should be understood, as a really finished dance is impossible without them.

The Charts will be found most useful in checking the alignment of the various figures. This feature of dancing is so often overlooked by competition dancers.

There is no short cut to championship rank in dancing. The standard of competition dancing in England at the present time is so high that there is not the slightest chance of a dancer attracting the judge's eye with a series of tricky variations that are not based on a sound technique.

It is possible to learn much from a book, but a few lessons from a good teacher are essential: it is so difficult to visualize the general effect of one's own dancing.

The keen amateur who shrinks from the publicity of competition dancing will be well advised to enter the Amateur Medal Tests which are held quite frequently in London and the Provinces. These Tests are of a similar nature to the Ice Skating Tests, and bronze, silver, and gold medals are awarded according to the standard of the entrant. The Tests are held in private, and they afford an excellent opportunity for enthusiastic dancers to test their proficiency. The fees for these Tests are quite moderate, and the board of examiners includes the most famous teachers of dancing in the world. Further notes on the Tests and on Competition Dancing will be found on pages 288 to 298.

## (3) The Student

The student who is training for a professional examination with a view to becoming a teacher of dancing should obviously be able to derive the most benefit from this book, for it contains all the technical information necessary for a student's or teacher's examination. A big mistake, however, would be made by the student who thinks that, with a mere book knowledge of the technique of dancing, plus a reasonably good practical demonstration of the standard dances, a competent examiner can be cheated into believing a candidate is fit to hold the diploma of a Teachers' Society.

The secret of the successful study of this book has nothing to do with the ability to remember such technical details as the numbers of the steps on which C.B.M., Rise and Sway occur. Rather, it is the ability to understand *why* they occur. The student reader who tackles his or her studies in this way will never have the mortification of going "blank" in the examination room and not being able to "repeat" those lines which have been so carefully committed to memory. The descriptions and technical details should be learned thoroughly, *and applied in practice*. Where slight alternatives to the standard technique have been given, these should be noted, and, more important still, the reason for such alternatives being suggested should be understood.

Remember also that a technical knowledge of dancing is not even a half of the requirements of a successful teacher. The ability to give a good practical demonstration of dancing and to speak firmly and clearly (but not dictatorially) will always inspire confidence.

## THE HOLD

### Gentleman's Hold for the Quickstep, Waltz, and Foxtrot

Careful attention should be paid to the hold in ballroom dancing. A bad hold will not only give a dancer an appearance of bad style, but will also seriously affect the balance and the guiding.

Stand in an upright position with the feet close together. The body should be braced slightly at the waist, but not at the shoulders, which should remain free and at the normal level.

Although the position of the arms is to some extent a matter of individual style, the following hints, together with the accompanying illustration, will help the dancer to avoid anything that is ungainly.

1. The LEFT ARM should slope *slightly* downwards from the shoulder to the elbow, otherwise the shoulder will be lifted. This part of the arm should be kept well back so that the elbow is in a line with the man's back. A common fault is to allow the elbow to move forward, towards the lady, thus forcing the lady's Right arm backwards.

2. The LEFT ARM should bend quite sharply at the elbow, the forearm pointing upwards and *slightly* forwards from the elbow to the hand. The forearm may be taken slightly inwards from the elbow, so that the hand is nearer the head than the elbow. This must not be exaggerated otherwise the hold will be too compact and breadth lost. The arm should be definitely angled at the

THE HOLD
Shown by Richard and Janet Gleave,
World professional champions

elbow. Held in this way it is much smarter and not so likely to annoy other dancers as when allowed to extend outwards.

3. The PALM of the LEFT HAND should be facing forward in a direction diagonally to the floor. The lady's Right hand should be held in a comfortable and "unfussy" manner. Most men hold the lady's fingers between the thumb and first finger, and then close the fingers over the side of her hand.

4. The LEFT WRIST must not bend. There should be an unbroken line from the elbow to the wrist, with the knuckles of the hand very slightly higher than the wrist. The hand should never bend downwards from the wrist.

5. The RIGHT ARM should slope downwards from the shoulder to the elbow in as near as possible the same line as the Left arm. This will depend to a great extent upon the height of the partner. The Right elbow will be more forward than the shoulder, owing to the hand being on the lady's back. It must not go too far forward nor must it be dropped close to the man's Right side.

6. The RIGHT HAND should be placed below the lady's Left shoulder blade. It should not be placed too far round the lady's back, or the Right shoulder will tend to drop.

7. The HEAD should be held in an easy upright position, and the man should normally look over the lady's Right shoulder.

8. POSITION WITH PARTNER. The man should endeavour to hold the lady in a position directly in front of him, although this is not quite possible. She will always tend to stand *very slightly* to his Right side, but care must be taken not to let this position become too pronounced.

## The Hold for the Lady

The hold for the lady must always depend somewhat upon the man, but the following points should be observed—

1. Stand in an upright position, slightly braced at the waist, without raising the shoulders.

2. Stand as near as possible in front of the man. The tendency will be to move slightly to his Right side, but do not exaggerate this.

3. Raise the RIGHT HAND with the fingers together, and allow the man to take it to his normal position. The man generally holds the lady's fingers between his thumb and first finger. When he has taken his position, the thumb is closed over the thumb of his Left hand.

4. The RIGHT ARM may slope slightly downwards from the shoulder to the elbow and then upwards from the elbow to meet the man's hand.

5. The LEFT ARM should rest *lightly* on the man's Right arm and must not bear downwards.

6. The FINGERS of the LEFT HAND should be grouped neatly on the man's Right arm between the elbow and the shoulder, but nearer the latter.

The hold for the Tango is described in the Tango Section of this book.

## THE POISE, BALANCE AND GENERAL OUTLINE OF THE WALK

To be able to walk properly in a forward and backward direction is the basis of ballroom dancing, and with it are allied such important points as the Poise or Carriage of the body, the Balance, or correct distribution of weight, and the alignment of the feet.

The following notes should be studied very carefully.

### The Forward Walk—Gentleman

*Poise.* Stand in an upright position as described in the notes on the hold. The knees should be slightly relaxed, but not definitely bent. Now let the body incline forwards from the feet upwards, until the weight of the body is felt mainly on the balls of the feet, but not letting the heels leave the floor. In doing this take care not to alter the upright position of the body from the hips upwards. You are now in the correct position to commence the Walk.

*Movement of the Legs and Feet.* Note. For the purpose of this description the Walk is being commenced with the Right foot. There is no rule on this point. The man may commence with either Right foot or Left foot but must indicate his intention to his partner. This is dealt with under the heading of "Leading and Following."

Take the weight on to the Left foot only and proceed as follows. Swing the Right leg forward from the hips, first with the ball of the Right foot touching the floor, and then the heel skimming the floor with the toe slightly raised.

As the Right foot passes the toe of the Left foot, the Left heel will be released from the floor, so that at the full extent of the stride the ball of the Left foot and the heel of the Right foot will be touching the floor. Lower the Right toe immediately so that the foot is flat on the floor.

With the body still moving forward, bring the Left foot forward with just a little pressure on the ball of the foot, and swing it past the Right foot to repeat the whole movement described above.

*Distribution of the Weight in the Walk.* When commencing a Walk from a closed position, the weight must always be brought forward over the balls of the feet before a foot is moved.

In the actual Walk the weight is first on the stationary foot. At the full extent of the stride it is divided for a moment between the heel of the front foot and the ball of the rear foot. It is taken immediately on to the front foot as this foot becomes flat.

Points to remember are—

From a stationary position, always feel that the *body* commences to move slightly *before* the foot. Remember that the speed of the foot is always greater than the speed of the body. If the foot is moved before the body, the weight will be kept too far back and a "sitting down" effect will result.

The KNEES should be easily and naturally relaxed throughout the Walk. The legs are only straight at the full extent of the stride, but even then the knees are not rigid. They are most relaxed as the moving foot passes the supporting foot.

The ANKLES and INSTEPS should be kept free to allow a slight downward "flick" of the foot as the toe is lowered at the end of each forward walk.

The FEET must be kept straight, the insides of the feet at both the toes and heels brushing past each other every time the feet pass.

*Important Note.* Although standard technique demands that some part of the foot is kept in contact with the floor in all forward steps, the majority of advanced dancers do not adhere to this rule. When moving the back foot to a forward position the heel does not actually touch the floor until it reaches the full extent of the stride. The movement thus becomes softer and lighter than could be achieved with the heel in contact with the floor.

## The Backward Walk—Lady

The Backward Walk for the lady is much more difficult than the Forward Walk of the man. The movement for the man is but little removed from a natural walking step, whilst the lady is using her legs and

THE HOLD
Another view shown by Richard and Janet Gleave

muscles in a manner that is not employed in any other sport or recreation. For this reason it is not always possible for a novice, especially the middle-aged novice, immediately to adopt the poise and balance of an accomplished dancer. In the following notes the correct poise and balance are given first; some useful advice to the beginner who has difficulty in maintaining this poise and balance in the early stages is given later.

*Poise and Balance.* Stand in an upright position as described in the notes on the Hold. The knees should be slightly relaxed, but not definitely bent. The body should now be poised slightly backwards. This position in no way assists the balance, but certainly makes the couple look much more attractive. Care should be taken not to lean backwards too much, or an ugly arching of the back will result.

Now let the body incline slightly backwards from the feet upwards, until some of the weight of the body is felt over the heels. At this point, the man's body is commencing to incline forwards, and the backward inclining of the body by the lady must be taken from the man. Although the lady's body is inclining backward she should endeavour to resist the man's forward movement slightly, this resistance being felt at the lower part of the body. It should not be felt entirely at the hips as this will tend to impede the man's forward movement and make outside steps very difficult. The lady should not lean forward, or endeavour to keep her weight forward over the balls of the feet when she is moving backward. If this is done the resistance to the man's forward movement will be felt at the chest, and this will not only check the even flow of the walk but will make the lady feel heavy to her partner.

This poise is the most difficult thing for the lady to acquire, and is only possible if she has such control over the muscles of her legs as to enable her to lower her back heel at an even speed. This is explained in the following notes on the "Movement of the Legs and Feet." The beginner would be well advised to try to master this correct poise, but, as it is sometimes physically impossible with a middle-aged dancer, an alternative poise is given on page 14.

*Movement of the Legs and Feet.* Note. For the purpose of this description the Walk is being commenced with the Left foot. There is no rule on this point. It is always left to the man to determine and indicate to his partner the commencing foot.

Take the weight on to the Right foot only and proceed as follows—

Swing the Left foot back from the hips, first with the ball of the foot and then the toe skimming the floor. When the Left foot has passed the Right heel, the ball of the Right foot will be gradually released from the floor.

At the full extent of the stride, lower on to the *ball* of the Left foot, so that at this point the ball of the back foot and the heel of the front foot are touching the floor.

Continuing to move backward, draw the Right foot back to the Left foot, and at the same time *slowly* lower the Left heel to the floor, *making sure that it does not touch the floor until the Right foot is level with it.* The Right foot is drawn back with the heel on the floor, the ball of the foot being lowered as it reaches the Left foot. Continue the Walk with the Right foot.

The most important feature of the Backward Walk is the gradual lowering of the back heel, and it is the careful control of this that ensures the lady keeping contact with the man whilst maintaining a backward poise.

*Distribution of the Weight in the Walk.* When commencing a Walk from a closed position, the weight must always be taken back over the heels before a foot is moved.

In the actual Walk the weight is first on the stationary foot. At the full extent of the stride it is divided for a moment between the heel of the front foot and the ball of the back foot. It is then taken on to the back foot, with slight pressure retained on the heel of the front foot.

Points to remember are—

From a stationary position, always feel that the *body* commences to move slightly *before* the foot.

Do not cling to the floor with the ball of the front foot, but release it gradually as the moving leg goes back.

The KNEES should be easily and naturally relaxed throughout the Walk. The legs are only straight at the full extent of the stride, but even then the knees are not rigid. The greatest relaxation is when the moving foot passes the supporting foot.

The ANKLES and INSTEPS should be kept free. If the ankles are stiff when the foot moves back, the stride will be considerably curtailed.

The FEET must be kept straight, the insides of the feet at both the toes and heels brushing past each other every time the feet pass. The usual fault is for the lady to allow her Left foot to move slightly to the Left instead of straight back. This causes her weight to be thrown against the man's Right arm and gives a definite feeling of heaviness.

## Alternative Poise for the Lady and Hints to the Beginner

The Poise described on page 12 is not easy to acquire, and the novice who has commenced dancing rather late in life would be well advised not to attempt to poise herself backward, unless the balance of the body can be controlled and kept in that position without the feeling of pulling away from the partner. A good method of practising the balance of the Walk is as follows—

Take a long step backward with the Left foot and stand balanced with the weight evenly divided between the heel of the front foot and the ball of the rear foot. Now slowly draw the front foot back, and make sure that the heel of the back foot does not touch the floor until the Right foot closes. Keep the arms extended sideways and, if necessary, keep the fingers of one hand touching the wall to assist the balance at first. When this can be done with ease, try to move backwards round the room, making sure to check any tendency to topple backwards.

If difficulty is experienced it is advisable not to attempt a backward poise when dancing with a partner, but to stand upright, and endeavour to keep the weight forward as long as possible.

Although, danced in this way, the Walk will not feel so easy to the partner as when danced in the correct manner, it will feel much more comfortable than the heavy "pulling away" effect that must inevitably result when the weight is dropped back to the heel too quickly.

## The Backward Walk—Man

Normally the man does not do a succession of Backward Walks except in the Foxtrot. Although the actions of the feet and legs are similar to those described for the Backward Walk of the lady, the man must remember to retain the same poise of the body as for a Forward Walk. In moving forward the man tends to be slightly "over" the lady. The positions are *not* reversed when the man moves backward and it would be quite wrong for the lady to adopt a forward poise and take control over the man.

**The Forward Walk—Lady**

Although the actions of the feet and legs are similar to those described for the Forward Walk of the man, the lady must not alter the poise of her body. She can materially assist the man's backward movements by pressing forward on forward steps, but any attempt to do this with a forward poise of the body would completely upset the man's balance. The man must retain control whether moving forward or backward.

## CONTRARY BODY MOVEMENT

Contrary Body Movement is the action of turning the opposite hip and shoulder towards the direction of the moving leg, and is used to commence all turning movements.

To the novice, the term "Contrary Body Movement" may appear rather frightening. In many cases, the term "Body Swing" would probably convey this turning action more clearly, for it should be noted at once that an excess of Contrary Body Movement will produce a dance that is more ugly and unbalanced than one entirely devoid of it.

Since it is essential that even the beginner should understand the elementary factors that govern turning movements in dancing, the following points should be noted.

There are four ways of turning in dancing. A turn to either the Right or the Left can be made when moving forwards, and also a turn to the Right or Left when moving backwards. The Contrary Body Movement in these turns would be as follows—

1. *Forward Turn to the Right.* Step forward with the

Right foot and at the same time swing the Left hip and shoulder forward.

2. *Forward Turn to the Left.* Step forward with the Left foot and at the same time swing the Right hip and shoulder forward.

3. *Backward Turn to the Right.* Step back with the Left foot and at the same time swing the Right hip and shoulder backward.

4. *Backward Turn to the Left.* Step back with the Right foot and at the same time swing the Left hip and shoulder backward.

It should be remembered that, with the exception of the pivot type of movement, this contrary swing of the body is in no way a "stationary" action. If a forward turn to the Right is being made it is far more important to feel a *forward swing* of the Left side of the body than a conscious twist of the body to the Right.

Although Contrary Body Movement must embrace the turning of both the hip and the shoulder, it is sometimes helpful to try to feel that, in forward turns, the movement is initiated in the shoulders, and, in backward turns, from the hips. This subtle difference in the mental approach of these two different turns should prove helpful to the novice.

Care must be taken not to turn the shoulders independently or an ugly dipping movement will result.

A most important point to remember is that Contrary Body Movement does not alter the direction of a step. A common fault with many dancers is to alter the alignment of a step as Contrary Body Movement is used. An example of this is—

*Facing the Line of Dance with the Right foot free, ready to make a forward turn to the Right.* As the Right foot moves forward and the body turns to the Right many dancers allow the Right foot to travel in a direction diagonal to the wall. This is wrong. It is only the body that turns away from the Line of Dance. The Right foot must move straight forward, or, if anything, cover in slightly in front of the other foot. The same rule applies to backward turning steps, although to step directly behind the stationary foot is not often possible when moving backwards.

## Contrary Body Movement Position

Contrary Body Movement, as described above, is a movement of the body. Contrary Body Movement *Position* is the position attained when either foot is placed across the front or the back of the body without the body turning. It is, therefore, a foot position, but in some cases Contrary Body *Movement* is used at the same time.

Even the novice should remember that every step taken outside partner, or with the partner outside, must be placed across the body in *C.B.M.P.* to ensure that the two bodies are kept in close contact.

Contrary Body Movement Position also occurs frequently in the Tango and in all Promenade figures.

## FOOTWORK

The term *Footwork* in Ballroom Dancing now has a definite technical meaning. Previously, Footwork was almost entirely governed by Rise and Fall, but the recent revisions to the standard technique have (quite soundly) separated these two headings. *Rise and Fall* now refers to the upward lift and lowering felt by advanced dancers in the *body* (which includes the legs, of course), and *Footwork* has been simplified to convey which part of the foot is in contact with the floor on each step.

Body Rise has been dealt with in the following pages and is of little interest to the beginner. Footwork, however, has a definite practical value, and the simple manner in which it is described will make it very easy for the beginner to gain an elementary knowledge of the correct placing of the feet in all steps. The more advanced dancer and the student should endeavour to understand the basic principles of this method of describing Footwork, and these are given below. They refer to Footwork used in the Quickstep, Waltz, and Foxtrot only. The Tango footwork is dealt with in the section dealing with that dance.

Only the terms *Heel* and *Toe* are used. The use of the term *Ball of Foot* has been omitted, and *Toe* now includes the ball of the foot as well as the higher position on the toes.

The use of the term Heel or Toe is meant to convey which part of the foot is in actual contact with the floor. Note, however, the following rules—

1. A forward walk on R.F., then on L.F. would be described as 1. Heel, 2. Heel. The fact that the whole of the R.F. lowers to the floor immediately is assumed, but not mentioned. It is also obvious that when the L.F. moves forward, the heel of the R.F. will naturally leave the floor, as described in the Forward Walk of the man. Again this is assumed, but not mentioned.

2. A forward step on R.F. followed by a forward step or side step on the L.F., *taken on the toes*, would be given as: 1. Heel, Toe; 2. Toe.

3. Two backward walks, on L.F. then R.F. would be described as: 1. Toe, Heel; 2. Toe. This indicates that the Toe of the L.F. is in contact with the floor first, then lowering to the Heel. On the second step only Toe is mentioned as the R. Heel does not lower until the L.F. passes the R.F. to continue with another step.

4. A backward step on the R.F. followed by a backward or side step on the L.F., taken with a *rise to the Toes*, would be: 1. Toe, Heel, Toe; 2. Toe. This indicates that the R. Heel will

leave the floor as the L.F. passes the R.F. for the next step. This footwork seldom occurs.

5. A backward step on the R.F. followed by a side step on the L.F., which is taken on the Toes would be: 1. Toe, Heel; 2. Toe. This indicates that the R. Heel is still on the floor until the L.F. has been placed in position on the Toe. It is, however, most important to remember that when a foot begins to close to a side step, it must be done with the toe in contact with the floor. This means that although the footwork of 1 (R.F.) is Toe, Heel; as the R.F. closes towards the L.F. for the 3rd step, it must close with the R. Toe in contact with the floor.

It may be thought by some students that it would be clearer to give the footwork on 1 as Toe, Heel, Toe, but this would be quite wrong as it would indicate that the R. Heel leaves the floor as the L.F. passes it on its way to the second step. To do this would result in an early rise and a stilted movement. The following example will help students to understand this method.

Reverse Turn (Waltz)—Lady; Footwork—
1. Toe, Heel.
2. Toe.
3. Toe, Heel.
4. Heel, Toe.
5. Toe.
6. Toe, Heel.

Although this method of giving Footwork makes it quite clear which part of the foot is in contact with the floor when a step is taken, it does not adequately cover the passage of the foot from one step to another. While this is fairly obvious in forward movements, it is not always clear when moving backwards. Two good rules to remember are—

1. Any time a foot is moved to close to a step that has been taken sideways it moves with the Toe in contact with the floor. Not only should the toe be in contact with the floor but firm pressure should be placed on it. Some advanced dancers tend to let this toe leave the floor as it closes to a side step (for instance, between 1 and 3 of a Lady's Natural Turn, Waltz) and the consequent lack of control results in an untidy closing of the feet.

2. In a succession of backward movements as used in the Fox-trot, if the Footwork on 1. (L.F.) is Toe, *Heel*, when the L.F. moves back for the third step it will be drawn back with the *Heel* on the floor, and with the Toe slightly raised as in a normal backward walk.

If the Footwork on 1. (L.F.) is *Toe* (or Toe, Heel, *Toe*) when the

L.F. moves back for the third step, it will be drawn back with the *Toe* in contact with the floor.

Less normal, but quite important, terms also used in describing Footwork are *Inside edge of Toe* and *Inside edge of Foot*. Such terms will be found self-explanatory.

Additional notes on the correct use of the feet, especially after a rise, will be found in the following notes on Rise and Fall.

## RISE AND FALL—BODY

Perhaps the greatest advance made in the revised technique is the adoption of the principle that Rise and Fall is felt in the body. Previously, Rise and Fall referred to the feet only with the result that the dancing of many fairly advanced dancers was completely lacking in expression. The rise and fall used in the feet is now covered by Footwork, although it is to be regretted that the new method of describing Footwork hardly gives a clear or true picture of the subtle uses of the ball of the foot as well as the toes.

As mentioned in the previous section, Footwork will cover the early requirements of the beginner. Body Rise is something that must be studied by the keen dancer wishing to reach a high standard, and it is not too much to say that no dancer can hope to be first class unless the subject is understood.

It must be remembered that the legs are a part of the body and, in fact, much of the Body Rise used in dancing is the result of the bracing of the muscles of the legs. The reaction to this will be felt in the body far more than any elevation taken from the feet without the co-ordinated use of these muscles. In addition, there are steps where the dancer should feel a slight "stretch" in the trunk of the body, but this upward stretch, if overdone, can have bad results. Normally, as mentioned in the remarks on the Walk, the dancer should be slightly braced at the waist at all times, and any effort to stretch or lift the body higher is likely to result in the shoulders being raised when attempted by inexperienced dancers.

There are three different types of Body Rise used in the Waltz, Foxtrot, and Quickstep, and if the student will endeavour to learn and understand these, the subject will present no difficulties when applying Body Rise to any figure in these dances. It will be noticed in the following examples that the term *No Foot Rise* has been used, and this denotes a later rise in the feet on the inside of all turns. It is a sound point and its use makes the Body Rise far easier to understand. The different types of Body Rise now in use are as follows.

## Natural Turn—Waltz

### Man

*Commence* to rise at the end of 1.
Continue to rise on 2 and 3.
Lower at the end of 3.
*Commence* to rise at the end of 4. (No foot rise.)
Continue to rise on 5 and 6.
Lower at the end of 6.

The words "Continue to rise" indicate that most of the rise is felt towards the end of each part of the turn; between 2 and 3 and then between 5 and 6. The term *no foot rise* makes it clear that the Left Heel is kept in contact with the floor until the Right Foot is in position.

## Natural Turn—Quickstep

### Man

*Rise* at the end of 1.
*Up* on 2 and 3.
Lower at the end of 3.
No more rise.

## Lady

*Rise* at the end of 1.  (No foot rise.)
*Up* on 2 and 3.
Lower at the end of 3.
No more rise.

The use of "Up" on 2 denotes an earlier rise than in a Closed Turn in the Waltz, which is due to the faster speed of the Quickstep music.  This type of rise is used in all Chassé Turns in the Quickstep.  Exceptions are the first part of the Quarter Turns and the Progressive Chassé, where the rise is continued for three steps instead of two steps as in other turns.  In these figures, and in a Lock step which also has a rise for three steps, the Body Rise is:  commence to rise at end of 1;  *continue* to rise for 2 and 3; up on 4.  The rise is thus more gradual than in normal Chassé Turns.

## Natural Turn—Foxtrot

### Man

Rise at the end of 1.
Up on 2 and 3.
Lower at the end of 3.
No more rise.

### Lady

*Rise slightly* at the end of 1.  (No foot rise.)
Continue to rise on 2.
Up on 3.
Lower at the end of 3.
No more rise.

Once again the use of *up* denotes an early rise for the man, who is on the outside of the turn.

The lady is on the inside of the turn and the slight bracing of the muscles of the L. leg at the end of the first step will cause her to rise slightly.  This rise is continued as the legs are braced further on the actual Heel Turn.  *No foot rise* is used to indicate that the feet are flat even though a slight body rise is used.  She will be *up* and feel the body well braced as the third step is taken.  Care must be taken to release the Heel of the foot supporting the weight, very gradually, and not rise abruptly to the toes as the third step moves forward.

This type of rise is used in all Open Turns in the Foxtrot, and in Open Turns in the Quickstep. Any Open Turn in the Waltz, such as the Double Reverse Spin, will also be danced with this rise.

These specimen rises cover practically all the turns in the moving dances, and careful study will show that they are comparatively easy to understand.

One further point which should be understood by the student is what is meant by the "end of a step." The following notes will be of assistance—

1. *A Forward Step.* The end of this step is when the moving foot is passing the foot supporting the weight, and the heel of the supporting foot will then be released from the floor.

2. *A Backward Step.* The end of this step is when the moving foot is passing the foot supporting the weight.

3. *A Side Step.* The end of a Side Step, such as the 2nd step of a Natural Turn in the Waltz when the feet are to close on the 3rd step, is approximately when the third step has closed half-way towards the second step. The end of a Side Step which is to be followed by a step forward or backward is when the moving foot is passing the foot supporting the weight.

## No Foot Rise

It has been explained in the preceding notes that the term *no foot rise* has been added in cases where a Body Rise is used while the foot supporting the weight of the body is still kept flat. It will help students if they appreciate that no foot rise occurs between 1 and 2 of all *Inside* Turns. (In the Natural Turn in the Waltz, the man is on the outside of the turn on the first part and on the inside of the turn on the second part.) Even in the Progressive Chassé (Quickstep) the man's R. heel is still down when the L.F. is in position on the 2nd step. The one notable exception to this rule is between steps 4 and 5 of the man's Reverse Turn in the Foxtrot. In this figure, although the man is on the inside of the turn he will rise with *the feet and body* between steps 4 and 5.  His forward poise and desire to swing forward into the Feather Finish are the reasons for this earlier rise.

In all forward movements in the Foxtrot, such as the Feather-step and Three-step, the man's forward poise and swing will again result in the lady having no foot rise, although she will feel a body rise by·bracing the legs.  This does not apply in a Forward Lock step in the Quickstep where the direction of the steps is more diagonally forward in relation to the body.  In such figures she will have no foot rise on the first step only.

No foot rise for the lady will also occur between steps 1 and 2 of such figures as the Closed Change in the Waltz and the Cross Chassé in the Quickstep.  The forward poise of the man is again responsible for this, even though no turn is being made.

## An Important Note

Although the revised technique has dealt comprehensively with the Rise and Fall and with the Footwork of all basic figures, one most important point has been completely neglected.

With very few exceptions a Rise is preceded by a softening of the knee of the supporting leg.  As an example, it would be quite wrong to assume that in a Natural Turn in the Waltz the first step is taken forward with the leg straight and that the following rise is immediately achieved by further bracing of the muscles of the R. leg, or by "lift" in the feet or body.

It is most important to remember that any leading step, forward or backward, is followed by a softening of the knee as the weight is taken on to that step. This will mean that the dancer *lowers* slightly before commencing any rise. This softening of the knee on a leading step is to some extent even more important than the following rise, which in many cases will occur naturally if the correct forward swing and footwork have been used.

The relaxation of the knee must not be sharp. As the weight is taken over a step the knee will soften to prevent any "jar" in the movement. The subsequent straightening of the knee will materially assist the dancer to achieve a soft and flowing movement during the following turn.

The degree of relaxation will very much depend on the speed of the music. Greatest relaxation of the knee is felt on the first step of Waltz Turns. In the Foxtrot it will be noted that there is more relaxation on the first step of a Feather-step than on the first step of a Natural Turn, where too much relaxation would seriously impede the swing into the turn.

## AMOUNT OF TURN

For examination work it is necessary for students to know the amount of turn made on each figure and, in some cases, between each step. This is of little interest to the beginner as the amount of turn is covered by the descriptions and the diagrams.

It is obvious, however, that a teacher or student training for the profession should be able to state how much turn is made between each step when a turn is used. The use of the fractions *one-eighth* and *three-eighths* may appear complicated at first but they are necessary to ensure accuracy.

It should be noted that the amount of turn is now measured from the positions of the feet, which is a little disconcerting at first. It would appear to be easier to take the amount of turn from where the body is facing, but in practice this becomes even more complicated.

An instance of how the amount of turn is assessed can be taken from the first three steps of the lady's Natural Turn in the Waltz. After stepping back diagonally to wall on the first step, her second step is placed to the side with the R. toe pointing down the L.O.D. The amount of turn is, therefore, given as three-eighths of a turn, although the body has turned slightly less.

The keen student will soon observe that although the turn is continued with the feet on the outside of every turn, on the inside of the turns the feet are always placed with the toe pointing to the required position, and no swivel of the foot is used. This can be seen quite clearly in the diagrams and it is very important to observe this rule when dancing. The few exceptions to the rule are noted in the descriptions.

The following example is given to assist students—

## Natural Turn (Waltz), Man—Amount of Turn

$\frac{1}{4}$ turn between 1 and 2.
$\frac{1}{8}$ turn between 2 and 3.
$\frac{3}{8}$ turn between 4 and 5, the body having turned less.
Body completes the turn between 5 and 6.

The man is on the outside of the turn on steps 1 to 3, and has a greater distance to travel, hence the continuing of the turn with the feet on this part of the figure. On steps 4 to 6 he is on the inside of the turn and will need no foot swivel.

## ALIGNMENT

The general meaning of the word *Alignment* has been given in the section on Definitions of Technical Terms on page 30.

In the revised technique *Alignment* is assumed to refer

to the position or direction the *feet* are pointing in relation to the room.

The alignment of each step is made clear in the descriptions or diagrams of each figure, and has not been given in detail in the technical notes following each description.

Students should note that three terms are used in connection with alignment. They are *Facing*, *Backing*, and *Pointing*. Facing and Backing are self-explanatory. Pointing is used on side steps when the foot is *pointing* in a direction different from the way the body is facing. The following example will help students to understand these terms—

## Natural Turn (Waltz), Man—Alignment

1. Facing diag. to wall.
2. Backing diag. to centre.
3. Backing L.O.D.
4. Backing L.O.D.
5. *Pointing* diag. to centre.
6. Facing diag. to centre.

Pointing is used on step 5 because the R.F. is pointing diag. to centre while the body is facing centre.

Pointing is also used in some Promenade steps to give a clearer picture of the position of the foot.

## BODY SWAYS

Body Sways in ballroom dancing are used chiefly for effect, although in a few turns even the novice may find them of practical value. The following notes regarding Sways should be helpful—

Sways should be made by inclining the body to the Left or Right.

Sways can be used on nearly all turns. Exceptions are all Spins, where the turn is too quick to permit Sway to be used with comfort. Sway is also used on figures that curve or wave and in some side figures such as the Cross Chassé.

All turns are initiated by a Contrary Body Movement step, and Sway is taken directly following this step. If the Contrary Body Movement step is with the Right foot, the inclination of the Sway will be to the Right; if with the Left foot, then the Sway will be to the Left, whether this step has been taken forward or backward. The Sway is usually held for the following two steps and will be corrected at the next Contrary Body Movement step. Sways sometimes occur on one step only. Details of the correct steps on which the body should sway are given with the descriptions of each figure.

The main principle of swaying is to incline the body towards the centre of the turn. Thus the practical value of swaying would be found in its assistance in preventing the dancer from overbalancing or overturning. This is most marked in the Waltz, and even the beginner may find that a slight inclination of the body *against* the direction he is moving will prove helpful and assist in preserving balance.

The greatest value of swaying, however, is purely decorative, and the keen dancer will find that a careful study of the correct Sways in the descriptions of the various figures will make the resultant dance much more attractive. To oversway, however, is a much worse fault than not swaying at all.

## LEADING AND FOLLOWING

There being no set sequence of steps in modern dancing the responsibility of leading from one figure to another rests *entirely* with the man. The lady's part is to follow, whether the man is dancing a figure correctly or not.

Most of the leading for the turns is done by the turning action of the man's body combined with a *very slight* pressure with his Right hand. The Right hand must not be used to pull or push the partner, but rather to keep an even pressure, thus ensuring that the lady feels from the man's body action the amount of turn that is being made. This pressure should be obtained by a slight inward movement of the forearm and not from the hand alone. The base of the Right hand and the Right fingers are only used to turn the lady into, and back from, Promenade Position. The Left hand and arm must not be used in guiding. They must be kept still.

It will be seen that it is of the utmost importance for the lady to keep contact with the man and to keep her body perfectly still from the hips upward, in order to feel the lead for a turn at the proper moment. She must not anticipate—she must not have a mind of her own. She must just follow whatever the man does and not attempt to correct him.

Contact with the partner should not be at the hips only, but from the hips and the lower part of the body— the diaphragm. If the lady presses her hips forward so that the only contact with the man is at the hips, the lady's body will tend to be poised backward far too much and the forward movement of the man will be seriously restricted.

When commencing to dance it is most important that the man should indicate which foot he is using first. There is no rule; it is for the man to use the foot that seems most natural. To practise this, stand with a partner in the normal commencing position with the feet together. If wishing to commence with the Right foot move the Left foot very slightly to the Left and take the weight on to it. At the same time, move the lady slightly to her Right and she will automatically take her weight on to that foot and be ready to commence with her Left foot.

Here are a few more hints for men—

Don't hold your partner with a vice-like grip; you will interfere with her balance.

Don't hold your partner so loosely that she cannot

feel your lead. A constant and even pressure is
required.

Don't take very long steps if your partner is
physically incapable of doing so. Adapt your stride
to the normal length of your partner's.

Don't try intricate steps in a crowded ballroom.

## ABBREVIATIONS

used in this book and in Ballroom Dancing Descriptions.

| | |
|---|---|
| S. A slow step. | N.F.R. No foot rise. |
| Q. A quick step. | C.B.M. Contrary Body |
| R. Right. |     Movement. |
| L. Left. | C.B.M.P. Contrary Body |
| R.F. Right foot. |     Movement Position. |
| L.F. Left foot. | L.O.D. Line of Dance. |
| B. Ball of foot. | P.P. Promenade Position. |
| H. Heel. | O.P. Outside partner. |
| T. Toe(s). | P.O. Partner outside. |
| I.E. Inside edge. | Diag. Diagonal(ly). |

*Note.* Descriptions of many of these terms are included in
"Definitions of Technical Terms," which follows.

## DEFINITIONS OF TECHNICAL TERMS

**Alignment.** This word has several meanings in
dancing. It may refer to the position of the feet in a
forward or backward step, when the feet should be
perfectly in line, turned neither in nor out, and with
the inside edge of each foot touching an imaginary line
drawn through the middle of the body. It is also used
to refer to the directional line of some part of a figure.

Its technical meaning for examination work is
described on page 26.

**Amalgamation.**\* A combination of two or more
figures.

               \* See note on page 34.

**Balance.** The correct distribution of the weight of the body when dancing.

**Basic Figure.** A figure that is considered to form a part of the basis of a particular dance.

**Brush.** When the moving foot is being taken from one open position to another open position, the word *Brush* is used to indicate that this foot must first close up to the foot supporting the weight of the body, but without the weight being changed.

**Chassé.** A figure of three steps in which the feet are closed on the 2nd step.

**Chassé Turn** or **Closed Turn.** A turn that is danced with a Chassé or with the feet closing on the 2nd or 3rd step.

**Contrary Body Movement.** The action of the body in turning figures. See pages 15–17.

**Contrary Body Movement Position.** A term used when the body is not turned, but the leg placed across the front or back of the body, so giving an appearance of Contrary Body Movement. See page 17.

**Fallaway Position.** A position used in advanced variations in which the man and lady move backwards in Promenade Position.

**Figure.*** A completed set of steps.

**Footwork.** This is dealt with on pages 17–20.

**Heel Pivot.** A turn on the heel of one foot only, in which no change of weight occurs. The Heel Pivot might be termed a "compact Chassé," and is used instead of a Chassé in the last part of the Quarter Turns in the Quickstep. A full description is—

After stepping back with the R.F., turning the body to the L. (S), close the L.F. to the R.F., at the same time turning on

* See note on page 34.

the heel of the R.F. (QQ). The L.F. is brought back with first
the heel and then the ball of the foot skimming the floor. When the
feet are closed, the ball of the L.F. should be touching the floor
and the heel very slightly raised. The feet must be kept parallel
throughout the turn with the L.F. slightly in advance.

The following step must be taken forward with the L.F. (S).

**Heel Turn.** A turn on the heel of the stepping foot,
the closing foot being kept parallel to it throughout.
The weight is transferred to the closing foot at the end
of the turn. It should be noted that, although the
major part of the turn is on the heel, it is actually
commenced on the ball of the foot. This will occur
naturally and is shown in the charts.

A Heel Turn is the backward part of an Open Turn.

**Hesitation.** A figure or part of a figure in which
progression is temporarily suspended, and the weight
retained on one foot for more than one count.

**Hover.** A part of a figure in which the moving or
turning of the body is checked, while the feet remain
almost stationary.

**Line of Dance.** The normal line of forward progression along each of the four sides of the room.

**Natural Turn.** A turn to the R.

**Open Turn.** A turn in which the third step passes
the second step instead of closing. The lady's counter-
part to a man's Open Turn is usually a Heel Turn.

**Outside Partner.** This indicates a step taken forward by the lady or man that does not follow the partner's opposite foot but is taken to the R. of both his (or
her) feet. In such steps the bodies must keep close
contact, the outside movement being achieved by
stepping rather across the front of the body. The
partner's step would be described "Partner Outside,"
and must be taken across the body at the back. Thus

all such steps are placed in C.B.M.P. In some advanced variations the outside step is taken on the Left side of the partner.

**Partner in Line, Partner Square, Square to Partner.** Terms used to indicate that the couple are standing in the normal dance position, i.e. facing each other and with the man's and lady's feet approximately opposite each other.

**Pivot.** A turn on the ball of one foot, the other foot being kept in front or behind in C.B.M.P.

**Poise.** The position of the body in relation to the feet.

**Promenade Position.** The position in which the man's R. side and the lady's L. side are kept in close contact, and the opposite sides of the bodies turned out to form a "V" shape. The feet are usually turned to the same direction as the body.

**Pull Step (Heel Pull).** This is a type of Heel Turn used by the man in some backward Natural Turns. The feet may be kept apart instead of closed, and the weight is more forward than in a Heel Turn.

**Quick.** A term used in timing steps. A quick step always occupies half the time of a slow step.

**Reverse Turn.** A turn to the L.

**Rhythm.** The word "Rhythm" is used in a broad sense, and usually refers to the accented beats of the music which recur regularly and give character to the music. Rhythm, however, is something much more subtle than this. It might be likened to colour. There are basic colours from which the expert can produce an infinite variety of beautiful shades. Similarly we have basic rhythms in all our dance music. The expert musician will produce numerous subsidiary rhythms from these, thus giving the music an entirely different character, which the expert dancer will endeavour to express in his dancing.

**Rise and Fall.** This is dealt with on pages 20–25.

**Step.*** This usually refers to one movement of the foot, although from a "time value" point of view this is incorrect. In the case of a walk forward or backward, for instance, the time value of the step is not completed until the moving foot is drawn up to the foot supporting the weight, ready to commence another step. Thus, when instructed to rise at the end of a step the dancer should not commence to rise until the moving foot is passing the foot supporting the weight of the body.

**Sway.** This is dealt with on pages 27–28.

**Swivel.** A turn on the ball of one foot.

**Tempo.** This indicates the speed of the music. The approved speeds for the standard dances are—

| | |
|---|---|
| Waltz  31 bars a minute | Quickstep 50 bars a minute |
| Foxtrot 30 bars a minute | Tango     33 bars a minute |

**Time.** The number of beats in each bar of music.

**Variation.** A varied and more advanced figure, additional to the basic figures.

## HOW TO READ THE CHARTS

The diagrams will be found to be of great assistance to readers if the following points are understood—

The squares on which the feet are placed represent a size of 2 ft by 2 ft for each square. The feet have been drawn to the same scale.

---

* The following analogy provides an easy method of remembering the meaning of the terms "step," "figure," and "amalgamation." Think of a step as a "syllable," a figure as a "word," and an amalgamation as a "sentence." A complete dance could be compared to a paragraph.

The distances between the steps have been made as far as possible mathematically correct, so that the exact length of a step can be gauged. The distances shown represent an average step. When the dancer is proficient, the steps can be lengthened considerably, but only to a length that is consistent with ease of movement.

*Each figure was drawn in the first place with both the man's and the lady's steps on the same chart, so that if a chart is drawn to scale on the floor it should be possible for a couple to dance together using the exact positions shown in this book.*

The L.O.D. is shown by an arrow on each chart. The right-hand edge of the page will represent the wall of the side of the room along which the dancer is moving.

When using the charts always hold the book so that the *toe* of each step you are looking at is pointing *away from you*. If a turn is made, turn the book also.

The R.F. is shown in black; the L.F. is outlined only. They are also marked "R." and "L."

When a foot is shown in dotted outline, this indicates a swivel on the ball or the heel of the foot to which it is connected, and shows the finishing position of that foot when that part of the turn has been made. Where only a slight swivel has been made this has been omitted.

It will be noted that in Heel Turns two dotted outlines are shown, indicating that the turn commences on the ball of the foot and continues on the heel of the same foot. No attempt should be made to commence the turn on the ball of the foot; this will occur naturally when dancing. It was necessary to include this to make the charts correspond with actual practice.

The lines connecting the feet give some idea of the path of the foot when moving to the next step.

## Special Notes

*Alignment.* The keen student of dancing should note that, technically, the leading step of any turning figure should be taken either straight forward or straight backward from the body, but in practice this is not quite possible in the case of *backward* turning steps, which tend to move *very slightly* outwards. The 4th step of the man's Natural Turn (Waltz) is an example.

In drawing the man's and lady's steps on one chart it was found necessary to show this slight loss of alignment; it was not possible to place the feet correctly without doing so.

The dancer should, however, take great care to keep such steps in alignment when possible.

*Parallel Positions.* Students are also warned that in the standard technique the 2nd step of some turns is described as being in a *parallel position*.

In practice, this parallel position of the feet is not possible when the feet are apart, as in the 2nd and 5th steps of the Natural and Reverse Turns in the Waltz. On most side steps the feet are turned slightly outwards, and any attempt to keep them parallel would seriously restrict the ease and flow of the turn.

It is also most important to remember that when taking a step to the side no attempt must be made to turn *on* the preceding step. To make an actual foot swivel on the first step would impede the movement.

The body should swing forward over the first step, and this will result in the heel leaving the floor quite naturally. It will then turn *as* the second step moves to the side.

## THE DESCRIPTIONS

The descriptions of each figure have been written in the simplest possible manner for the novice to understand them; and this happens to be the best way for the student to give an oral description of the figures.

Details of the Contrary Body Movement, Rise and Fall, the amount of turn used, and useful hints regarding guiding and amalgamations are given afterwards.

It should be noted that in all turning figures the turn should be gradual. It is only in Pivots that the full amount of turn is completed on one step.

A number of positional and directional terms are used in the descriptions, and it is essential for the reader to commit these to memory. They are shown in the accompanying diagrams.

It is most important to remember that the positions of the steps in Diagram 1 are in relation to the body only. This means that such steps always move in the same direction from the body, irrespective of the position of the dancer in the room.

Diagram 2 indicates the various positions of the body and the directions of the steps *in relation to the room*.

Thus, the description "R.F. forward, diag. to wall" would mean a step taken straight forward from the body, and in a direction diagonally to the wall.

# POSITION OF STEPS IN RELATION TO THE BODY

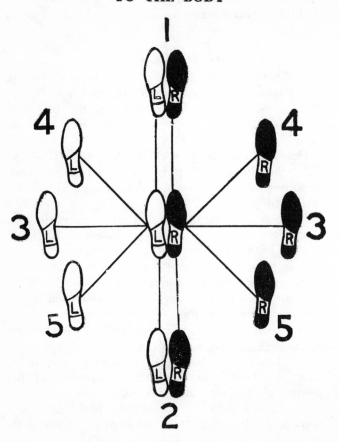

DIAGRAM I

1. R.F. or L.F. forward
2. R.F. or L.F. back
3. R.F. or L.F. to side

4. R.F. or L.F. diagonally forward
5. R.F. or L.F. diagonally back

# DIRECTIONS OF STEPS OR POSITIONS OF BODY IN RELATION TO THE ROOM

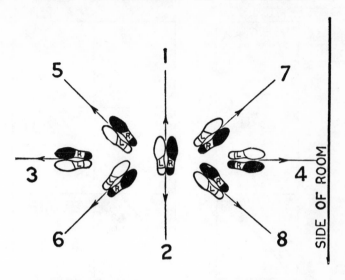

DIAGRAM 2

*Positions of Body in the Room*
1. Facing L.O.D.
3. Facing Centre.
4. Facing Wall.
5. Facing Centre Diagonally.
7. Facing Wall Diagonally.

*Directions of Steps*
1. Down the L.O.D.
2. Against the L.O.D.
3. To Centre.
4. To Wall.
5. Diagonally to the Centre.
6. Diagonally to the Centre against the L.O.D.
7. Diagonally to the Wall.
8. Diagonally to the Wall against the L.O.D.

**"Across the L.O.D."** Another term that has been used is "across the L.O.D." This term can easily be understood by referring to the diagram on page 40.

## DIAGRAM ILLUSTRATING THE TERM—
## "ACROSS THE L.O.D."

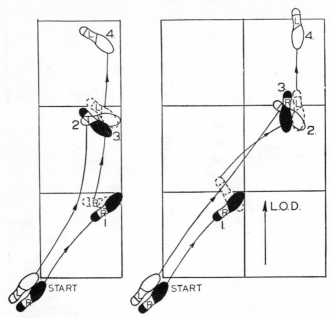

THE QUARTER TURNS (MAN)
The second step has been taken
to the side on the same L.O.D.
as the first step.

THE NATURAL TURN (MAN)
The second step has been taken
"across the L.O.D." of the first
step.

**"Centre."** Note that the "centre," as used in such
expressions as "diagonally to the centre," is not the
actual centre point of the room, but that part of the
room which is on the man's L. when he is facing the
L.O.D.

# SECTION I

## THE QUICKSTEP

THIS dance might be termed the "joy" dance of modern dancing. Whilst the basic figures are quite simple, the tempo of the music and the whole character of the dance seem to invite a care-free interpretation of its bright rhythm. The beginner will find the basic steps easy to learn and easy to fit to music. The advanced dancer will discover that the music lends itself to an infinite variety of steps.

In most sports and pastimes, a sound knowledge of the basic work is necessary before the "frills" can be indulged in with any degree of pleasure. The dancer who masters the fundamentals of the Quickstep will have command of a dance that can never grow stale, a dance that is unquestionably the most attractive expression of rhythm the world has ever known.

### General Notes

*Time*. 4/4. Four beats in a bar. The 1st and 3rd beats are accented.

*Tempo*. Music should be played between 48 and 52 bars a minute.

*Basic Rhythms*. Slow, Slow. Quick, Quick, Slow. Each "Slow" has 2 beats of music. The "Quicks" have 1 beat each.

*Figures*. Walk, Quarter Turns, Progressive Chassé, Natural Turn, Natural Pivot Turn, Chassé Reverse Turn, Zig Zag, Cross Chassé, Lock Step, Reverse

Pivot, Progressive Chassé to Right, Zig Zag, Back Lock and Running Finish, Tipple Chassé to the Right, Double Reverse Spin, Natural Spin Turn, Change of Direction, Cross Swivel, Running Right Turn, Fish Tail, Quick Open Reverse, Four Quick Run, Flicker, Telemark, Open Telemark, Impetus Turn, Open Impetus Turn.

### For the Beginner

The foundation of the Quickstep is the Walk and the Chassé, this latter figure usually being included as a part of the basic figures. The following suggestion regarding the order in which to learn the basic figures should prove useful to the beginner.

After the Walk—

*Quarter Turns.* These should be learned first.

*Natural Turn.* This is excellent groundwork for other figures and should be learnt in preference to the Natural Pivot Turn, which is the alternative turn to use at corners.

*Reverse Turns.* The Chassé Reverse Turn is the most useful Reverse Turn; it is compact and easier to dance in a crowded room.

*Progressive Chassé and Forward Lock Step.* These two figures follow the above in popularity and it is advisable to learn them next.

Further details of how to amalgamate these figures and to introduce other standard variations are given after the descriptions of each figure.

## THE WALK, FORWARD AND BACKWARD

A full description of the Walk is given on pages 9–15,

and, although the ultimate aim of the dancer should be to construct the dance so that the Walk as a separate figure is eliminated, it is most essential to learn this first.

When the basic principles of the Walk have been mastered, put on a gramophone record at a fairly slow tempo—about 40 bars per minute—and gradually increase the speed as confidence is acquired.

The Walk should be practised alone, and then with a partner until it can be danced with ease and comfort in a forward and backward direction.

Special points to note in the Quickstep Walk are—

1. The steps will be slightly shorter than in the Foxtrot, owing to the quicker music.

2. For the same reason the knees will not relax quite so much as in the slower tempo.

Whilst practising the Walk pay careful attention to the Hold and the Poise of the body. If they are wrong now, they will most likely get worse when the more difficult figures are attempted.

## THE QUARTER TURNS

### Man

The Quarter Turns are a progressive figure, and constitute the most important basic figure in the Quickstep.

They consist of a Chassé Turn, making a quarter turn to the R., followed by a compact type of turn to the L. known as a Heel Pivot. The Heel Pivot is rather too difficult for beginners, but the method of turning described below is similar to a Heel Pivot, and is better than substituting a Chassé Turn, which was formerly considered to be the only alternative open to a novice. A full description of the Heel Pivot is given on page 31.

The Quarter Turns are normally commenced and finished facing diagonally to the wall. They may be commenced facing the L.O.D. when preceded by a figure ending in that direction and finished facing the L.O.D. when a reverse figure is to follow.

1. R.F. forward, diag. to wall, turning body to R.  S
2. L.F. to side, on same L.O.D., body facing wall.  Q
3. Continue turning slightly and close R.F. to L.F.  Q
4. L.F. to side and slightly back. Body now backing diag. to centre.  S
5. R.F. back, diag. to centre, body turning to L.  S
6. Bring L.F. back to R.F., heels together, L. toe pointing diag. to wall.  Q
7. With slight pressure on *ball* of L.F., close R.F. parallel to L.F. by turning on R. heel.  Q
8. L.F. forward, diag. to wall.  S

*Contrary Body Movement.* C.B.M. on 1 and 5. Slight C.B.M. on 8.

*Rise and Fall (Body).* Commence to rise at end of 1; continue to rise on 2 and 3; up on 4. Lower at end of 4. Slight rise between 5 and 7 (N.F.R.). Note the gradual rise on the first part of the figure.

*Body Sway.* Sway to R. on 2 and 3; level on 4. Sway to R. on 6 and 7.

*Amount of Turn.* Starting and finishing diagonally to wall a quarter turn is made on each four steps. If either part is started or finished on the L.O.D. three-eighths of a turn is made on that part.

*Footwork.* 1. H. T. 2. T. 3. T. 4. T. H. 5. T. H. 6. H. 7. H. (R.F.) pressure on T. of L.F. 8. H.

*General Notes.* It should be noted that the fourth step (L.F.) moves in a sideways direction along the L.O.D. Its actual position in relation to the body, however, will be side and slightly back.

## THE QUARTER TURNS

### Lady

The Quarter Turns are a progressive figure, turning alternately to R. and L. by means of Chassé Turns.

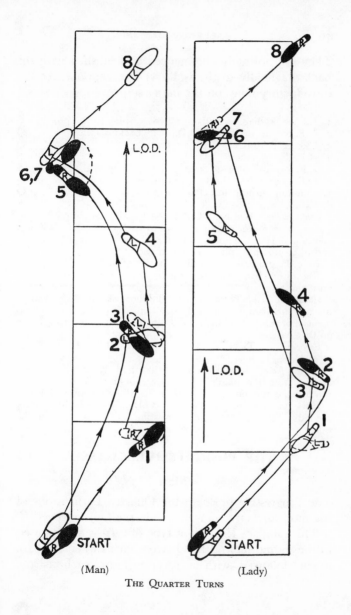

THE QUARTER TURNS

They are normally commenced and finished with the back diagonally to the wall. (For exceptions, see the introductory notes on the man's steps.)

1. L.F. back, diag. to wall, with body turning to R.            S
2. R.F. to side, on same L.O.D., body backing to wall          Q
3. Close L.F. to R.F. (face diag. centre).                     Q
4. R.F. diag. forward.                                          S
5. L.F. forward, diag. to centre, turning body to L.            S
6. R.F. to side, body backing towards wall.                    Q
7. Continue turning and close L.F. to R.F.                     Q
8. R.F. back, diag. to wall.                                    S

*Contrary Body Movement.* C.B.M. on 1 and 5; slight on 8.

*Rise and Fall (Body).* Commence to rise at end of 1 (N.F.R.); continue to rise on 2 and 3; up on 4. Lower at end of 4. Rise at end of 5; up on 6 and 7. Lower at end of 7.

Note the gradual rise on the first part of the figure.

*Body Sway.* Sway to L. on 2 and 3. Level on 4. Sway to L. on 6 and 7.

*Amount of Turn.* Starting and finishing diagonally to wall a quarter turn is made on each four steps. If either part is commenced or finished on the L.O.D. three-eighths of a turn is made on that part.

*Footwork.* 1. T. H.  2. T.  3. T.  4. T. H.  5. H. T.  6. T. 7. T. H.  8. T.

*General Notes.* It will be noticed that the lady's 4th step differs slightly from the man's. The lady should tend to step "in" towards the man on the 4th step, ending slightly between his feet.

If the man is turning to face the L.O.D. at the end of the figure, the lady's 6th step must move across the L.O.D. as it goes to the side.

## THE PROGRESSIVE CHASSÉ

### Man

The Progressive finish to the Quarter Turns is one of the most attractive movements in the Quickstep.

The compact Heel-pivot type of turn is always used in the second half of the Quarter Turns when they are to be followed with a reverse figure such as the

Zig-Zag or Double Reverse Spin. The Progressive finish will be found more suitable when the Quarter Turns are to be followed by a natural figure, or a variation that is commenced with the R.F. outside the partner.

Commence facing diagonally to the wall, and then dance steps 1 to 4 of the Quarter Turns. SQQS. Continue—

1. R.F. back, diag. to centre, with body turning to L.          S
2. L.F. to side, along the L.O.D., body facing wall              Q
3. Close R.F. to L.F.                                            Q
4. L.F. to side, and slightly forward.                          S
5. R.F. forward, outside partner, diag. to wall.                S

*Contrary Body Movement.* C.B.M. on 1 and 5. The 5th step is placed in C.B.M.P.

*Rise and Fall (Body).* Commence to rise at end of 1 (N.F.R.); continue to rise on 2 and 3; up on 4. Lower at end of 4. Note the gradual rise which is completed only on the 3rd step.

*Body Sway.* There is no sway.

*Amount of Turn.* Make a quarter turn to the L.

*Footwork.* 1. T. H.  2. T.  3. T.  4. T. H.  5. H.

*General Notes.* Care should be taken not to turn too much when dancing the wide Chassé (steps 2, 3, 4.) Keep the body practically square to the wall the whole time, otherwise the bodies will become out of alignment on the outside step.

The Progressive Chassé could be danced after the Natural Spin Turn; 1, 2, 3 of the Chassé Reverse Turn, or 1, 2, 3 of the Quick Open Reverse Turn.

Follow the Progressive Chassé with—

(1) Use the 5th step as the 1st step of a Natural Turn, or any natural figure. (2) Lock Step. This is described on pages 66–67. (3) Any advanced variation, such as the Fish Tail.

## THE PROGRESSIVE CHASSÉ

### Lady

The Progressive finish to the Quarter Turns is one of the most attractive movements in the Quickstep. It is usually danced when the man wishes to follow the Quarter Turns with a figure that commences with a turn to the R. When a reverse figure follows the

Quarter Turns, the normal ending to the Quarter Turns must be used.

Commence with the back diagonally to the wall, and then dance steps 1 to 4 of the Quarter Turns. Finish facing diagonally to the centre. SQQS. Continue—

| | |
|---|---|
| 1. L.F. forward, diag. to centre, body turning to L. | S |
| 2. R.F. to side, along the L.O.D., body facing centre. | Q |
| 3. Close L.F. to R.F. | Q |
| 4. R.F. to side, and slightly back. | S |
| 5. L.F. back, partner outside, diag. to wall. | S |

*Contrary Body Movement.* C.B.M. on 1 and 5. The 5th step is placed in C.B.M.P.

*Rise and Fall (Body).* Commence to rise at end of 1; continue to rise on 2 and 3; up on 4. Lower at end of 4. Note the gradual rise.

*Body Sway.* There is no sway.

*Amount of Turn.* Make a quarter turn to the L.

*Footwork.* 1. H. T. 2. T. 3. T. 4. T. H. 5. T.

*General Notes.* The lady should have no difficulty in knowing which ending to the Quarter Turns is being used. When using the Progressive finish, the man's body will not turn so much to the L. on the first step as when a Heel Pivot is employed.

## THE NATURAL TURN

### Man

The most useful figure to use at corners. It is sometimes more difficult to master than the Natural Pivot Turn (described later), but is excellent groundwork for similar figures in other dances.

It consists of a Chassé Turn and a type of Heel Turn called a Pull Step.

Commence facing the L.O.D. or diagonally to the wall, the latter being the more comfortable position.

| | |
|---|---|
| 1. R.F. forward, turning body to R. | S |
| 2. L.F. to side, across the L.O.D. | Q |
| 3. Continue turning on ball of L.F. and close R.F. to L.F. | Q |
| 4. L.F. back, down the L.O.D. and turning body to R. | S |

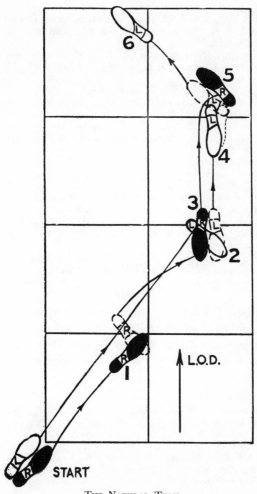

THE NATURAL TURN
(Man)

5. Pull R.F. back to L.F., at the same time turning to R.
   on L. heel. Transfer weight to R.F. at end of step.   S
6. L.F. forward.   S

*Contrary Body Movement.* C.B.M. on 1 and 4; slight on 6.

*Rise and Fall (Body).* Rise at end of 1; up for 2 and 3; lower at end of 3.

*Body Sway.* Sway to the R. on 2 and 3.

*Amount of Turn.* When commenced diagonally to the wall near a corner, make three-eighths of a turn on the first three steps. On the Pull Step (4, 5, and 6) make either a quarter turn to face the new L.O.D. or three-eighths to face diagonally to the wall of the new L.O.D.

*Footwork.* 1. H. T. 2. T. 3. T. H. 4. T. H. 5. H., I.E. of foot, whole foot. 6. H.

*General Notes.* Advanced dancers will keep the feet slightly apart in the Pull Step. If the Natural Turn is used along the side of the room, it is advisable to make the 5th step fairly wide, and then brush L.F. to R.F. with an extra "S" count. Rhythm will then be SQQSSSS. Follow with the Chassé Reverse Turn, or a Progressive Chassé to R.

## THE NATURAL TURN

### Lady

This figure is used at corners.

It consists of a Chassé Turn and a Brush Step.

Commence with the back to the L.O.D. or diagonally to the wall, the latter being the more comfortable position.

1. L.F. back, turning body to R.   S
2. R.F. to side, across the L.O.D.   Q
3. Close L.F. to R.F.   Q
4. R.F. forward down L.O.D., turning body to R.   S
5. L.F. to side.   S
6. Brush R.F. up to L.F. and then step back with R.F.   S

*Contrary Body Movement.* C.B.M. on 1 and 4; slight on 6.

*Rise and Fall (Body).* Rise at end of 1 (N.F.R.); up on 2 and 3. Lower at end of 3.

*Body Sway.* Sway to the L. on 2 and 3.

*Amount of Turn.* When commenced diagonally to the wall near a corner, make three-eighths of a turn on the first three steps.

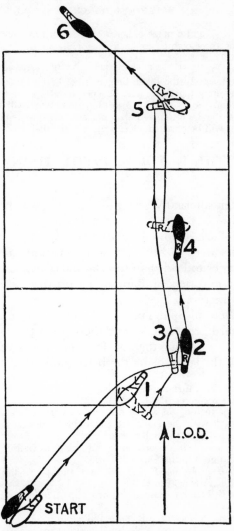

6

5

4
3 2
1

L.O.D.

START

THE NATURAL TURN
(Lady)

On steps 4, 5, and 6 make either a quarter turn to back the new L.O.D. or three-eighths to back diagonally to the wall of the new L.O.D.

*Footwork.* 1. T. H. 2. T. 3. T. H. 4. H. T. 5. T. H. 6. T.

*General Notes.* In the Brush Step it is not necessary for the feet to be absolutely together. The R. knee should be slightly more relaxed than the L., and in brushing, the R. toe will be about level with the L. instep. If the toes are brought together, the movement will be checked. Keep the feet parallel.

## THE NATURAL PIVOT TURN

### Man

This is an alternative Right-hand turn which should be used at a corner. It consists of 1, 2, and 3 of the Natural Turn, followed by a Pivot. Although difficult to dance well, a beginner will sometimes find this figure easier to lead than the Natural Turn. It can be used by experienced dancers to progress along the sides of the room.

The Natural Spin Turn is a better figure to employ for forward progression along the sides of the room.

Commence facing the L.O.D. or facing diagonally to the wall, the latter being the better position.

1. R.F. forward, turning body to R.         S
2. L.F. to side, across the L.O.D.         Q
3. Continue turning on ball of L.F. and close R.F. to L.F.   Q
4. Step back with the L.F., and pivot three-eighths of a turn to R. on the ball of L.F. Keep R.F. in front.   S

To continue, step forward on to R.F. diag. to wall of the new L.O.D. and go into the Quarter Turns.

*Contrary Body Movement.* C.B.M. on 1 and 4. As the pivot is made, the R.F. is held in C.B.M.P.

*Rise and Fall (Body).* Rise at end of 1; up on 2 and 3. Lower at end of 3.

*Body Sway.* Sway to the R. on 2 and 3.

*Amount of Turn.* From a diagonal position make three-eighths turn on the first three steps. The 4th step is made with the back to

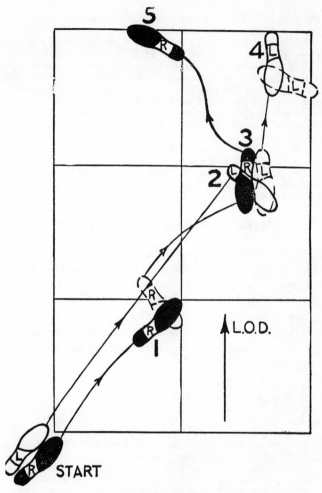

THE NATURAL PIVOT TURN
(Man)

the L.O.D. Make three-eighths of a turn on the pivot. To continue along the same L.O.D., pivot a half-turn.

*Footwork.* 1. H. T. 2. T. 3. T. H. 4. T. H. T. Note: a though footwork of step 4 is given as T. H. T. the turn is made on the ball of the foot and with the heel in contact with the floor.

*General Notes.* The 4th step of the Pivot Turn is shorter than the 4th step of the Natural Turn and the knees are more relaxed. Beginners will find the Pivot quite easy to lead, by making the step back on the L.F. quite small, not letting the heel touch the floor, and keeping the weight forward. As this step is taken the man guides the lady with his R. hand, so that her forward impetus is received on his R. side. He will then turn quite easily to the R. on the ball of the L.F., and if the R.F. is kept forward, it will be ready to commence the Quarter Turns. Advanced dancers, with more control on the actual Pivot, will be able to get a slight forward thrust on the R.F. to swing into the Quarter Turns.

# THE NATURAL PIVOT TURN

## Lady

This is an alternative right-hand turn which should be used at a corner. It consists of 1, 2, and 3 of the Natural Turn, followed by a Pivoting action. Some notes on this will be found below.

Commence with the back to the L.O.D. or diagonally to the wall, the latter position being the more comfortable.

1. L.F. back, turning body to R.                          S
2. R.F. to side, across the L.O.D.                        Q
3. Close L.F. to R.F.                                     Q
4. R.F. forward and turn three-eighths of a turn to R. with a Pivoting action.                                S

To continue, step back on to L.F. diagonally to wall of the new L.O.D. and go into the Quarter Turns.

*Contrary Body Movement.* C.B.M. on 1 and 4. As the turn is made on the 4th step the L.F. is not held in C.B.M.P.

*Rise and Fall (Body).* Rise at end of 1 (N.F.R.); up on 2 and 3. Lower at end of 3.

*Body Sway.* Sway to the L. on 2 and 3.

*Amount of Turn.* If commenced from a diagonal position make

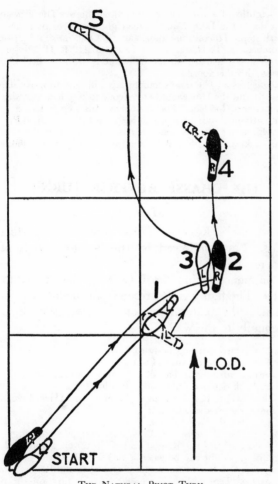

THE NATURAL PIVOT TURN
(Lady)

three-eighths of a turn on the first three steps. The 4th step is taken down the L.O.D. and three-eighths of a turn is made on the 4th step. To continue along same L.O.D. make a half-turn.

*Footwork.* 1. T. H. 2. T. 3. T. H. 4. H. T. H. Note: the turn on step 4 is made on the ball of R.F. with the heel in close contact with the floor.

*General Notes.* The man's fourth step will tend to move slightly leftwards and the lady should endeavour to step forward with her R.F. between his feet. The action on this step is like a pivot, but no attempt must be made to hold the L.F. in C.B.M.P. The L.F. will move slightly leftwards during the turn, but should move backwards, with C.B.M. for the first step of the following figure.

# THE CHASSÉ REVERSE TURN

## Man

The Chassé Reverse Turn consists of a forward Chassé Turn, followed by the last four steps of the Quarter Turns.

Commence facing the L.O.D. or diagonally to the centre. The figure is described from the latter position, which is the better (see notes below). Finish facing diagonally to the wall.

1. L.F. forward, turning body to L.                                        S
2. R.F. to side, across the L.O.D.                                         Q
3. Continue turning on ball of R.F. and close L.F. to R.F.                 Q
4. R.F. back down L.O.D., body turning to L.                               S
5. ⎰ Close L.F. to R.F., turning to L. on R. heel (Heel Pivot).           Q
6. ⎱ Finish facing diag. to wall.                                          Q
7. L.F. forward, diag. to wall.                                            S

*Contrary Body Movement.* C.B.M. on 1 and 4; slight on 7.

*Rise and Fall (Body).* Rise at end of 1; up on 2 and 3. Lower at end of 3. Slight rise between 4 and 6 (N.F.R.).

*Body Sway.* Sway to the L. on 2 and 3, to the R. on 5 and 6.

*Amount of Turn.* Make three-eighths of a turn on the first 3 steps and three-eighths on the last part.

*Footwork.* 1. H. T. 2. T. 3. T. H. 4. T. H. 5. H. 6. H. (R.F.) pressure on T. of L.F. 7. H.

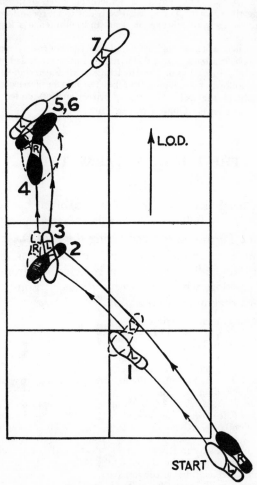

THE CHASSÉ REVERSE TURN
(Man)

*General Notes.* This figure is sometimes taken immediately following the Quarter Turns, but this is not to be recommended. The lady is likely to mistake the lead and commence a Zig-Zag instead.

Commence when facing diagonally to the centre. Beginners should take it after a Natural Turn that has been ended in this position by turning less on the Heel Pull. Advanced dancers will find the following amalgamation best: Quarter Turns, ended diagonally to the wall; Change of Direction step, ended diagonally to the cover; Chase Reverse Turn.

# THE CHASSÉ REVERSE TURN

## Lady

The Chassé Reverse Turn consists of a backward Chassé Turn followed by the last four steps of the Quarter Turns commenced facing the L.O.D.

Commence with the back to the L.O.D. or to the centre diagonally. The figure is described from the latter position, which is easier and nicer. Finish with the back diagonally to the wall.

1. R.F. back, turning body to L.                                    S
2. L.F. to side, across L.O.D.                                      Q
3. Close R.F. to L.F.                                               Q
4. L.F. forward, turning body to L.                                 S
5. R.F. to side, on same L.O.D.                                     Q
6. Close L.F. to R.F., continuing to turn to back diag. to wall.    Q
7. R.F. back, diag. to wall.                                        S

*Contrary Body Movement.* C.B.M. on 1 and 4; slight on 7.

*Rise and Fall (Body).* Rise at end of 1 (N.F.R.); up on 2 and 3. Lower at end of 3. Rise at end of 4; up on 5 and 6. Lower at end of 6.

*Body Sway.* Sway to R. on 2 and 3. Sway to L. on 5 and 6.

*Amount of Turn.* Make three-eighths of a turn on the first 3 steps and three-eighths on the last part.

*Footwork.* 1. T. H. 2. T. 3. T. H. 4. H. T. 5. T. 6. T. H. 7. T.

*General Notes.* Please refer to the notes on the man's step.

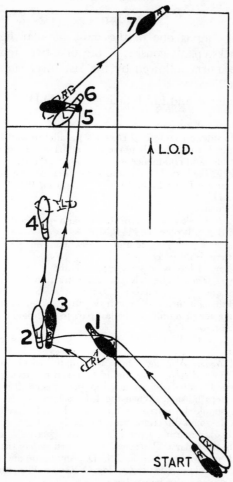

THE CHASSÉ REVERSE TURN
(Lady)

# THE ZIG-ZAG

## Man

The Zig-Zag is one of the most popular figures in the Quickstep. It consists of the first two steps of the Reverse Turn, followed by the last three steps of the Natural Turn.

Commence and finish facing the L.O.D.

1. L.F. forward, turning body to L.      S
2. R.F. to side, on same L.O.D., back parallel to wall.      S
3. Continue turning slightly to the L., step back L.F., partner outside, and commence to turn body to the R.      S
4. Pull R.F. back to L.F., at the same time turning to the R. on the L. heel. Finish with weight on R.F., facing L.O.D.      S
5. L.F. forward.      S

*Contrary Body Movement.* C.B.M. on 1 and 3. Slight C.B.M. on 5. The 3rd step is placed in C.B.M.P.

*Rise and Fall (Body).* The 2nd step is taken on the ball of the foot but there is no body rise.

*Body Sway.* There is no sway in this figure.

*Amount of Turn.* There is a quarter turn to L. on the first two steps and then a further slight turn to L. before making three-eighths of a turn to R. on steps 3 to 5. When near a corner make a quarter turn only on the last part to end diagonally to the wall of the new L.O.D.

*Footwork.* 1. H. T. 2. T. H. 3. T. H. 4. H., I.E. of foot, whole foot. 5. H.

*General Notes.* Although there is a slight swivel on the ball of the R.F. (2nd step), care should be taken not to overturn the body to the L., otherwise an ugly hip movement will result when the lady steps outside. When the L.F. is back on the 3rd step, the body should be square to the wall, the L.F. having moved back in a diagonal direction across the body.

The Zig-Zag is usually preceded by the Quarter Turns. The last step of the Quarter Turns will be the first step of the Zig-Zag, and is taken straight down the L.O.D. Any figure ending with a Heel Pivot could precede the Zig-Zag. A Reverse Pivot and Double Reverse Spin can also be used as entries.

*Zig-Zag and Backward Lock.* After 1, 2 of the Zig-Zag, the Backward Lock may be used. See page 71.

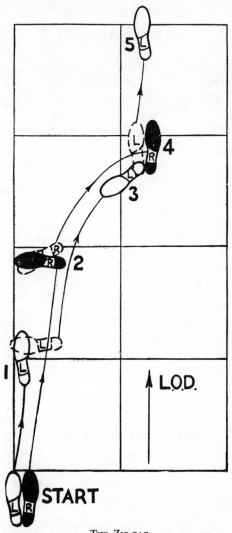

THE ZIG-ZAG
(Man)

# THE  ZIG-ZAG

## Lady

The Zig-Zag is a very popular figure consisting of a Heel Turn followed by the last three steps of the Natural Turn.

Commence and finish with the back to the L.O.D.

1. R.F. back, turning body to L.                                  S
2. Close L.F. to R.F. turning on R. heel.  Finish with weight on L.F., having made three-eighths of a turn to L.        S
3. R.F. forward, diag. to wall outside partner.  Take this step across the body, beginning to turn to R.               S
4. L.F. to side, across the L.O.D.                               S
5. Brush R.F. to L.F. and then step back R.F. down L.O.D.        S

*Contrary Body Movement.* C.B.M. on 1 and 3.  Slight C.B.M. on 5. The 3rd step is placed in C.B.M.P.

*Rise and Fall (Body).* The 4th step is taken on the ball of the foot, but there is no body rise.

*Body Sway.* There is no sway in this figure.

*Amount of Turn.* Make three-eighths of a turn to the L. on the first two steps and three-eighths to the R. on the last part.  If near a corner it is permissible to underturn the last part to end backing diagonally to the wall of the new L.O.D.

*Footwork.*  1. T. H.  2. H.  3. H. T.  4. T. H.  5. T.

*General Notes.* When stepping to the side of the man on the 3rd step, endeavour to keep contact by stepping well across the body with the R.F.  The body should be facing the wall when the R.F. is forward.


# THE  CROSS  CHASSÉ

## Man

The Cross Chassé is a popular figure consisting of a Chassé taken to the man's R. side and finishing forward outside the lady.

It is normally commenced and finished facing diagonally to the wall.

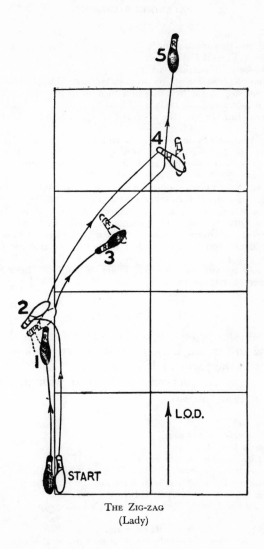

THE ZIG-ZAG
(Lady)

1. L.F. forward.     S
2. R.F. to side—small step.     Q
3. Close L.F. to R.F.     Q
4. R.F. forward, outside partner.     S

*Contrary Body Movement.* Slight C.B.M. on 1. C.B.M. on 4 when using this step as the first step of a turning figure. The 4th step is taken well across the body in C.B.M.P.

*Rise and Fall (Body).* Rise at end of 1; up on 2 and 3. Lower at end of 3.

*Body Sway.* Sway to the L. on 2 and 3.

*Amount of Turn.* Normally there is no turn in this figure. A turn to the L. is sometimes made in advanced variations.

*Footwork.* 1. H. T. 2. T. 3. T. H. 4. H.

*General Notes.* Care should be taken to keep contact with the partner when the R.F. is taken outside the lady on the 4th step.

The Cross Chassé is usually preceded by the Quarter Turns. End the Quarter Turns facing diagonally to the wall and use the last step of the Quarter Turns as the first of the Cross Chassé.

Any figure ending with a Heel Pivot can precede the Cross Chassé, also a Double Reverse Spin or Reverse Pivot. Follow the Cross Chassé with any Natural figure or with the Lock Step, described on pages 66–67.

## Lady

An easy and popular figure in which the lady does a Chassé to her L., finishing with a step back on the L.F. with the partner's R.F. outside.

Normally commenced and finished with the back diagonally to the wall.

1. R.F. back.     S
2. L.F. to side—small step.     Q
3. Close R.F. to L.F.     Q
4. L.F. back, with partner outside.     S

*Contrary Body Movement.* Slight C.B.M. on 1. C.B.M. on 4 when following the Cross Chassé with a turning figure. The 4th step is taken well across the body in C.B.M.P.

*Rise and Fall (Body).* Rise at end of 1 (N.F.R.); up on 2 and 3. Lower at end of 3.

*Body Sway.* Sway to the R. on 2 and 3.

*Amount of Turn.* Normally there is no turn in this figure. A

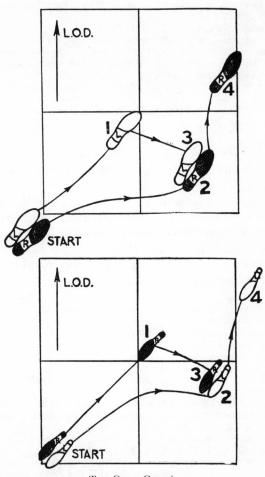

THE CROSS CHASSÉ
(*Top:* Man; *Below:* Lady)

turn to the L. may be made in advanced variations, but this should never be done by beginners.

*Footwork.* 1. T. H. 2. T. 3. T. H. 4. T.

*General Notes.* The lady should make sure that her 4th step is taken well across the body, otherwise an ugly hip movement will result when the man steps outside. Keep the hips well forward as this step is taken.

## THE LOCK STEP

### Man

The Lock Step is a very popular figure.

It consists of a forward Chassé in which the feet are crossed on the second quick step.

It commences with a step forward on the R.F., which must be taken outside the partner. The last step of the Progressive Chassé or the Cross Chassé would form an excellent entry to this figure.

The Lock Step is normally commenced and finished facing diagonally to the wall.

1. R.F. forward, outside partner, diagonally to wall.      S
2. L.F. diag. forward.      Q
3. Cross R.F. behind L.F. (not tightly).      Q
4. L.F. diag. forward.      S
5. R.F. forward, outside partner, diag. to wall.      S

*Contrary Body Movement.* Steps 1 and 5 will be placed in C.B.M.P. Use C.B.M. on the 5th step of the Lock Step when following with a turn.

*Rise and Fall (Body).* Commence to rise at end of 1; continue to rise on 2 and 3. Up on 4. Lower at end of 4. Note the gradual rise.

*Body Sway.* There is no sway.

*Footwork.* 1. H. T. 2. T. 3. T. 4. T. H. 5. H.

*General Notes.* Although the figure travels diagonally to wall the body should be facing between the wall and diagonally to wall so that contact with partner is kept. The Lock Step is often danced backwards by the man after 1, 2, of a Zig-Zag. It would be followed with a Heel Pull or a Running Finish. In the latter case the complete rhythm would be SSSQQSQQSS or SSSQQSSQQS. Either rhythm for the Running Finish is correct. It is a matter of personal expression. The description of a Lock Step taken backwards would be the same as given in the lady's Lock Step below. Please also refer to page 71.

# THE LOCK STEP

## Lady

The Lock Step consists of a backward Chassé in which the feet are crossed on the second quick step.

It is danced when the man has taken a step forward with his R.F. outside the lady. The last step of the Progressive Chassé or the Cross Chassé forms an excellent entry to this figure.

Normally commenced backing diagonally to the wall, in which position the above figures are ended.

1. L.F. back, diag. to wall, partner outside.        S
2. R.F. backward, and slightly to the R.        Q
3. Cross L.F. in front of R.F. (not tightly).        Q
4. R.F. diag. back.        S
5. L.F. back diag. to wall, partner outside.        S

*Contrary Body Movement.* Steps 1 and 5 will be placed back in C.B.M.P. Use C.B.M. on the 5th step of the Lock Step when following with a turn.

*Rise and Fall (Body).* Commence to rise at end of 1 (N.F.R.); continue to rise on 2 and 3; up on 4. Lower at end of 4. Note the gradual rise.

*Body Sway.* There is no sway.

*Footwork.* 1. T. H. 2. T. 3. T. 4. T. H. 5. T.

*General Notes.* Although the rise commences at the end of 1 there is no foot rise, and care should be taken to have the L. heel in contact with the floor when this foot commences to draw back to cross in front of R.F. on the third step.

The lady may dance a Lock Step forward after steps 1 and 2 of a Zig-Zag, when the description would be the same as given in the man's steps of the Lock Step.

## THE REVERSE PIVOT
### Man

This is a most useful and attractive figure of only one step and is used in place of a Heel Pivot to make a quick turn to the left. Notes on its uses are given below. See also the diagram on page 94.

Commence backing the L.O.D.

1. Slip R.F. back, under the body (small step) in a direction
   diag. to centre, with the toe turned in. Now pivot to L.
   on ball of R.F., holding L.F. forward in C.B.M.P.     S

   *Contrary Body Movement.* C.B.M. on 1. This step is also placed in C.B.M.P. and the L.F. is held forward in C.B.M.P.

   *Rise and Fall (Body).* There is no rise.

   *Body Sway.* There is no sway.

   *Amount of Turn.* An eighth of a turn to L. is made between the preceding step and the pivot and up to a further three-eighths of a turn on the R.F.

   *Footwork.* 1. T.H.T. (but R.F. is kept practically flat).

   *General Notes.* It is important to remember that the body commences to turn to L. *as* the R.F. moves back, and this results in the R.F. moving in a direction diag. to centre and ending well under the body in C.B.M.P. The weight should be kept forward. If the Pivot is commenced backing diag. to centre after a Spin Turn or 4 steps of the Quarter Turns, the R.F. will move back in a direction to centre on the pivot. In some amalgamations the Reverse Pivot can be counted Q or "&".

   The Reverse Pivot could be preceded by 4 steps of the Quarter Turns, the Spin Turn, or Quick Open Reverse Turns, etc. Figures that could follow the pivot are—

   (*a*) If ended facing diag. to wall. Cross Chassé, Cross Swivel, Change of Direction.

   (*b*) If ended facing L.O.D. The best endings are the Double Reverse Spin, a Quick Open Reverse Turn or a Progressive Chassé to R.

### Lady

Commence facing the L.O.D.

1. Slip the L.F. forward (small step), in a direction diag. to
   centre, with body turning to L. Now pivot to L. on ball
   of L.F. holding the R.F. at back in C.B.M.P.           S

*Contrary Body Movement.* C.B.M. on 1. The L.F. is also placed in C.B.M.P. and the R.F. held in C.B.M.P.

*Rise and Fall (Body).* There is no rise.

*Body Sway.* There is no sway.

*Amount of Turn.* An eighth of a turn to L. is made between the preceding step and the pivot and up to a further three-eighths of a turn on the L.F.

*Footwork.* 1. T.H. (Turn is made on the ball of foot with the foot practically flat.)

*General Notes.* The man should hold the lady firmly as he commences the pivot and she will then feel his body turn to the L. The lady will then automatically follow the direction of his R.F. with her L.F. Amalgamations are given under the man's steps.


# PROGRESSIVE CHASSÉ TO THE RIGHT

## Man

This is a delightful and most useful figure. It is similar to the Progressive Chassé described on page 46 but danced moving to the right instead of to the left. It can be taken after a Natural Turn danced with a hesitation on step 5 or after a Change of Direction.

Commence facing diagonally to centre.

1. L.F. forward, diag. to centre, turning to L.                    S
2. R.F. to side, with body backing towards wall.                Q
3. Close L.F. to R.F., now backing diag. to wall.              Q
4. R.F. to side and slightly back, still moving sideways along L.O.D.                    S
5. L.F. back, diag. to wall, partner outside.                    S

*Contrary Body Movement.* C.B.M. on 1 and 5. The 5th step is placed in C.B.M.P.

*Rise and Fall (Body).* Commence to rise at end of 1; continue to rise on 2 and 3; up on 4. Lower at end of 4.

*Body Sway.* There is no sway.

*Amount of Turn.* Make a quarter turn to L.

*Footwork.* 1. H.T. 2. T. 3. T. 4. T. H. 5. T.

*General Notes.* Although a quarter turn to L. is made with the feet it is better to turn the body slightly less so that the body is backing between wall and diag. to wall on steps 3 to 5. Note the gradual rise which is most important. The best amalgamations are—

(*a*) Quarter Turns ended diag. to wall. Change of Direction, ended diag. to centre. Progressive Chassé to R., followed by a Back Lock with the Heel Pull or Running Finish.

(*b*) Natural Turn with Hesitation, SQQSSS (see page 50) ended diag. to centre. Progressive Chassé to R., Back Lock and Running Finish.

(*c*) Make a half turn to L. on the Progressive Chassé to R. to end backing diag. to centre SQQSS. Now step back R.F. with the Lady in line and dance steps 1 to 7 of the Four Quick Run but counting these steps QQQQQQS. This is the Six Quick Run.


# PROGRESSIVE CHASSÉ TO THE RIGHT
## Lady

Commence backing diagonally to centre. (See notes above.)

1. R.F. back, diag. to centre, turning to L.                    S
2. L.F. to side, along L.O.D., body facing wall.               Q
3. Close R.F. to L.F.                                          Q
4. L.F. to side and slightly forward.                          S
5. R.F. forward, diag. to wall, outside partner.               S

*Contrary Body Movement.* C.B.M. on 1 and 5. The 5th step is placed in C.B.M.P.

*Rise and Fall (Body).* Commence to rise at end of 1 (N.F.R.); continue to rise on 2 and 3; up on 4; Lower at end of 4.

*Body Sway.* There is no sway.

*Amount of Turn.* Make a quarter turn to L.

*Footwork.* 1. T.H. 2. T. 3. T. 4. T. H. 5. H.

*General Notes.* On step 2 the L.F. will be pointing diag. to wall but when the R.F. closes, the body should be held between the wall and diag. to wall to ensure good contact with partner.

# THE ZIG ZAG, BACK LOCK AND RUNNING FINISH

## Man

The figure known as the Running Zig Zag is now seldom danced. Most dancers use the first part of the Zig Zag followed by a Backward Lock, ending with a Running Finish. It is an important figure for the keen dancer to master as parts of it recur in more advanced variations.

Commence facing the L.O.D.

1. L.F. forward, turning body to L.                                S
2. R.F. to side, on same L.O.D., back parallel to wall.           S
3. Continue turning slightly to L., and step back L.F., partner
   outside, diag. to wall.                                        S
4. R.F. back.                                                     Q
5. Cross L.F. in front of R.F.                                    Q
6. R.F. diag. back, still moving back diag. to wall.              S

   Now into the Running Finish:

7. L.F. back, partner outside, turning body to R.                 Q
8. R.F. to side and slightly forward with body almost facing
   the L.O.D.                                                     Q
9. L.F. forward, preparing to step outside partner, L. shoulder
   leading.                                                       S
10. R.F. forward, outside partner.                                S

*Contrary Body Movement.* C.B.M. on 1, 3 (slight), 7 and 10. Steps 3, 7 and 10 are placed in C.B.M.P.

*Rise and Fall (Body).* There is no rise on steps 1 and 2. Commence to rise at end of 3 (N.F.R.) continue to rise on 4 and 5; up on 6; lower at end of 6. Rise at end of 7; up on 8 and 9; lower at end of 9. Note that the rise is taken from the ball of foot on step 7. The L. heel does not lower to the floor.

*Body Sway.* Sway to L. on 8 and 9.

*Amount of Turn.* There is a quarter turn to L. between steps 1 and 2 and a slight turn to L. between 2 and 3. Make three-eighths turn to R. between 7 and 8. The body will turn slightly less and will complete the turn between steps 8 and 9.

*Footwork.* 1. H. T.  2. T. H.  3. T. H.  4. T.  5. T.  6. T. H. 7. T.  8. T.  9. T. H.  10. H.

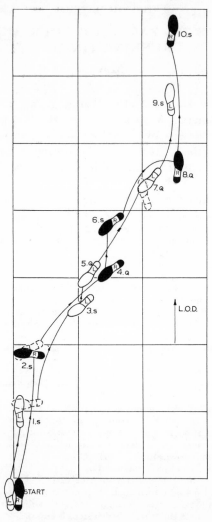

ZIG ZAG, LOCK AND RUNNING FINISH

(Man)

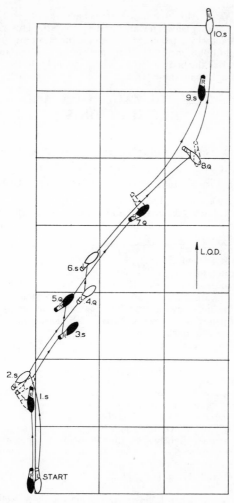

ZIG ZAG, LOCK AND RUNNING FINISH
(Lady)

*General Notes.* Although step 3 moves back diag. to wall the body should be backing between wall and diag. to wall. This will ensure better contact with partner. Steps 7 to 10, the Running Finish, can be counted QQSS or SQQS. Both are correct. Try to use an upward stretch of the body on step 7 which will help the man to move freely and lightly on these steps.

# THE ZIG ZAG, LOCK AND RUNNING FINISH

## Lady

This is a very popular figure, consisting of the first part of the Zig Zag, a Forward Lock Step ending with a Running Finish. Commence backing the L.O.D.

| | |
|---|---|
| 1. R.F. back, turning body to L. | S |
| 2. Close L.F. to R.F. turning on R. heel and making a heel turn to face diag. to wall. | S |
| 3. R.F. forward, outside partner, diag. to wall. | S |
| 4. L.F. diag. forward. | Q |
| 5. Cross R.F. behind L.F. | Q |
| 6. L.F. diag. forward, still moving diag. to wall. | S |

Now into the Running Finish:

| | |
|---|---|
| 7. R.F. forward, outside partner, turning body to R. | Q |
| 8. L.F. to side, body backing diag. to centre. | Q |
| 9. Still turning to R., step back R.F., R. shoulder leading. Now moving back down L.O.D. | S |
| 10. L.F. back, partner outside. | S |

*Contrary Body Movement.* C.B.M. on 1, 3 (slight), 7 and 10. Steps 3, 7 and 10 are placed in C.B.M.P.

*Rise and Fall (Body).* Commence to rise at end of 3: continue to rise on 4 and 5; up on 6; lower at end of 6. Rise at end of 7; up on 8 and 9; lower at end of 9.

*Body Sway.* Sway to R. on 8 and 9.

*Amount of Turn.* Turn three-eighths to L. between steps 1 and 2, the body turning slightly less, thus ensuring good contact when stepping outside on step 3. Turn a quarter to R. between 7 and 8 and an eighth between 8 and 9.

*Footwork.* 1. T. H. 2. H. 3. H. T. 4. T. 5. T. 6. T. H. 7. H. T. 8. T. 9. T. H. 10. T.

*General Notes.* When taking step 7 swing the body well forward into the step. This will help the man to dance the Running Finish with a free and flowing movement.

Micky and Momo Kezuka, Japanese Latin American
Champions, show an attractive line

# THE TIPPLE CHASSÉ TO RIGHT
## Man

The Tipple Chassé to Right is a newer ending to the Natural Turn and is a free moving figure to use at corners.

It consists of 1, 2, 3 of a Natural Turn, followed by the Tipple Chassé to Right, ended with steps 2 to 5 of a Forward Lock Step along the new L.O.D.

Commence facing diagonally to wall near a corner.

1. R.F. forward, turning body to R.     S
2. L.F. to side, across the L.O.D.     Q
3. Continue turning on ball of L.F. and close R.F. to L.F.   Q
4. L.F. back, down the L.O.D. and turning body to R.   S
5. R.F. to side, now facing new L.O.D.     Q
6. Close L.F. to R.F.     Q
7. Turning slightly to R., R.F. to side and slightly forward.   S
8. L.F. diag. forward, L. shoulder leading and moving diag. to wall.     Q
9. Cross R.F. behind L.F.     Q
10. L.F. diag. forward.     S
11. R.F. forward, outside partner, diag. to wall.   S

*Contrary Body Movement.* C.B.M. on 1, 4, and 11. The 11th step is placed in C.B.M.P.

*Rise and Fall (Body).* Rise at end of 1; up for 2 and 3; lower at end of 3. Commence to rise at end of 4 (N.F.R.); continue to rise on 5 and 6; up on 7 (see note below); up on 8, 9, and 10; lower at end of 10.

*Note.* A slight flexing of the knees may be used on step 7, straightening as step 8 is taken. The R. heel should not lower to the floor.

*Body Sway.* Sway to R. on 2 and 3.

*Amount of Turn.* Make three-eighths turn to R. on the first three steps. Make a quarter to R. between steps 4 and 5 and an eighth between steps 6 and 7.

*Footwork.* 1. H. T.   2. T.   3. T. H.   4. T. H.   5. T.   6. T.   7. T. 8. T.   9. T.   10. T. H.   11. H.

*General Notes.* The body will turn a little quicker than usual between steps 4 and 5 to completely face the new L.O.D. After turning slightly to R. as step 7 is taken diag. forward, remember to soften the knee slightly before moving diag. forward into the

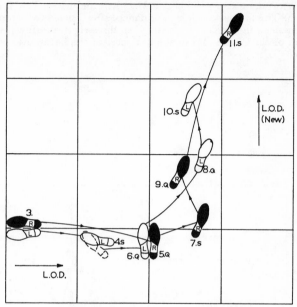

TIPPLE CHASSÉ TO THE RIGHT
(Man)

Forward Lock Step. An alternative method of dancing the figure
is given below.

*Tipple Chassé to R. with R. Sway.* Dance steps 1, 2, 3 of the Natural
Turn as usual but when dancing steps 4 to 7, turn only a quarter
turn to R. to end facing the new L.O.D. Step 7 will be taken to
side—not side and slightly forward. Turn the head to the R. for
steps 5, 6, 7 and sway to the R. The rise will be: Slight rise on 5
and 6; lower on 7. Rise for the following Forward Lock Step,
which will be danced down the new L.O.D. or diag. to centre of
the new L.O.D., will be: Commence to rise at end of 7; continue
to rise on 8 and 9; up on 10; lower at end of 10 (see page 78).

Footwork on step 7 will be: T. H. of R.F. and I.E. of T. of L.F.

The Tipple Chassé to R. can be danced after 4 steps of a Natural Turn along the side of the room, when three-eighths turn will be made on the Chassé. It can also be danced after a Backward Lock Step.

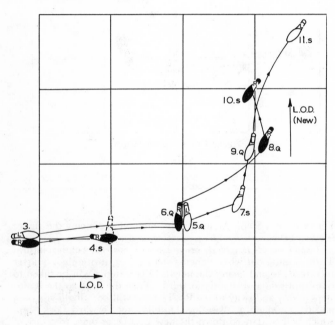

TIPPLE CHASSÉ TO THE RIGHT
(Lady)

# THE TIPPLE CHASSÉ TO RIGHT
## Lady

The Tipple Chassé to Right is normally used after three steps of a Natural Turn.

Commence backing diagonally to wall near a corner.

1. L.F. back, turning body to R.    S
2. R.F. to side, across the L.O.D.    Q
3. Close L.F. to R.F.    Q
4. R.F. forward, down L.O.D. turning body to R.    S
5. L.F. to side, now backing new L.O.D.    Q
6. Close R.F. to L.F.    Q
7. Turning slightly to R., step to side and slightly back with L.F.    S
8. R.F. back, R. shoulder leading and moving diag. to wall.    Q
9. Cross L.F. in front of R.F.    Q
10. R.F. diag. back.    S
11. L.F. back, partner outside, diag. to wall.    S

*Contrary Body Movement.* C.B.M. on 1, 4, and 11. The 11th step is placed in C.B.M.P.

*Rise and Fall (Body).* Rise at end of 1 (N.F.R.); up on 2 and 3; lower at end of 3. Commence to rise at end of 4; continue to rise on 5 and 6, up on 7 (see note below); up on 8, 9, and 10; lower at end of 10.

*Body Sway.* Sway to L. on 2 and 3.

*Amount of Turn.* Make three-eighths turn to R. on the first three steps. Make a quarter between steps 4 and 5 and an eighth between steps 6 and 7.

*Footwork.* 1. T. H. 2. T. 3. T. H. 4. H. T. 5. T. 6. T. 7. T. 8. T. 9. T. 10. T. H. 11. T.

*General Notes.* If the man uses the slight flexing of the knees on step 7, the lady will soften her L. knee on step 7, straightening again as the R.F. moves back for the Lock Step. The L. heel should not lower to the floor.

When the man underturns the Tipple Chassé, as explained below the description of the man's steps, the lady will turn her head more to her L. and sway to the L. on steps 5, 6, 7. She will use only a slight rise on steps 5 and 6 and will lower on 7. Rise for the following Backward Lock Step will be: Commence to rise at end of 7; continue to rise on 8 and 9; up on 10; lower at end of 10. Footwork on step 7 will be: T. H. of L.F. and I.E. of T. of R.F.

## THE DOUBLE REVERSE SPIN
### Man

Originally a Waltz variation, this figure is now much used in the Quickstep. The name is rather misleading as there is no double spin, neither is it danced twice as its name might imply.

Commence facing the L.O.D. Finish facing diagonally to the wall, or down the L.O.D. if wishing to continue into another reverse movement.

1. L.F. forward, turning body to L.                                    S
2. R.F. to side, across L.O.D.                                         S
3, 4. Continue turning on ball of R.F. and close L.F.
    to R.F. without weight (toe pivot).                                QQ
   Then step forward with L.F. diag. to wall.                          S

*Contrary Body Movement.* C.B.M. on 1.

*Rise and Fall (Body).* Rise at end of 1; up on 2, 3, and 4. Lower at end of 4.

*Body Sway.* There is no sway.

*Amount of Turn.* Make a complete turn or slightly less on the whole figure. The turn must be gradual. Do not force the turn on the 1st step. Most of the "swing" of the turn should be felt as the L.F. is closing. Three-eighths of a turn should be made on the first 2 steps.

*Footwork.* 1. H. T. 2. T. 3. T. (both feet). 4. T. H. (R.F.).

*General Notes.* The Double Reverse Spin is usually preceded by the Quarter Turns, which should be turned to face the L.O.D. Follow with a Cross Chassé or Cross Swivel. If the figure is turned to finish on the L.O.D. go into any Reverse Figure.

A chart of this figure appears in the Waltz Section.


## THE DOUBLE REVERSE SPIN

### Lady

Commence backing the L.O.D.

1. R.F. back, turning body to L.                                       S
2. Close L.F. to R.F., turning on R. heel (Heel Turn).
   Finish facing L.O.D.                                                S

3. Continue turning on ball of L.F. and take a small step
   to the side and slightly back with R.F.　　　　　　Q
4. Still turning slightly, cross L.F. in front of R.F.　　Q
   Then step back R.F., diag. to wall.　　　　　　　　S
   *Contrary Body Movement.* C.B.M. on 1.
   *Rise and Fall (Body).* Rise slightly at end of 1 (N.F.R.); continue
   to rise on 2; up on 3 and 4. Lower at end of 4.
   *Body Sway.* There is no sway.
   *Amount of Turn.* Make a complete turn or slightly less on the
   whole figure. A half turn is made on the first 2 steps.
   *Footwork.* 1. T. H. 2. H. T. 3. T. 4. T. H.
   A chart and further notes appear in the Waltz Section.

# THE NATURAL SPIN TURN

## Man

The Spin Turn is in some respects a continuation of
the Natural Pivot Turn. It is most used in the Waltz.
A chart and fuller notes are included in the description
of the figure in that dance.

Commence facing diagonally to the wall.

1, 2, 3. First three steps of Natural Turn. Finish with
   back to L.O.D.　　　　　　　　　　　　　　　SQQ
4. L.F. back (medium-length step) and pivot half a turn
   to R. on the ball of the L.F. Keep R.F. in front in
   C.B.M. position.　　　　　　　　　　　　　　　S
5. R.F. forward, down L.O.D., body still turning to R.　S
6. L.F. to side and slightly back. Finish with back to centre
   diagonally.　　　　　　　　　　　　　　　　　S
   To continue, step back with R.F. into 5, 6, 7, and 8
   of Quarter Turns, or into the Reverse Pivot on R.F.
   *Contrary Body Movement.* C.B.M. on 1, 4, and 5. The 5th step
   is in C.B.M.P.
   *Rise and Fall (Body).* Rise at end of 1; up on 2 and 3. Lower
   at end of 3. Rise at end of 5; up on 6. Lower at end of 6.
   *Body Sway.* Sway to the R. on 2 and 3. No sway on actual spin.
   *Amount of Turn.* On steps 1 to 3 make three-eighths of a turn, a
   half-turn on 4, and three-eighths of a turn between steps 5 and 6.
   Less turn will be made on the pivot when taken at a corner.

*Footwork.* 1. H. T. 2. T. 3. T. H. 4. T. H. T. 5. H. T. 6. T. H. The turn is made on the ball of foot on step 4, with the heel in contact with the floor.

*General Notes.* In leading the Spin remember not to let the weight go too far back on 4.

## Lady

Commence backing diagonally to the wall.

| | |
|---|---|
| 1, 2, 3. First three steps of Natural Turn. | SQQ |
| 4. R.F. forward, and turn about half a turn to R. on the ball of R.F. with a pivoting action. | S |
| 5. Still turning, move the L.F. back and leftwards, down the L.O.D. | S |
| 6. Continue turning on ball of L.F. and take a small step diagonally forward with R.F. Body facing diag. to centre. | S |

To continue, step forward with L.F. into 5, 6, 7, 8 of Quarter Turns or into the Reverse Pivot.

*Contrary Body Movement.* C.B.M. on 1 and 4.

*Rise and Fall (Body).* Rise at end of 1 (N.F.R.); up on 2 and 3. Lower at end of 3. Rise at end of 5; up on 6. Lower at end of 6. The rise is taken from the ball of L.F. on 5.

*Body Sway.* Sway to L. on 2 and 3.

*Amount of Turn.* On steps 1 to 3 make three-eighths of a turn. Make a half a turn on step 4 and three-eighths of a turn between 5 and 6.

*Footwork.* 1. T. H. 2. T. 3. T. H. 4. H. T. 5. T. 6. T. H. Note: the moving of the L.F. leftwards at the end of the pivoting action will result in the R. heel leaving the floor and this heel will not lower again as it does when a back step, with C.B.M., is to follow.

*General Notes.* On the 6th step, the R.F. should brush lightly up to the L.F. before stepping diagonally forward.

## THE CHANGE OF DIRECTION

### Man

Originally a Foxtrot variation, this figure is now used frequently in the Quickstep as a lead into the Chassé Reverse Turn or the Progressive Chassé to R.

Commence facing diagonally to the wall. Finish facing diagonally to the centre.

1. L.F. forward, diag. to wall, body turning slightly to the L.   S
2. Slide the R.F. diag. forward, R. shoulder leading, with
   the R. toe pointing towards the L.O.D.   S
3. Turning on the ball of R.F. but with foot flat, brush L.F.
   to R.F. without weight, and with knees well relaxed.   S
4. L.F. forward, diag. to centre, across the body in C.B.M.P.   S

*Contrary Body Movement.* C.B.M. on 1 and 4. The 4th step is placed in C.B.M.P.

*Rise and Fall.* There is no rise.

*Body Sway.* Sway to the L. on 3.

*Amount of Turn.* Up to half a turn can be made on this figure, but normally a quarter turn is used in the Quickstep.

*Footwork.* 1. H. 2. I.E. of T. H. 3. I.E. of T. (L.F.). 4. H.

*General Notes.* When closing the L.F. keep pressure on the inside of the L. toe, to control the turn. It should be closed with the L. toe a little in advance of the R. toe. Avoid turning too much on the 1st step or the lead will be mistaken by the lady for that of a Zig-Zag. Precede with any Heel Pivot. Follow with the Chassé Reverse Turn or Progressive Chassé to R.


# THE CHANGE OF DIRECTION

## Lady

1. R.F. back, diag. to wall, body turning slightly to L.   S
2. L.F. diag. back, L. shoulder leading. Not a long step.   S
3. Turning on the ball of L.F., but with foot flat, brush R.F.
   to L.F. without weight and with knees well relaxed.   S
4. R.F. back, diag. to centre, across the body in C.B.M.P.   S

*Contrary Body Movement.* C.B.M. on 1 and 4. The 4th step is placed in C.B.M.P.

*Rise and Fall.* There is no rise.

*Body Sway.* Sway to R. on 3.

*Amount of Turn.* The same as in the man's steps.

*Footwork.* 1. T. H. 2. T., I.E. of T., H. 3. I.E. of T. (R.F.). 4. T.

*General Notes.* When the R.F. brushes up to the L.F., the R. toe will be level with the L. instep, not toe to toe.

# THE CROSS SWIVEL

## Man

A delightful variation for experienced dancers only. The steps are easy, but the figure requires good balance to dance effectively. A diagram appears on page 90.

Commence facing diagonally to the wall. Finish facing diagonally to the centre.

1. L.F. forward turning body to L.                                           S
2. Swivelling to L. on ball of L.F., close (or nearly close)
    R.F. to L.F. without weight.                               S
3. Forward R.F. outside partner.                                             S

*Contrary Body Movement.* C.B.M. on 1 and 3. The 3rd step is placed in C.B.M.P.

*Rise and Fall (Body).* There is no rise.

*Body Sway.* Sway to L. on 2.

*Amount of Turn.* Normally a quarter turn is made. It is possible to make up to half a turn.

*Footwork.* 1. H. 2. Pressure on T. of L.F. with foot flat, pressure on I.E. of T. of R.F. 3. H.

*General Notes.* A good Cross Swivel depends on the first step. This should be long and *bold*, with a confident swing to the L. L.F. should be kept quite flat, and when R.F. closes, balance will be assisted if it is kept slightly back and a few inches apart at the end of the turn. The pressure on the inside edge of R.F. will also assist the balance. Precede with the Quarter Turns, the Double Reverse Spin, or the Reverse Pivot. Follow with—

(a) The Running Finish. Transfer the weight back to the L.F. with a slight turn to the R., making this the first step of the Running Finish, counting SQQS or QQSS. See page 71.

(b) The "Fish Tail." This is described on page 89.

(c) Any advanced variation that is suitable.

## Lady

1. R.F. back, turning body to L.                                             S
2. Swivelling a quarter turn to L. on ball of R.F., close L.F.
    to R.F. without weight.                                 S
3. L.F. back, partner outside                                                S

*Contrary Body Movement.* C.B.M. on 1 and 3. The 3rd step is placed in C.B.M.P.

*Rise and Fall (Body).* There is no rise.
*Body Sway.* Sway to R. on 2.
*Amount of Turn.* The same as in the man's steps.
*Footwork.* 1. T. H. 2. H., then I.E. of T. of L.F. 3. T. Note that the heel of R.F. on step 1 does not lower until the turn is completed.
*General Notes.* If the L.F. closes to R.F. *slightly forward*, balance will be assisted and it will help to avoid hurrying into the 3rd step.

# THE RUNNING RIGHT TURN

## Man

The Running Right Turn is a composite figure, embracing the Natural Pivot Turn, followed by 1, 2, and 3 of a Foxtrot Natural Turn (danced SSS rhythm), and ended with the Running Finish.

This figure is best taken near a corner. The notes on page 87 should be read carefully.

Commence facing diagonally to the wall.

| | |
|---|---|
| 1, 2, 3, 4. Do the Natural Pivot Turn. Finish facing the L.O.D. (This amount of turn can be modified.) | SQQS |
| 5. R.F. forward, in C.B.M.P., turning body to R. | S |
| 6 L.F. to side, across the L.O.D. | S |
| 7. Continue turning on the ball of L.F. and step back with R.F., R. shoulder leading. | S |
| Now follow with the Running Finish— | |
| 8. L.F. back, turning body to the R., partner outside. | Q |
| 9. Small step to side and slightly forward with R.F., facing the *new* L.O.D. | Q |
| 10. L.F. forward, preparing to step outside partner, L. shoulder leading. | S |
| 11. R.F. forward, outside partner. | S |

*Contrary Body Movement.* C.B.M. on 1, 4, 5, 8, and 11. Steps 5, 8, and 11 are placed in C.B.M.P.
*Rise and Fall (Body).* Rise at end of 1; up on 2 and 3. Lower at end of 3. Rise at end of 5; up on 6 and 7. Lower at end of 7. Rise at end of 8; up on 9 and 10. Lower at end of 10.
*Body Sway.* Sway to the R. on 2 and 3; to the R. on 6 and 7; to the L. on 9 and 10.

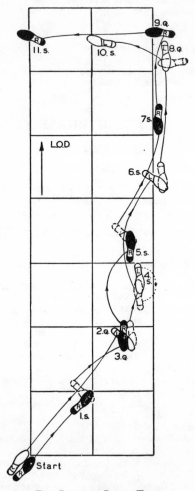

THE RUNNING RIGHT TURN
(Man)

86

*Footwork.* 1. H. T. 2. T. 3. T. H. 4. T. H. T. 5. H. T. 6. T. 7. T. H. 8. T. 9. T. 10. T. H. 11. H.

*Amount of Turn.* 1¾ turns to R. or less. Fuller details are given below.

There are four main alignments of the Running Right Turn, when the amount of turn used is as follows—

1. *Round one corner.* Make a half turn on the pivot; half turn on the Natural Turn; a quarter on the Running Finish to end down the new L.O.D.

2. *Across a corner.* Make three-eighths turn on the pivot; half turn on the Natural Turn to cut across the corner; three-eighths on the Running Finish to end down the new L.O.D.

3. *Round two corners.* Make a three-eighths turn on the pivot; three-eighths on the Natural Turn to end backing the new L.O.D.; a quarter on the Running Finish to end down the 3rd L.O.D.

4. *Along side of room.* Make a half turn on the pivot; a half turn on the Natural Turn; three-eighths turn on the Running Finish to end facing diagonally to centre. Follow, in this case, with a Fish Tail or a Quick Open Reverse Turn.

## THE RUNNING RIGHT TURN

### Lady

The Running Right Turn is a composite figure embracing the Natural Pivot Turn, followed by 1, 2, and 3 of a Foxtrot Natural Turn (danced SSS rhythm), and ended with the Running Finish.

This figure is best taken near a corner.

Commence with the back diagonally to the wall.

| | |
|---|---|
| 1, 2, 3, 4. Do the Natural Pivot Turn. Finish with back to L.O.D. | SQQS |
| 5. L.F. back, down L.O.D., turning body to the R. | S |
| 6. Close R.F. to L.F., turning on L. heel (Heel Turn). | S |
| 7. L.F. forward down L.O.D., preparing to step outside partner, L. shoulder leading. | S |
| 8. R.F. forward, outside partner, turning body to R. | Q |
| 9. L.F. to side. | Q |
| 10. R.F. back, down new L.O.D., R. shoulder leading. | S |

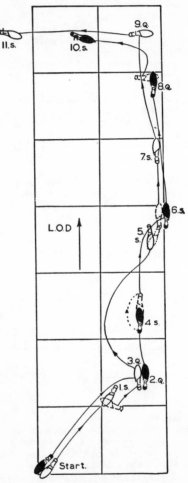

THE RUNNING RIGHT TURN
(Lady)

11. L.F. back, down new L.O.D., partner outside.                    S

*Contrary Body Movement.* C.B.M. on 1, 4, 5, 8, and 11. Steps 8 and 11 are placed in C.B.M.P.

*Rise and Fall (Body).* Rise at end of 1 (N.F.R.); up on 2 and 3. Lower at end of 3. Rise slightly at end of 5 (N.F.R.); continue to rise on 6; up on 7. Lower at end of 7. Rise at end of 8; up on 9 and 10. Lower at end of 10.

*Body Sway.* Sway to the L. on 2 and 3; to the L. on 6 and 7; to the R. on 9 and 10.

*Amount of Turn.* 1¾ turns to R. or less. Full details are given following the description of the man's steps.

*Footwork.* 1. T. H. 2. T. 3. T. H. 4. H. T. H. 5. T. H. 6. H. T. 7. T. H. 8. H. T. 9. T. 10. T. H. 11. T.

*General Notes.* The lady will use a "pivoting action" on the 4th step and step back with C.B.M. on step 5.


## THE FISH TAIL

### Man

The Fish Tail is one of the most popular standard variations in the Quickstep.

The most attractive position to commence it is diagonally to the centre (after a Cross Swivel). Finish facing diagonally to the wall. Another amalgamation is given in the general notes below. When taken from a Cross Swivel, the last step of the Cross Swivel becomes the first step of the Fish Tail.

Dance 1, 2 of the Cross Swivel. Finish facing diagonally to the centre and continue as follows—

1. R.F. forward, outside partner, diag. to centre.                    S
2. Move the L.F. slightly forward so that it is crossed (but not tightly) behind the R.F. Body commences to turn to R.                    Q
3. Move the R.F. forward and slightly to the R. Body now facing diag. to wall. Small step outside partner.                    Q
4. L.F. diag., forward, L. shoulder leading.                    Q
5. Cross R.F. behind L.F., but not tightly.                    Q
6. L.F. diag. forward.                    S

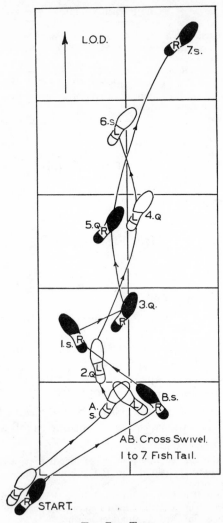

THE FISH TAIL
(Man)

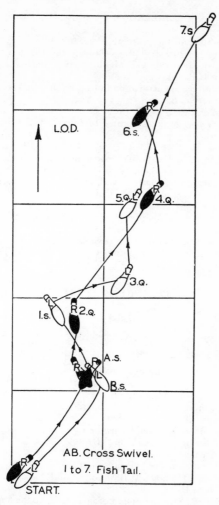

THE FISH TAIL
(Lady)

91

7. R.F. forward, outside partner. Diag. to wall.                    S
  Continue into Quarter Turns or any Natural figure.

*Contrary Body Movement.* C.B.M. on 1 and 7. Both of these steps
are placed in C.B.M.P.

*Rise and Fall (Body).* Rise at end of 1; remain up for steps 2 to
6. Lower at end of 6.

*Body Sway.* Sway to the R. on 2.

*Amount of Turn.* Make a quarter turn to R. between 1 and 3.
No more turn.

*Footwork.* 1. H. T.  2. T.  3. T.  4. T.  5. T.  6. T. H.  7. H.

*General Notes.* The Fish Tail can be danced at any time the man
has taken a step outside the lady with his R.F. It should be noted
that if he is facing diagonally to wall on this step, no turn will be
made on steps 1 to 3 of the Fish Tail.

Good amalgamations are—

(*a*) Quarter Turns. Double Reverse Spin, Cross Swivel, Fish
Tail.

(*b*) Natural Spin Turn, Progressive Chassé, Fish Tail.

(*c*) Open Impetus Turn, Wing, Closed Telemark, Fish Tail.
Rhythm: SQQSSS SQQ SSS SQQQQSS.

# THE FISH TAIL

## Lady

Dance 1, 2 of the Cross Swivel. Finish backing
diagonally to the centre. Continue as follows—

1. L.F. back, partner outside. Diag. to centre.                    S
2. Draw the R.F. back across the front of L.F. (feet slightly
     apart). Turn body to the R.                                   Q
3. L.F. back, and slightly to side (small step) now backing
     diag. to wall.                                                Q
4. R.F. diag. back, R. shoulder leading.                           Q
5. Cross L.F. in front of R.F. (not tightly).                      Q
6. R.F. diag. back.                                                S
7. L.F. back, diag. to wall. Partner outside.                      S

*Contrary Body Movement.* C.B.M. on 1 and 7. Both are also
placed in C.B.M.P.

*Rise and Fall (Body).* Rise at end of 1; remain up for steps 2 to 6.
Lower at end 6.

*Body Sway.* Sway to the L. on 2.

*Amount of Turn.* Make a quarter turn to R. between 1 and 3.

*Footwork.* 1. T.  2. T.  3. T.  4. T.  5. T.  6. T. H.  7. T.

# THE QUICK OPEN REVERSE TURN
## Man

This is an advanced standard variation that is most attractive to dance, but it looks very untidy if it is danced badly. The man's steps are similar to the first 4 steps of a Foxtrot Reverse Turn, but danced in a quicker rhythm and with the lady outside on the 3rd step.

Suggested entries and endings are given in the general notes.

Commence facing the L.O.D.

1. L.F. forward, turning body to L.                                    S
2. R.F. to side, across the L.O.D.                                     Q
3. Continue turning on the ball of R.F. and step back with
      L.F., partner outside.                                            Q
4. R.F. back, down the L.O.D. (See notes below.)                       S

*Contrary Body Movement.* C.B.M. on 1 and 4. The 3rd step is placed in C.B.M.P.

*Rise and Fall (Body).* Rise at end of 1; up on 2 and 3. Lower at end of 3.

*Body Sway.* Sway to L. on 2 and 3.

*Amount of Turn.* A half turn is made on the first three steps.

*Footwork.* 1. H. T. 2. T. 3. T. H. 4. T.

*General Notes.* In leading into this figure a strong swing forward on the first step (L.F.) should be used. This will result in an early rise and give that lightness which is necessary for the speed of the figure. The 3rd step should be rather "cut under" the body in C.B.M. Position, and this will accentuate the sway.

*Amalgamations.* The figure may be danced after a Heel Pivot, after a Reverse Pivot and after a Double Reverse Spin. It can also be danced after a step forward on R.F. outside partner. A good amalgamation would be: Impetus Turn (or underturn a Spin Turn to end backing diagonally to centre against the L.O.D.), Progressive Chassé, ending with R.F. forward, outside partner and moving diagonally to centre; Quick Open Reverse.

*Endings—*

(*a*) The Progressive Chassé. The last step of the Quick Open Reverse will be the first step of the Progressive Chassé.

(*b*) A Four Quick Run. (See page 95).

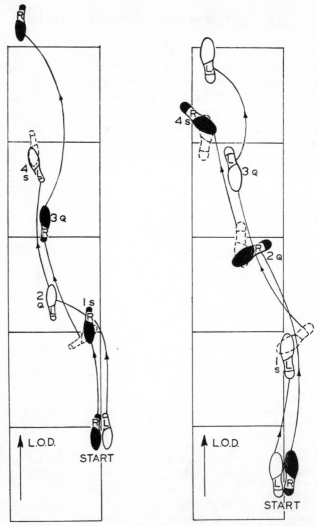

QUICK OPEN REVERSE TURN ENDING WITH A REVERSE PIVOT
(Lady)

(c) Use a Reverse Pivot on the 4th step. Turn three-eighths on the pivot and follow with the Cross Swivel. Turn a half on the pivot and follow with another Quick Open Reverse or any Reverse figure.

# THE QUICK OPEN REVERSE TURN

## Lady

This is a most attractive advanced variation.

For suitable entries and endings please refer to the amalgamations given in the notes on the man's steps.

Commence backing the L.O.D.

| | |
|---|---|
| 1. R.F. back, turning body to L. | S |
| 2. Small step to side and slightly forward with L.F. | Q |
| 3. R.F. forward, down the L.O.D. Outside partner. | Q |
| 4. L.F. forward, in line with man. | S |

*Contrary Body Movement.* C.B.M. on 1 and 4. The 3rd step is placed in C.B.M.P.

*Rise and Fall (Body).* Rise at end of 1 (N.F.R.); up on 2 and 3. Lower at end of 3.

*Body Sway.* Sway to R. on 2 and 3.

*Amount of Turn.* A half turn is made on the first 3 steps.

*Footwork.* 1. T. H. 2. T. 3. T. H. 4. H.

*General Notes.* Please refer to the amalgamations given in the man's notes.

# THE FOUR QUICK RUN

## Man

This is one of the most popular and useful variations in the Quickstep. It is used after a step back on R.F., and the Quick Open Reverse Turn is one of the best entries. Other suggested entries and amalgamations are given below. Commence backing the L.O.D.

| | |
|---|---|
| 1. R. F. back, turning to the L. | S |
| 2. Step to side and slightly forward, along the L.O.D. with L.F. Facing wall. | Q |

3. Small step forward with R.F. outside partner. Diag. to
   wall.                                                        Q
4. L.F. diag. forward.                                         Q
5. Cross R.F. behind L.F. (not tightly).                       Q
6. L.F. diag. forward.                                         S
7. R.F. forward, outside partner, diag. to wall.              S

*Contrary Body Movement.* C.B.M. on 1 and 7. The 3rd and 7th
steps are placed in C.B.M.P.

*Rise and Fall (Body).* Rise at the end of 1, remain up for steps 2
to 6. Lower at end of 6.

*Body Sway.* There is no sway.

*Amount of Turn.* Make three-eighths of a turn to L. between
1 and 2.

*Footwork.* 1. T.H.T. 2. T. 3. T. 4 T. 5 T. 6 T.H.. 7. H.

*General Notes.* In all steps the feet are pointing diagonally to wall,
but the figure will tend to travel more sideways, along the L.O.D.,
with the body facing between the wall and diagonally to wall.

*Best Amalgamations—*

(*a*) Quick Open Reverse Turn into Four Quick Run.

(*b*) Three steps of the Chassé Reverse Turn into Four Quick
Run (for average dancers).

(*c*) Dance a Progressive Chassé. End with R.F. forward,
outside partner diag. to wall. Then—

Bring L.F. near to R.F. and "Flicker" the feet as
described on page 97.                                          S
L.F. back, towards centre, partner outside.                   S
R.F. back, towards centre, partner in line.                   S
With a slight turn to L. rise to toes and continue
with the Four Quick Run.                              QQQQSS

## Lady

### Commence facing the L.O.D.

1. L.F. forward, turning to L.                                 S
2. Step to side R.F. with back towards wall.                  Q
3. Still turning slightly, step back L.F. (small step) partner
   outside. Diag. to wall.                                     Q
4. R.F. diag. back.                                           Q
5. Cross L.F. in front of R.F. (not tightly).                 Q
6. R.F. diag. back.                                          S
7. L.F. back, diag. to wall, partner outside.                S

*Contrary Body Movement.* C.B.M. on 1 and 7. The 3rd and 7th
steps are placed in C.B.M.P.

*Rise and Fall (Body).* Rise at the end of 1. Remain up for steps 2 to 6. Lower at end of 6.

*Body Sway.* There is no sway.

*Amount of Turn.* Three-eighths turn to L. between 1 and 3.

*Footwork.* 1. H.T. 2. T. 3. T. 4. T. 5. T. 6. T.H. 7 T.

*General Notes.* See notes under man's steps.

## THE FLICKER

### Man

The Flicker is not a standard figure in the Quickstep, but the action of "flickering" the feet is extensively used by advanced dancers. The action of the feet in the Flicker is the same as the twist in the original Charleston. The following description gives the actual twists of the feet in relation to the music.

|  | Count |
|---|---|
| 1. R.F. forward, outside partner. Feet straight. | 1 |
| 2. Relax knees, and twist toes inwards. | 2 |
| 3. Point L.F. forwards, and twist toes outwards. | 3 |
| 4. Twist toes inwards. | 4 |

Now step back with L.F. with partner outside into any usual ending. (See amalgamation below.)

A more effective type of twist is the Double Flicker, in which the feet are twisted twice in the same musical time as the single Flicker.

|  | Count |
|---|---|
| 1. R.F. forward, outside partner. | 1 |
| 2. Relax knees, and twist toes inwards. | 2 |
| 3. Point L.F. forward, and twist toes outwards. | 3 |
| 4. Twist toes inwards. | "and" |
| 5. Twist toes outwards. | "a" |
| 6. Twist toes inwards. | 4 |

7. ⎫ As the L.F. is being taken backwards with the
8. ⎭ partner stepping outside, quickly twist the R.F. *only* outwards and then inwards, counting "and" "a," the L.F. stepping back on the 1st beat of the next bar.

The count of "and" and "a" indicates the splitting of a beat. Thus movements 3, 4 and 5 will occupy the 3rd beat, and movements 6, 7 and 8 will be made on the 4th beat. The Flicker for the lady is the normal opposite to the man's step.

## THE TELEMARK
## THE OPEN TELEMARK
## THE IMPETUS TURN
## THE OPEN IMPETUS TURN

These four standard variations are frequently used in Quickstep, Waltz, and Foxtrot. The method of dancing them is the same in each dance, but the rhythm is changed to suit the tempo of the music.

Descriptions of each variation are given in the section of the book to which the figure originally belonged. In the following notes, the alternative rhythms are given, together with notes on the best way of amalgamating them into each dance.

### The Telemark (Closed)

This was originally a Foxtrot variation, and a description will be found on page 187.

*Rhythm.* When danced in the Quickstep the Rhythm is SSSS. It can be danced SQQS, but it is not advisable for beginners to attempt this quicker rhythm. When danced in the Waltz, each step has one beat. Other technical details are unaltered.

*Amalgamation (Quickstep).* The Telemark is usually danced when the man is stepping outside the lady on her *left* side. If it is used directly following the Quarter Turns, the lady may mistake the lead for that of a Double Reverse Spin. A good amalgamation is—Open Impetus Turn, Wing, Telemark, Fish Tail. Complete rhythm would be: SQQSSS SQQ SSSS QQQQSS. A good Waltz amalgamation would be—Open Telemark, Wing, Telemark (see Waltz Section).

## The Open Telemark

This is more popular in Waltz and Foxtrot, and descriptions will be found on pages 138 and 191. A diagram is given on page 142.

*Rhythm.* When danced in Quickstep the rhythm is SSSS. The quicker rhythm of SQQS could be used by advanced dancers. Other technical details are unaltered.

*Amalgamation.* Open Telemark, Open Natural Turn, ending with an Impetus Turn or Running Finish. Complete rhythm for the latter amalgamation would be: SSS SQQ SQQS.

## The Impetus Turn

This was originally a Foxtrot variation, and a description will be found in the Foxtrot Section on page 184.

*Rhythm.* When danced in the Quickstep the rhythm, including the first 3 steps of the Natural Turn, would be: SQQSSSS. When danced in the Waltz, each step has one beat. Other technical details remain unaltered.

*Amalgamation.* The Impetus Turn can be used in place of the Natural Spin Turn in both the Quickstep and Waltz. Many good dancers prefer this figure to the Natural Spin Turn, especially in the Waltz. It should be noted, however, that only five-eighths of a turn is made on the Impetus Turn so that if it is danced along the sides of the room, the last step will be taken diagonally to centre against the L.O.D. A Progressive Chassé into a Quick Open Reverse Turn could follow.

## The Open Impetus Turn

This was originally a Waltz variation, and a description will be found in the Waltz Section on page 144.

*Rhythm.* When danced in the Foxtrot the rhythm is SQQS. When danced in the Quickstep the rhythm, including the first 3 steps of the Natural Turn, would be: SQQSSSS. A good amalgamation is included in the notes on the Telemark on the preceding page. Other technical details remain unaltered.

*Amalgamation. Foxtrot.* Dance 1, 2, 3 of Natural Turn.     SQQ
Follow with the Open Impetus Turn finishing in Pro-
   menade Position moving diag. to the centre.            SQQS
Turn the lady square and go into steps 2, 3, 4 of a
   Feather-step, taken diag. to centre.                   QQS
Follow with a Reverse figure.

## SUGGESTED QUICKSTEP AMALGAMATIONS

1. Quarter Turns—Cross Chassé—Lock Step—
Natural Turn at corner, continuing into the Tipple
Chassé to R. and a Lock Step down the new L.O.D.

2. Quarter Turns—Zig-Zag—Quarter Turn to R.
ending with the Progressive Chassé—Lock Step—
Natural Spin Turn.

3. Quarter Turns—Change of Direction—Chassé
Reverse Turn—Cross Chassé—Lock Step.

4. Natural Turn with Hesitation (extra S)—Progressive Chassé to R.—Backward Lock with Running
Finish—Natural Spin Turn—Progressive Chassé.

5. Quarter Turns—Double Reverse Spin—Cross
Swivel—Fish Tail.

6. Natural Spin Turn, underturning to face diag.
to wall—R.F. back into a Progressive Chassé, moving
towards centre and end facing diag. to centre—
Quick Open Reverse Turn—Four Quick Run—
Running Right Turn.

7. Natural Spin Turn—Reverse Pivot to face
L.O.D. or diag. to centre—Quick Open Reverse—
Progressive Chassé—Lock Step.

8. Quarter Turns—Zig-Zag, Backward Lock and
Running Finish—Natural Spin Turn—Progressive
Chassé—Flicker—Check back to a Four Quick Run.

9. Quarter Turns—Change of Direction—Progressive Chassé to R. overturning to end backing diag. to
centre—Six Quick Run.

# SECTION II

## THE WALTZ

THE steps of the modern Waltz are probably the easiest of the present-day dances to learn. Steps, however, are by no means the most important factor in modern dancing, and the dancer must pay very careful attention to several other details before the delightful rhythmic swing and lilt of the dance can be captured. The correct use of Contrary Body Movement resulting in an easy swing of the body into the turns, the correct relaxing and straightening of the knees, in conjunction with the Rises, and the controlled use of Body Sways, all play their part in producing a dance that is continuously flowing with a rhythmic, lilting movement. These points are dealt with under their respective headings and should be studied after the basic principles are understood.

### General Notes

*Time.* 3/4. Three beats in a bar.

*Tempo.* Music should be played at 31 bars a minute.

*Basic Rhythm.* There are no "Slows" and "Quicks" in the Waltz. Count 1, 2, 3. The first beat is accented.

*Figures.* The Closed Changes, Natural Turn, Reverse Turn, Hesitation Change, Outside Change, Natural Spin Turn, Reverse Corté, Back Whisk from Reverse Corté, Double Reverse Spin, Outside Spin, Open Telemark and Cross Hesitation, The Wing, Open Impetus Turn, Whisk and Chassé, Drag

Hesitation and Backward Lock, Progressive Chassé to R., Turning Lock, Weave from P.P.

For the novice there are but three basic figures in the Waltz, and the normal construction of the Waltz is made from these figures only. It must be understood that a complete circle in six steps is never danced, the construction being based on diagonal lines which require only three-eighths of a turn to be made on each three steps. Normally no turn is made on a Closed Change step, this figure being used to change the dancer from a Natural Turn to a Reverse Turn or *vice versa*.

The following method of practising is described for a man dancer. A lady should use the steps and directions that are the normal opposite.

The beginner should learn the Closed Change step first, commencing it first with the R.F. and then the L.F., and dancing it continuously in a straight line down the room. It is advisable, even at this early stage, to acquire some knowledge of the Rise and Fall, and even the Body Sway, as these details are easy to remember and will prove helpful when the turns are attempted.

Learn the Natural Turn next, and practise the two figures in this way—

Dance the Closed Change Steps when moving down the sides of the room. When near a corner, dance a full Natural Turn (six steps), finishing facing the next Line of Dance. Continue with the Change Steps to the next corner.

This, of course, is based on the assumption that the room is not very large. In a very large room it would be advisable to use one part of the room only, as it is only possible to regain the Line of Dance after a Natural Turn by departing from the normal lines of the dance.

The Reverse Turn should be learned next, and then

an attempt should be made to amalgamate the three figures in the following manner.

Commence facing diagonally to the wall.

Step forward with the R.F. and dance 1, 2, 3 of the Natural Turn. Finish with the back to the L.O.D.

Step backward with the L.F. and dance 4, 5, 6 of the Natural Turn. Finish facing diagonally to the centre.

Step forward with the R.F. and dance the Closed Change, making no turn.

Step forward with the L.F. diagonally to the centre and dance 1, 2, 3 of the Reverse Turn. Finish with the back to the L.O.D.

Step backward with the R.F. and dance 4, 5, 6 of the Reverse Turn. Finish facing diagonally to the wall.

Step forward with the L.F. and dance the Closed Change, making no turn, and still facing diagonally to the wall.

This is the same as the commencing position and the amalgamation can be repeated.

Remember that only a Natural Turn is danced round a corner. If the corner is acute, two complete turns could be danced. Care must be taken to adjust the amount of turn on each part so that the new L.O.D. is faced from a diagonal position. If this has not been done, a slight turn on a Closed Change will give the diagonal position from which all turns should be commenced. Remember, however, that a Closed Change commencing with the L.F. may only be turned to the L., and a R.F. Closed Change only turned to the R.

Naturally, an experienced dancer, with the use of variations, will not have to bother too much about the diagonal positions, but the beginner will be advised to pay careful attention to this point in the early stages.

Further details of how to amalgamate the basic figures with standard variations are given with the descriptions of the latter. The following notes should be very carefully read.

## Special Notes

*Contrary Body Movement.* The Contrary Body Movement on the first step of each turn must not be exaggerated. On the forward part of any turning figure it is much more important to feel a *forward swing*, rather than a conscious twist of the body on the first step. It should be remembered that the first step is the *strong* step, and from the swing of this step it should be possible to take a wide second step without further effort. The closing of the feet on the third step must be controlled by keeping the inside of the closing foot pressed firmly to the floor. It should never be lifted and allowed to close quickly.

*Knees.* When taking the weight on the first step of any turn or Closed Change allow the knee to relax slightly. This will prevent any jar or stop in the movement of the body, and also tend to make the subsequent rise softer.

*Sway.* The Sway is quite pronounced in turning figures in the Waltz.

## Footwork and Rises

In the Waltz, as in other dances, there is no foot rise on the backward half of any turn or in a Closed Change when danced backward. Any attempt to rise early with the feet or body would seriously impede the flow of the movement. The rise must be gradual and felt throughout the turns, the full extent of the rise not being reached until the feet are closed on the third step. The notes on Rise and Fall given in the early part of the book should be studied with care.

The correct footwork on the backward turns is also of great importance. The first step of a turn is taken back on to the toe, gradually lowering to the heel as the second step moves to the side. When the second step is in position—to the side—the heel of the first step is released from the floor and even then it must not be raised abruptly.

A common fault with more advanced dancers is found in the movement of the foot when it commences to close for the third step. In the Natural Turn (lady) when the L.F. commences to close for the third step it is most important that the Left toe, or inside edge of the toe, should be pressed firmly to the floor. Many advanced dancers allow the toe to leave the floor when the second step is in position, which results in the L.F. leaving the floor before closing for the third step. Much control is lost in this way and the result will be ugly footwork and very often the closing foot will pass the supporting foot instead of closing firmly to it.

Another important point should be observed when the feet are closed in the Closed Changes and the Natural and Reverse Turns. If a *forward* step is to follow, the normal footwork is for the heel of the foot supporting the weight to lower to the floor and then come up again as the forward step is taken. To do this, however, will often result in the weight being dropped back just at the moment when a good forward swing is required. The heel of the supporting foot should *always lower lightly* and be raised again immediately, but it is not absolutely essential that it should actually touch the floor. It is better that the heel should not quite touch the floor than to let it drop heavily, thus retarding the swing into the following step. To step forward without lowering the supporting heel at all would, of course, be equally bad.

# THE CLOSED CHANGE

## (From Natural Turn to Reverse Turn)

### Man

In the normal construction of the Diagonal Waltz the Closed Change is taken either diagonally to the centre or diagonally to the wall. There is, however, no reason at all why it cannot be danced straight down the L.O.D. for the purpose of practice.

The Natural Turn finishes facing diagonally to the centre. Commence the Closed Change from this position.

1. R.F. forward.
2. L.F. to side and slightly forward.
3. Close R.F. to L.F.
   Then go forward with L.F. into a Reverse Turn.
   *Contrary Body Movement.* Slight C.B.M. on 1.
   *Rise and Fall (Body).* Commence to rise at end of 1; continue to rise on 2 and 3. Lower at end of 3.
   *Body Sway.* Sway to R. on 2 and 3.
   *Footwork.* 1. H. T. 2. T. 3. T. H.
   *General Notes.* The beginner should endeavour to place the 2nd step *to the side*, as the swing on the first step will result in the correct position being achieved quite naturally. Care must be taken not to allow this step to move too much forward, otherwise alignment will be lost and the following turn made more difficult.
   It is permissible to make a slight turn to R. on this figure.

### Lady

1. L.F. back.
2. R.F to side and slightly back.
3. Close L.F. to R.F.
   Then go back with R.F. into a Reverse Turn.
   *Contrary Body Movement.* Slight C.B.M. on 1.
   *Rise and Fall (Body).* Commence to rise at end of 1 (N.F.R.); continue to rise on 2 and 3. Lower at end of 3.
   *Footwork.* 1. T. H. 2. T. 3. T. H.
   *Body Sway.* Sway to L. on 2 and 3.

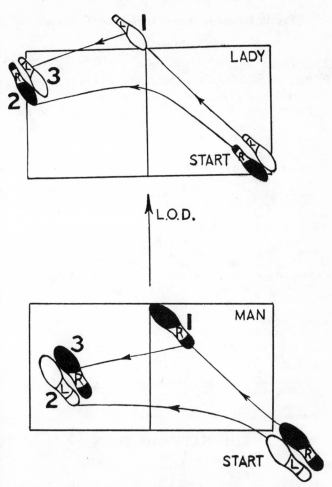

THE CLOSED CHANGE
(From Natural to Reverse Turn)

# THE CLOSED CHANGE

## (From Reverse Turn to Natural Turn)

### Man

This figure is similar to the Closed Change from Natural to Reverse Turns, described and illustrated on pages 106 and 107.

The Reverse Turn finishes facing diagonally to the wall. Commence the Closed Change from this position.

1. L.F. forward.
2. R.F. to side and slightly forward.
3. Close L.F. to R.F.
   Then go forward with R.F. into a Natural Turn.
   *Contrary Body Movement.* Slight C.B.M. on 1.
   *Rise and Fall (Body).* Commence to rise at end of 1; continue to rise on 2 and 3. Lower at end of 3.
   *Body Sway.* Sway to L. on 2 and 3.
   *Footwork.* 1. H. T. 2. T. 3. T. H.
   *General Notes.* The action for this Closed Change is the same as for a Closed Change from Natural Turn to Reverse Turn, and the general notes thereon apply also to this figure. A slight turn to the Left may be made.

### Lady

1. R.F. back.
2. L.F. to side and slightly back.
3. Close R.F. to L.F.
   Then go back with L.F. into a Natural Turn.
   *Contrary Body Movement.* Slight C.B.M. on 1.
   *Rise and Fall (Body).* Commence to rise at end of 1 (N.F.R.); continue to rise on 2 and 3. Lower at end of 3.
   *Body Sway.* Sway to R. on 2 and 3.
   *Footwork.* 1. T. H. 2. T. 3. T. H.

# THE NATURAL TURN

## Man

This figure is described as it is used in the normal construction of the Diagonal Waltz. Beginners

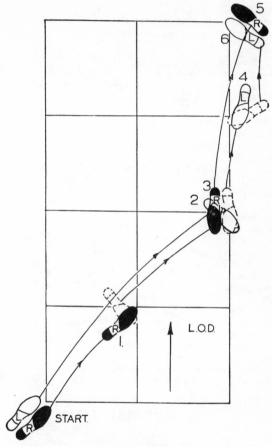

THE NATURAL TURN
(Man)

should read carefully the introductory notes on this dance.

Commence facing diagonally to the wall. Finish facing diagonally to the centre.

1. R.F. forward, turning body to R.
2. Long step to side with L.F. across the L.O.D.
3. Continue turning on ball of L.F. and close R.F. to L.F. (Back now to L.O.D.).
4. L.F. back, turning body to R.
5. R.F. to side, on the same L.O.D.
6. Close L.F. to R.F.

*Contrary Body Movement.* C.B.M. on 1 and 4.

*Rise and Fall (Body).* Commence to rise at end of 1; continue to rise on 2 and 3. Lower at end of 3. Commence to rise at the end of 4 (N.F.R.); continue to rise on 5 and 6. Lower at end of 6. Remember to relax the knee slightly on steps 1 and 4. This will soften the movement considerably.

*Body Sway.* Sway to R. on 2 and 3. Sway to L. on 5 and 6.

*Footwork.* 1. H. T. 2. T. 3. T. H. 4. T. H. 5. T. 6. T. H.

*Amount of Turn.* Make three-eighths of a turn on each three steps.

*General Notes.* It will be noticed in the description and in the diagram that the 2nd step of the forward turn is longer than the 2nd step (step No. 5) of the backward turn. This is owing to the fact that the person on the *outside* of a circle will necessarily have a longer distance to travel. For the same reason, there is a continuation of the turn on the ball of the foot on the 2nd step of the forward turn. On the backward turn the 5th step is placed with the R. foot turned outwards—pointing in the finishing direction. There will be only a slight body turn as the L. foot closes on 6.

Most good dancers tend to underturn on 4, 5, 6, of the Natural Turn, thus making slightly less than three-eighths of a turn. The following Closed Change is then turned slightly to the R.

# THE NATURAL TURN

## Lady

This figure is described as it is used in the normal construction of the Diagonal Waltz. Beginners should read carefully the introductory notes on this dance.

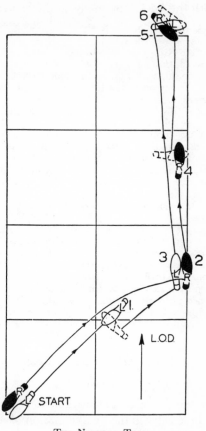

THE NATURAL TURN
(Lady)

111

Commence with the back diagonally to the wall. Finish with the back diagonally to the centre.

1. L.F. back, turning body to R.
2. R.F. to side, across the L.O.D.
3. Close L.F. to R.F., body now facing L.O.D.
4. R.F. forward, turning body to R.
5. Long step to side with L.F. on the same L.O.D.
6. Continue turning on ball of L.F. and close R.F. to L.F.

*Contrary Body Movement.* C.B.M. on 1 and 4.

*Rise and Fall (Body).* Commence to rise at end of 1 (N.F.R.); continue to rise on 2 and 3. Lower at end of 3. Commence to rise at end of 4; continue to rise on 5 and 6. Lower at end of 6. Remember to relax the knee slightly on steps 1 and 4. This will soften the movement considerably.

*Body Sway.* Sway to L. on 2 and 3; sway to R. on 5 and 6.

*Amount of Turn.* Make three-eighths of a turn on each three steps.

*Footwork.* 1. T. H. 2. T. 3. T. H. 4. H. T. 5. T. 6. T. H.

*General Notes.* It will be noticed in the description and in the diagram that the 2nd step of the forward part of the turn is longer than the 2nd step of the backward part of the turn. This is owing to the fact that the person on the *outside* of a circle will necessarily have a longer distance to travel. For the same reason there is a continuation of the turn on the ball of the foot on the 2nd step of the forward turn. On the backward half the 2nd step is placed with R. foot turned outwards, pointing down the L.O.D. There will only be a slight body turn as the L. foot closes on 3. Note also that the lady should use a good forward swing on the 4th step to assist the turn.

## THE REVERSE TURN

### Man

Beginners should read the introductory notes on this dance. These explain the amalgamation of steps which lead into this figure.

Commence facing diagonally to the centre. Finish facing diagonally to the wall.

1. L.F. forward, turning body to L.
2. Long step to side with R.F., across the L.O.D.

3. Continue turning on ball of R.F. and close L.F. to R.F. (Back now to L.O.D.)
4. R.F. back, turning body to L.
5. L.F. to side, on the same L.O.D.
6. Close R.F. to L.F.

*Contrary Body Movement.* C.B.M. on 1 and 4.

*Rise and Fall (Body).* Commence to rise at end of 1; continue to rise on 2 and 3. Lower at end of 3. Commence to rise at end of 4 (N.F.R.); continue to rise on 5 and 6. Lower at end of 6.

*Body Sway.* Sway to L. on 2 and 3; sway to R. on 5 and 6.

*Amount of Turn.* Make three-eighths of a turn on each three steps.

*Footwork.* 1. H. T. 2. T. 3. T. H. 4. T. H. 5. T. 6. T. H.

*General Notes.* The notes at the foot of the description of the Natural Turn, regarding the length of the 2nd step of each part of the turn, and the continuation of the turn on the ball of the foot, apply also to the Reverse Turn. (Diagram overleaf.)


# THE REVERSE TURN

## Lady

Commence with the back diagonally to the centre. Finish with the back diagonally to the wall.

1. R.F. back, turning body to L.
2. L.F. to side, across the L.O.D.
3. Close R.F. to L.F. (Body now facing L.O.D.)
4. L.F. forward, turning body to L.
5. Long step to side with R.F., on the same L.O.D.
6. Continue turning on ball of R.F. and close L.F. to R.F.

*Contrary Body Movement.* C.B.M. on 1 and 4.

*Rise and Fall (Body).* Commence to rise at end of 1 (N.F.R.); continue to rise on 2 and 3. Lower at end of 3. Commence to rise at end of 4; continue to rise on 5 and 6. Lower at end of 6.

*Body Sway.* Sway to R. on 2 and 3; sway to L. on 5 and 6.

*Amount of Turn.* Make three-eighths of a turn on each three steps.

*Footwork.* 1. T. H. 2. T. 3. T. H. 4. H. T. 5. T. 6. T. H.

*General Notes.* The notes at the foot of the description of the Natural Turn, regarding the length of the 2nd step of each part of the turn, and the continuation of the turn on the ball of the foot, apply also to the Reverse Turn. (Diagram overleaf.)

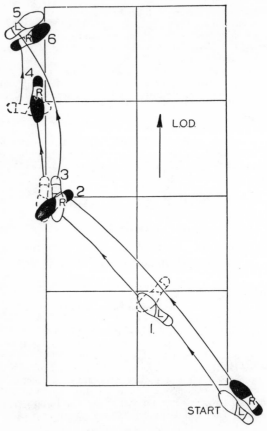

THE REVERSE TURN
(Man)

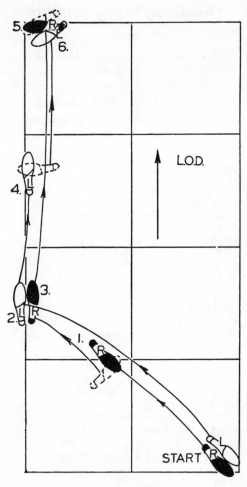

THE REVERSE TURN
(Lady)

## THE HESITATION CHANGE

### Man

A most useful and attractive variation which is used as a link between 1, 2, and 3 of the Natural Turn, and 1, 2, and 3 of the Reverse Turn.

Commence facing diagonally to the wall and dance 1, 2, and 3 of the Natural Turn. Finish with the feet together, and with the back to the L.O.D. Continue with—

4. L.F. back, turning body to R.
5. Pull R.F. back to the L.F. (about six inches apart), turning on L. heel. Finish facing diagonally to centre, weight on R.F.
6. Hesitate, and begin slowly to brush the L. heel past the R. toe. Then go forward with L.F. into a Reverse Turn.

*Contrary Body Movement.* C.B.M. on 1 and 4.

*Rise and Fall (Body).* Normal rise is used on steps 1, 2, 3 of the Natural Turn. There is no rise on steps 4, 5, 6.

*Body Sway.* Sway to R. on 2 and 3; sway to L. on 5 and 6.

*Amount of Turn.* Three-eighths of a turn on 1, 2, and 3. Three-eighths of a turn on 4, 5, and 6. Less turn may be made at a corner.

*Footwork.* 1. H. T. 2. T. 3. T. H. 4. T. H. 5. H., I.E. of foot, whole foot. 6. I.E. of T. of L.F.

*General Notes.* Care should be taken to "Pull" the R.F. back firmly on step 5, with pressure first on the heel and then on the inside edge of the R. foot. Advanced dancers will add greatly to the attraction of the figure by pulling the R. foot back very slowly, so that it takes nearly two beats to assume its position at the side of the L.F. As the L.F. brushes to R.F. the body will commence to turn to the L., thus maintaining a continuous movement of the body in spite of the hesitation effect of the figure. Both ways are correct. It is a matter of personal expression.

## THE HESITATION CHANGE

### Lady

This figure forms a useful link between 1, 2, and 3 of the Natural Turn, and 1, 2, and 3 of the Reverse Turn.

Commence with the back diagonally to the wall and dance 1, 2, and 3 of the Natural Turn. Finish with the feet together, facing the L.O.D.

4. R.F. forward, turning body to R.
5. L.F. to side, across the L.O.D. and let the R.F. begin to close towards it.
6. Let R.F. brush up to L.F. and hesitate with weight on L.F. Then step back on R.F. and go into the Reverse Turn

*Contrary Body Movement.* C.B.M. on 1 and 4.

*Rise and Fall (Body).* Normal rise is used on steps 1, 2, 3 of the Natural Turn. There is no rise on steps 4, 5, and 6 although the 5th step is taken on the ball of L.F.

*Body Sway.* Sway to L. on 2 and 3. Sway to R. on 5 and 6.

*Amount of Turn.* Three-eighths of a turn on 1, 2, and 3; three-eighths of a turn on 4, 5, and 6. Less turn may be made at a corner.

*Footwork.* 1. T. H. 2. T. 3. T. H. 4. H. T. 5. T. H. 6. I.E. of T. (R.F.).

*General Notes.* When the R.F. brushes to L.F. on the 6th step the R. toe should be level with the L. instep.

It should be noted that the 5th step is taken well across the L.O.D. with no continuation of the turn on the ball of L.F. as the R.F. brushes. The action of the man's Pull-step brings this foot across the L.O.D. instead of in the position shown for the 5th step of a Natural Turn (on the same L.O.D.).

# THE OUTSIDE CHANGE

## Man

The Outside Change is one of the most useful figures in the Waltz especially in a crowded room. When it has been found impossible to complete the full amount of turn on the first part of the Natural Turn so that these 3 steps end backing diagonally to centre, the Outside Change is easily the best figure to employ.

Dance steps 1, 2, 3 of a Natural Turn and end backing diagonally to centre, then—

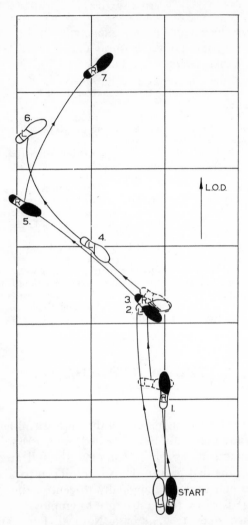

THE OUTSIDE CHANGE

(Man)

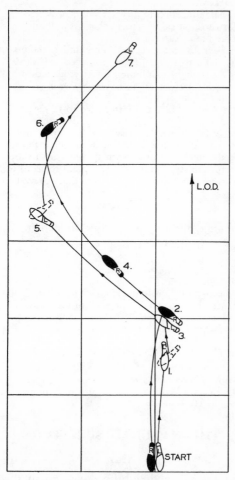

THE OUTSIDE CHANGE
(Lady)
119

1. L.F. back, diag. to centre. Lady in line.
2. R.F. back, turning slightly to L.
3. L.F. to side and slightly forward.
4. R.F. forward, outside partner, diag. to wall and make this the first step of a Natural Turn.

*Contrary Body Movement.* C.B.M. on 2 and 4 (the first step of the next Natural Turn). The 4th step is placed in C.B.M.P.

*Rise and Fall (Body).* Commence to rise at end of 1 (N.F.R.); continue to rise on 2; up on 3. Lower at end of 3.

*Body Sway.* There is no sway.

*Amount of Turn.* Make a quarter turn to L. between 2 and 3.

*Footwork.* 1. T. H. 2. T. 3. T. H. 4. H.

*General Notes.* The gradual rise between steps 1 and 3 makes the figure far more attractive to dance. Remember to draw the L.F. back with the heel in contact with the floor as it moves back for the 3rd step. On step 3 the L.F. will point diag. to wall but the body should be facing between wall and diag. to wall.

## Lady

Commence facing diagonally to centre after steps 1, 2, 3 of a Natural Turn. Then—

1. R.F. forward, in line with man.
2. L.F. forward, turning slightly to L.
3. R.F. to side and slightly back, now backing diag. to wall.
4. L.F. back, diag. to wall, partner outside, and make this the first step of a Natural Turn.

*Contrary Body Movement.* C.B.M. on 2 and 4. The 4th step is placed in C.B.M.P.

*Rise and Fall (Body).* Commence to rise at end of 1; continue to rise on 2; up on 3. Lower at end of 3.

*Body Sway.* There is no sway.

*Amount of Turn.* Make a quarter turn to L. between 2 and 3.

*Footwork.* 1. H. T. 2. T. 3. T. H. 4. T.

## THE NATURAL SPIN TURN

### Man

The Spin Turn is a delightful variation in the Waltz rhythm. Commence facing diagonally to the wall.

# Finish with the back diagonally to the centre.

1, 2, 3. First three steps of the Natural Turn. Finish with back to L.O.D.

4. L.F. back (medium-length step) and pivot half a turn to R. on the ball of the L.F. Keep R.F. in front in C.B.M. position whilst pivoting.

5. R.F. forward, down L.O.D., body still turning to R.

6. L.F. to side and slightly back, Finish with back to centre diagonally.

To continue, step back R.F. into 4, 5, 6 of Reverse Turn, making only a quarter of a turn. Finish facing diag. to wall.

*Contrary Body Movement.* C.B.M. on 1, 4, and 5. The 5th step is held in C.B.M.P.

*Rise and Fall (Body).* Commence to rise at end of 1; continue to rise on 2 and 3. Lower at end of 3. Rise at end of 5; up on 6. Lower at end of 6.

*Body Sway.* Sway to R. on 2 and 3. No sway on actual spin.

*Amount of Turn.* On steps 1 to 3 make three-eighths of a turn, half a turn on 4, and three-eighths of a turn between steps 5 and 6.

*Footwork.* 1. H. T. 2. T. 3. T. H. 4. T. H. T. 5. H. T. 6. T. H. Note: although the footwork on 4 is given as T. H. T. the turn is made on the ball of L.F. with the heel in contact with the floor.

*General Notes.* The Spin Turn should be used by beginners at the corners of the room, when three-eighths of a turn is made on 4 and a quarter turn between 5 and 6.

The Spin is a convenient step to use preceding a Double Reverse Spin or an Open Telemark. When the man commences the 4, 5, and 6 of the Reverse Turn which follows the Spin, his back is diagonally to the centre instead of down the L.O.D. Thus he can end this turn facing the L.O.D., which is the most attractive position to commence the Double Reverse Spin.

Two good amalgamations are—

(a) Natural Spin Turn followed by 4, 5, and 6 of the Reverse Turn. Finish facing the L.O.D.

Double Reverse Spin; finish facing diagonally to the wall. Closed Change, followed by a Natural Turn.

(b) Natural Spin Turn, followed by 4, 5, and 6 of the Reverse Turn. Finish facing the L.O.D.

Double Reverse Spin. Finish facing the L.O.D. Follow with an advanced figure such as the Open Telemark or Drag Hesitation.

(c) The Turning Lock may follow the Spin Turn.

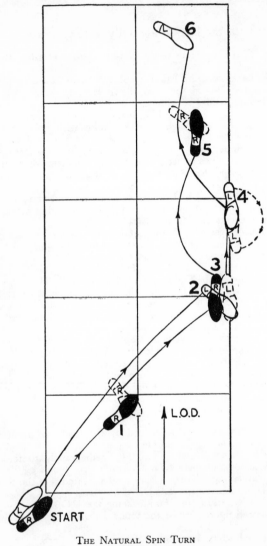

THE NATURAL SPIN TURN
(Man)

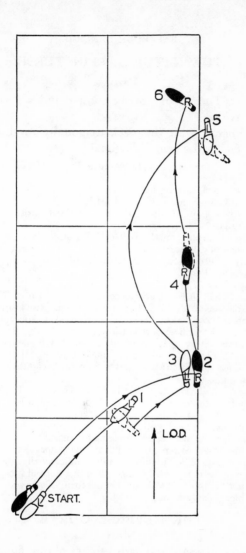

THE NATURAL SPIN TURN
(Lady)

## THE NATURAL SPIN TURN
### Lady

The Spin Turn is one of the most popular variations in the Waltz.

Commence with the back diagonally to the wall. Finish facing the centre diagonally.

1, 2, 3. First three steps of the Natural Turn. Finish facing the L.O.D.

4. R.F. forward, turning half a turn to R. with a pivoting action. The L. leg is not held in C.B.M.P.

5. Still turning, move the L.F. back and leftwards, down the L.O.D.

6. Continue turning on the ball of L.F., and take a small step diagonally forward with R.F., body facing centre diagonally. To continue, step forward with L.F. into 4, 5, 6 of Reverse Turn.

*Contrary Body Movement.* C.B.M. on 1 and 4.

*Rise and Fall (Body).* Commence to rise at end of 1 (N.F.R.); continue to rise on 2 and 3. Lower at end of 3. Rise at the end of 5; up on 6. Lower at end of 6. The rise is taken from the ball of L.F. on 5. The L. heel does not lower.

*Body Sway.* Sway to L. on 2 and 3. No sway on actual spin.

*Amount of Turn.* On steps 1 to 3 make three-eighths of a turn. Make half a turn between 4 and 5, and three-eighths of a turn between 5 and 6.

*Footwork.* 1. T. H. 2. T. 3. T. H. 4. H. T. 5. T. 6. T. H. Note the footwork on 4. Turn is made on the ball of R.F. and the heel does not lower as the 5th step is taken.

*General Notes.* On the 6th step, the R.F. should brush lightly up to the L.F. before stepping diagonally forward.

It is important to remember that the lady does not use a true pivot on step 4. The "pivoting action" indicates that the weight is held over the R.F. slightly longer than in a normal turn, but the L.F. is not held in C.B.M.P. during the turn. To do so is, in fact, impossible. (Diagram on page 123.)

## THE REVERSE CORTÉ
### Man

The steps of man and lady differ in this figure, the man making a hesitation movement whilst the lady turns with two extra steps. The Reverse Corté can be made much more attractive by departing from the orthodox amount of turn. Particulars of this are given under the general notes.

Commence facing diagonally to the centre and dance 1, 2, and 3 of the Reverse Turn. Finish with the back to the L.O.D.

1. R.F. back, body turning to L.
2. Turning on the ball or heel of the R.F., close L.F. to R.F. Finish with back diag. to centre against the L.O.D., weight on R.F.
3. Hesitate.
4. L.F. back, diag. to centre against L.O.D. (partner outside).
5. R.F. to side (no turn) getting into line with lady.
6. Close L.F. to R.F.
   Then go forward with R.F., diag. to wall, into a Natural Turn.
   *Contrary Body Movement.* C.B.M. on 1, slight C.B.M. on 4. The 4th step of the Corté is taken back in C.B.M.P.
   *Rise and Fall (Body).* Rise on 2; up on 3. Lower at end of 3. Commence to rise at end of 4 (N.F.R.); continue to rise on 5 and 6. Lower at end of 6.
   *Body Sway.* Sway to R. on 2 and 3. Sway to L. on 5 and 6.
   *Amount of Turn.* Three-eighths of a turn on preceding Reverse Turn. Three-eighths of a turn on first three steps of Corté. No turn on 4, 5, and 6.
   *Footwork.* 1. T. H. T. 2. Toes (both feet). 3. T. H. (R.F.). 4. T. H. 5. T. H. 6. T. H.
   *Note.* If the turn is made on the R. heel on 2 the footwork of the first three steps will be: 1. T. H. 2. H. (L.F.), then toes both feet. 3. T. H. (R.F.). Even when the turn is made on the ball of foot on 2, the feet should be kept flat, and the rise is taken on the 2nd beat in both cases.
   *General Notes.* The amount of turn given above is sometimes the easiest way for the novice to dance this figure. A more general method is to make half a turn on 1, 2, and 3 of the Corté, and then turn about an eighth of a turn to the R. on 4, 5, and 6 to regain the diagonal position necessary for the following Natural Turn.
   Advanced dancers make this figure much more attractive by overturning the first three steps, making five-eighths of a turn,

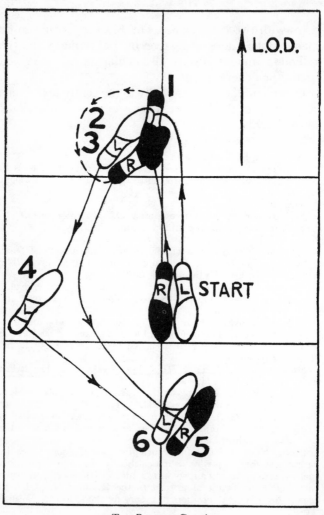

THE REVERSE CORTÉ
(Man)

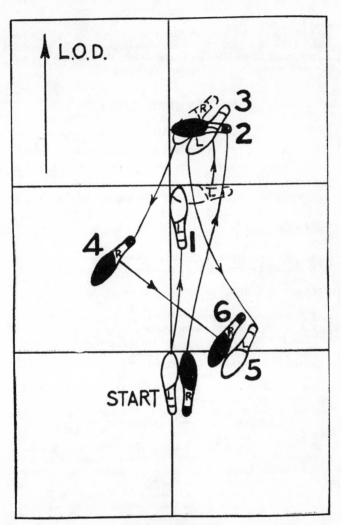

THE REVERSE CORTÉ
(Lady)

127

so that the 4th step is taken back diagonally to the *wall* against the L.O.D. A quarter turn must then be made on 4, 5, and 6 to regain the diagonal position necessary for the following Natural Turn. See page 129 for the Back Whisk ending.

# THE REVERSE CORTÉ

## Lady

The Reverse Corté is an attractive variation in which the lady takes a step to the side and then closes whilst the man is hesitating.

Commence with the back diagonally to the centre and dance 1, 2, and 3 of the Reverse Turn. Finish facing the L.O.D.

1. L.F. forward turning body to L.
2. Small step to side with R.F., on same L.O.D. and still turning to L.
3. Close L.F. to R.F. Finish facing diagonally to centre against the L.O.D.
4. R.F. forward, outside partner.
5. L.F. to side (no turn) partner getting into line.
6. Close R.F. to L.F.

Then go back with L.F., diag. to wall, into a Natural Turn.

*Contrary Body Movement.* C.B.M. on 1, slight C.B.M. on 4. The 4th step of the Corté is taken forward in C.B.M.P.

*Rise and Fall (Body).* Commence to rise at end of 1; continue to rise on 2 and 3. Lower at end of 3. Commence to rise at end of 4; continue to rise on 5 and 6. Lower at end of 6. It should be noted that the lady rises slightly earlier than the man on this figure.

*Body Sway.* Sway to L. on 2 and 3. Sway to R. on 5 and 6.

*Amount of Turn.* Three-eighths of a turn is made on the preceding Reverse Turn. Three-eighths of a turn on first three steps of the Corté. No turn on 4, 5, and 6.

*Footwork.* 1. H. T. 2. T. 3. T. H. 4. H. T. 5. T. 6. T. H.

*General Notes.* When the man overturns the first three steps of the Corté (described in notes on man's steps) the lady must take her 2nd step slightly across the L.O.D., and continue to turn as the 3rd step closes. (Diagram on p. 127.)

# THE BACK WHISK
## (From a Reverse Corté)
## Man

The Back Whisk is a very popular ending to the first three steps of the Reverse Corté and is described from this position. Other entries to the Back Whisk are given in the General Notes below.

Commence facing diagonally to centre and dance 1, 2, and 3 of a Reverse Turn. Finish backing the L.O.D.

1, 2, 3. Dance steps 1, 2, 3 of a Reverse Corté. Finish backing diag. to centre against the L.O.D.

4. L.F. back, partner outside.

5. R.F. diag. back. Commence to turn the lady to P.P. at the end of the step.

6. Cross L.F. behind R.F. Man and lady now in P.P.

Now step forward R.F., along the L.O.D. in P.P. and follow with the Chassé. p. 147.

*Contrary Body Movement.* C.B.M. on 1 and 4 (slight). Step 4 is placed in C.B.M.P.

*Rise and Fall (Body).* Commence to rise at end of 1 (N.F.R.) continue to rise on 2; up on 3; lower at end of 3. Commence to rise at end of 4 (N.F.R.); continue to rise on 5; up on 6; lower at end of 6.

*Body Sway.* Sway to R. on 2 and 3. Sway to L. on 5 and 6.

*Amount of Turn.* Make three-eighths turn to L. on steps 1, 2, 3 of the Reverse Corté. No turn on the Back Whisk.

*Footwork.* 1, 2, 3 (See notes on Reverse Corté footwork). 4. T. H. 5. T. 6. T. H.

*General Notes.* It is advisable to use the Footwork of T.H. on step 1 of the Reverse Corté, making the turn on the heel of the R.F. Do not drop backwards too quickly on the Back Whisk. Lower the L. heel softly on step 6 and release it again as the R.F. moves forward in P.P. for the following Chassé, details of which will be found on p. 147.

The Back Whisk can be danced after steps 1, 2, 3 of a Natural Turn, when the man will turn his body up to three-eighths of a turn to R. between steps 4 and 5. When turn is used, step 5 (R.F.) will be placed to side and slightly back instead of diag. back.

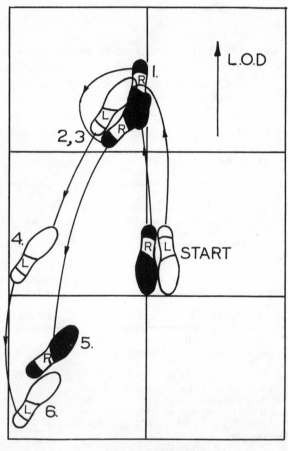

THE BACK WHISK
(From a Reverse Corté)
(Man)

130

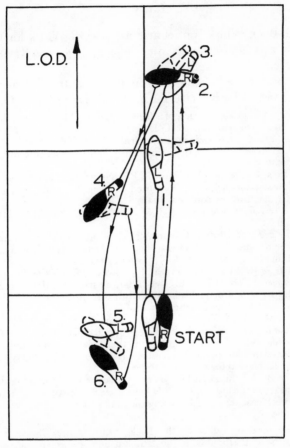

THE BACK WHISK
(From a Reverse Corté)
(Lady)

# THE BACK WHISK
## (From a Reverse Corté)
## Lady

The Back Whisk is of course a Forward Whisk for the lady and is often used after steps 1, 2, 3 of a Reverse Corté.

Commence backing diagonally to centre and dance 1, 2, and 3 of a Reverse Turn. Finish facing the L.O.D.

1, 2, 3. Dance steps 1, 2, 3 of a Reverse Corté. Finish facing diag. to centre against the L.O.D.

4. R.F. forward, outside partner, turning body to R.

5. L.F. to side, with body facing centre and commencing to turn to P.P.

6. Cross R.F. behind L.F. Now in P.P. facing diag. to centre.

Now step forward L.F., along the L.O.D. in P.P. and follow with the Chassé, turning square to man. See p. 150.

*Contrary Body Movement.* C.B.M. on 1 and 4. Step 4 is placed in C.B.M.P.

*Rise and Fall (Body).* Commence to rise at end of 1; continue to rise on 2 and 3; lower at end of 3. Commence to rise at end of 4; continue to rise on 5; up on 6; lower at end of 6.

*Body Sway.* Sway to L. on 2 and 3. Sway to R. on 5 and 6.

*Amount of Turn.* Make three-eighths of a turn to L. on steps 1, 2, 3 of the Reverse Corté. Make an eighth turn to R. between steps 4 and 5 and an eighth between 5 and 6.

*Footwork.* 1. H. T. 2. T. 3. T. H. 4. H. T. 5. T. 6. T. H.

*General Notes.* When dancing steps 4, 5, 6 of The Back Whisk, it is better style to tend to underturn the body, thus avoiding the tendency to turn outwards too much on step 6. The head may turn to the R. on step 6.

The Back Whisk can be danced after steps 1, 2, 3 of a Natural Turn, when the lady will usually have to turn more between steps 4 and 6. Please see notes following the man's steps.

The normal ending to the Back Whisk is the Chassé from Promenade Position with the lady turning square to the man. This is described on p. 150.

The Wing and the Weave from Promenade Position are two attractive but more advanced endings.

# THE DOUBLE REVERSE SPIN

## Man

This figure is rather misnamed as it is not a spin, nor is it necessary to dance it twice. The man does two steps and a "toe pivot" whilst the lady does four steps. It should only be attempted by advanced dancers.

The commencing position and the amount of turn depend on the preceding figure. It is described below as a complete turn. Commence facing the L.O.D.

|  |  | Beats |
|---|---|---|
| 1. | L.F. forward, turning body to L. | 1 |
| 2. | R.F. to side, across the L.O.D. | ½ |
| "and" | Continue turning on ball of R.F. and close L.F. to R.F. Keep weight on R.F. and finish facing approximately to outside wall. | ½ |
| 3. | Continue turning on ball of R.F. to face the L.O.D. Then step forward with L.F. into next figure. | 1 |

*Note.* Although the man has actually only two steps and a pivot on the R. toe, the exact timing of each part of the turn has been given, as it is necessary for the man to accelerate the closing of the L.F. to assist the lady's turn.

*Contrary Body Movement.* C.B.M. on 1.

*Rise and Fall (Body).* Rise at end of 1; up on 2 and 3. Lower at end of 3.

*Body Sway.* There is no sway.

*Amount of Turn.* Three-quarters, seven-eighths or a complete turn may be made.

*Footwork.* 1. H. T. 2. T. 3. T. (L.F.) then T. H. (R.F.).

*General Notes.* Positions from which this figure can be taken and the amount of turn used are—

(*a*) *The Easiest Amalgamation.* With R.F. do a Closed Change to centre diagonally. Double Reverse Spin, making only three-quarters of a turn to finish facing the wall diagonally. Forward with L.F. into a Closed Change or the Whisk.

(*b*) Closed Change commencing with R.F. as above. Double Reverse Spin finishing facing L.O.D. Follow with another Double Reverse Spin to face diagonally to wall and so into the Whisk.

(*c*) *The Best Amalgamation.* Do the Natural Spin Turn, 1 to 6. Finish with back diagonally to centre.

Now do 4, 5, and 6 of Reverse Turn, making three-eighths of a turn to finish facing L.O.D.

Double Reverse Spin, making a complete turn. Follow with:

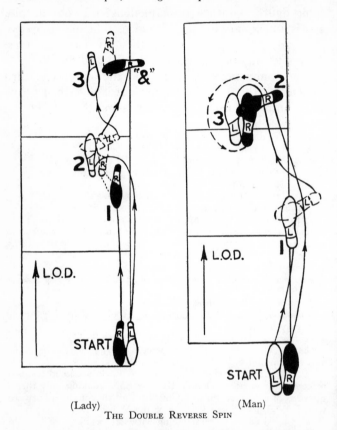

(Lady)                              (Man)
THE DOUBLE REVERSE SPIN

(1) Open Telemark, Cross Hesitation and Outside Spin;     (2) The Drag Hesitation and Backward Lock.

Amalgamations (a) and (b) could be danced following the Hesitation Change, instead of the R.F. Closed Change.

# THE DOUBLE REVERSE SPIN

## Lady

Commence with the back to the L.O.D. (See notes on the man's steps.)

|   |   | Beats |
|---|---|---|
| 1. | R.F. back, turning body to L. | 1 |
| 2. | Close L.F. to R.F., turning on R. heel. Finish facing L.O.D. Weight on L.F. | ½ |
| "and" | Continue turning on ball of L.F. as R.F. is moved to the side and slightly back. Finish with back diagonally to wall. | ½ |
| 3. | Still turning, cross L.F. in front of R.F. Finish with back to L.O.D. | 1 |
|   | Then step back with R.F. into next figure. | |

*Contrary Body Movement.* C.B.M. on 1.

*Rise and Fall (Body).* Rise slightly at end of 1 (N.F.R.); continue to rise on 2; up on 3 and 4. Lower at end of 4.

*Body Sway.* There is no sway.

*Amount of Turn.* Please see notes at the foot of the description of the man's steps.

*Footwork.* 1. T. H. 2. H. T. 3. T. 4. T. H.

*General Notes.* The lady will notice that she has four steps to dance in three beats of music. It is most important for her to get the acceleration on the 2nd step (Heel Turn) so that the *2nd and 3rd steps* are the quick ones. The 4th step must be firm and controlled, with the balance kept well over it, to enable the following step to be taken with ease.

Some advanced men dancers delay the speed of the turn. The lady will then use the rhythm of 1, 2, 3 "and", or one beat, one beat, half beat, half beat.

When the Double Reverse Spin is ended diagonally to wall, the lady should be backing towards wall on the 3rd step.

# THE OUTSIDE SPIN

## Man

This is a difficult variation, but is both useful and attractive. The man's steps are similar to those of the

Natural Spin Turn, but he leads his partner outside him on 1. It is usually danced after the hesitation on the 3rd step of the Reverse Corté.

The commencing position depends on the preceding

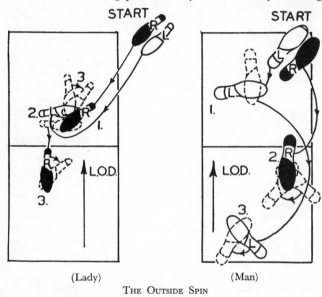

(Lady)    (Man)

THE OUTSIDE SPIN

figure. It is described below as following the 3rd step of the Reverse Corté, so that the commencing position will be facing diagonally to the wall.

1. Very small step back with L.F., partner outside, with the toe turned in, and pivot three-eighths of a turn to R. to face against the L.O.D.
2. R.F. forward, outside partner, still turning to the R.
3. Step to side L.F. with body facing diag. to centre, and then continue turning on ball of L.F. until body faces diag. to wall. The L.F. will then be directly behind the R.F.

To continue, step forward R.F. into a Natural Turn.

*Contrary Body Movement.* C.B.M. on 1 and 2.

*Rise and Fall (Body).* Rise at end of 2; up on 3. Lower at end of 3.

*Body Sway.* There is no sway.

*Amount of Turn.* A complete turn is made between 1 and 3.

*Footwork.* 1. T. H. T. 2. H. T. 3. T. H.

*General Notes.* Care should be taken to make the 1st step very small and it is better to *slip* this foot into position with firm pressure on it. The weight should be kept well forward as the step is taken. The position of the 3rd step is also important. If too much turn is made between the 2nd and 3rd steps there will be a stop in the flow of the movement before entering the following Natural Turn.

The Outside Spin may be underturned, and this type of Outside Spin is usually taken after a Drag Hesitation. Three-quarters of a turn is made, and the 3rd step will be placed to the side and slightly back, with the body backing diag. to centre. The following step will be a step *back* with R.F., into 4, 5, 6 of a Reverse Turn. The Turning Lock could follow this Outside Spin.

The Outside Spin can be danced in the Quickstep. The rhythm would be: SSS or QQS. The Quarter Turns would follow the Outside Spin.

## THE OUTSIDE SPIN

### Lady

This is an advanced variation, and difficult for the lady to do neatly. The lady's steps of this figure are entirely different from the Natural Spin Turn. It is usually danced after the 3rd step of the Reverse Corté, and is described from this position.

Commence with the back diagonally to the wall.

1. R.F. forward, outside partner, body turning to R.
2. Turning on ball of R.F., close L.F. to R.F. The weight should not be taken on to L.F. until body is facing the wall.
3. Continue turning on ball of L.F. and take a small step forward on R.F. between partner's feet.

*Note.* As the R.F. (3) is moving forward, both man and lady are still turning. The weight is not taken on to the R.F. until the lady's body is backing the L.O.D. She will continue to turn, so that by the time she is backing diagonally to the wall, her R.F. is forward and across the body in C.B.M.P. To continue, step back with the L.F. into a Natural Turn.

*Contrary Body Movement.* C.B.M. on 1. The lady turns into C.B.M.P. on 3.

*Rise and Fall (Body).* Commence to rise at end of 1; continue to rise on 2; up on 3. Lower at end of 3.

*Body Sway.* There is no sway.

*Amount of Turn.* A complete turn is made between 1 and 3. See also notes on the man's steps. When the Outside Spin is underturned the lady's 3rd step will be diagonally forward as in the Natural Spin Turn (6th step). The following step will be a step *forward* with L.F. into 4, 5, 6 of the Reverse Turn.

*Footwork.* 1. H. T. 2. T. 3. T. H.

*General Notes.* The lady must be careful not to take the small step forward on R.F. (3rd step) too quickly, otherwise she will be obstructed by the man's R. toe.

# THE OPEN TELEMARK

## (With Cross Hesitation Finish)

### Man

The Open Telemark is adapted from the Telemark figure, which is described in the Foxtrot Section. The term "Open" indicates that the figure is finished in Promenade Position. Many advanced variations are taken from the Open Telemark, but the normal finish is described below.

Commence facing diagonally to the centre, which is the easiest position.

1. L.F. forward, diag. to centre, turning body to L.
2. R.F. to side, across the L.O.D.
3. Continue turning on ball of R.F. until body is facing towards outside wall, and step to side and slightly forward with L.F. (Now in P.P. See note below.)

Follow with Cross Hesitation—
1. R.F. forward, diag. to wall in P.P., body still facing wall.
2. Close L.F. to R.F., turning body slightly to L.
3. Hesitate. (Body now facing diagonally to wall.) To continue, step back with L.F. diag. to centre against the L.O.D. (partner outside) into 4, 5, and 6 of Natural Turn danced with *no turn*, or an Outside Spin, or step forward with L.F. into a Closed Change or Whisk.

*Contrary Body Movement.* C.B.M. on 1 of Open Telemark. The 1st step of the Cross Hesitation is in C.B.M.P.

*Rise and Fall (Body).* Open Telemark: rise at end of 1; up on 2 and 3. Lower at end of 3. Cross Hesitation: commence to rise at end of 1; continue to rise on 2 and 3. Lower at end of 3.

*Body Sway.* Open Telemark: Sway to L. on 2. No sway on the Cross Hesitation.

*Amount of Turn.* Turn of man and lady differs in these figures. Open Telemark: man turns three-quarters of a turn, the body turning slightly less. Cross Hesitation: man turns an eighth of a turn with the body.

*Footwork.* Open Telemark: 1. H. T. 2. T. 3. T. H. Cross Hesitation: 1. H. T. 2. Toes (both feet). 3. T. H. (R.F.).

*General Notes.* As the man continues to turn on his second step of the Open Telemark, he must guide the lady by applying pressure with the *base* of his R. hand on her L. *side*. He must endeavour to indicate that *he* is turning to Promenade Position and that she is not to continue the turn with him. The man's L.F. should be pointing diagonally to wall on the 3rd step. His body is facing the wall. On the first step of the Cross Hesitation the R.F. is pointing diagonally to wall.

A more attractive way of dancing the Cross Hesitation is to make a quarter turn to the L. on 1, 2, and 3, so that the following 4th step of the Natural Turn is commenced with the man stepping back with the L.F. diagonally to the wall against the L.O.D. He must then turn a quarter turn to the R. on 4, 5, and 6 of the Natural Turn. A Back Whisk may follow the Cross Hesitation.

Note that when more turn is to be made on the Cross Hesitation, or if the Wing variation is to follow, the 3rd step of the Open Telemark should be placed to the side *and slightly back*.

Entries (a), (b), and (c) given in the notes on the Double Reverse Spin, may be used as entries to the Open Telemark.

The Cross Hesitation may be danced diagonally to centre after an Open Impetus Turn.

# OPEN TELEMARK

## (With Cross Hesitation Finish)

### Lady

The Open Telemark can be commenced backing the L.O.D. or backing diagonally to the centre. It is described from the latter position.

1. R.F. back, diag. to centre, turning body to L.
2. Close L.F. to R.F., turning on R. heel (Heel Turn). Finish facing the L.O.D.
3. R.F. diag. forward in P.P., R. shoulder leading. Follow with Cross Hesitation—

1. L.F. forward, across the body in P.P., turning body to L.
2. R.F. to side, still turning to get square to partner.
3. Close L.F. to R.F.

To continue, step forward with R.F. outside partner into 4, 5, and 6 of Natural Turn, etc. (See man's notes.)

*Contrary Body Movement.* C.B.M. on 1 of Open Telemark. C.B.M. and C.B.M.P. on the 1st step of Cross Hesitation.

*Rise and Fall (Body).* Open Telemark: rise slightly at end of 1 (N.F.R.); continue to rise on 2; up on 3. Lower at end of 3. Cross Hesitation: commence to rise at end of 1; continue to rise on 2 and 3. Lower at end of 3.

*Body Sway.* Open Telemark: sway to R. on 2. Cross Hesitation: sway to the L. on 2, 3.

*Amount of Turn.* Turn of lady and man differs in this figure. Open Telemark: three-eighths of a turn between 1 and 2, with a slight body turn to L. on 3. Cross Hesitation: three-eighths of a turn to L.

*Footwork.* Open Telemark: 1. T. H. 2. H. T. 3. T. H. Cross Hesitation: 1. H. T. 2. T. 3. T. H.

*General Notes.* The R. shoulder lead on 3 of the Open Telemark will tend to keep the position compact, a desirable feature. On this step the lady may turn her head to the R. to face the direction of the 3rd step, or may leave it in the normal position. It is a matter of personal taste.

The Wing ending to the Open Telemark is described on page 144.

# THE WING

## Man

This is an advanced variation that has become very popular. The steps for the man are similar to the Cross Hesitation, but no rise is made. The man makes a slight turn to the L., while the lady walks round him to his L. side.

Dance 1, 2, and 3 of the Open Telemark, ending in Promenade Position. In this case, the 3rd step of the Open Telemark is to the side and *back* slightly across the L.O.D. Continue as follows—

1. R.F. forward and across the body in P.P., with the body turning to the L. R.F. should be pointing down the L.O.D. and body facing diag. to wall.
2. With the weight on R.F. let body turn slightly to L. to face the L.O.D. and L.F. commences to close.
3. L.F. closes to R.F. without weight, and at the same time turn the R.F. and body to face diag. to centre.
   Now step forward L.F., outside the lady on her L. side, into: (a) Closed Telemark; (b) Double Reverse Spin; (c) a Progressive Chassé to R...

*Contrary Body Movement.* The 1st step is taken in C.B.M.P

*Rise and Fall.* There is no rise and no body sway.

*Amount of Turn.* Up to a quarter turn to L. may be made.

*Footwork.* 1. H. 2. 3. Pressure on T. of R.F. with foot flat, and pressure on I.E. of T. of L.F.

*General Notes.* In leading this figure, the man must keep a slight pressure with his R. hand on the lady's L. side, and definitely lead her to his L. side. The hold should be loosened slightly, but complete contact with partner should not be lost.

The man may end the Wing facing the L.O.D. but the diag. to centre position will be found more natural.

The Wing is also danced after the Open Impetus Turn and the Whisk. A diagram appears on page 142.

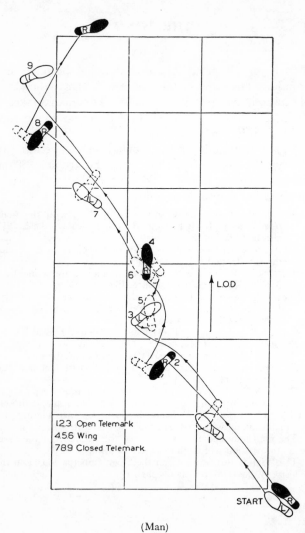

123 Open Telemark
456 Wing
789 Closed Telemark

START

LOD

(Man)

142

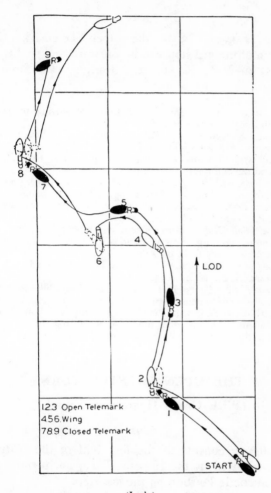

12.3 Open Telemark
4.5.6. Wing
7.8.9 Closed Telemark

L.O.D

START

(Lady)

143

## THE WING

### Lady

Dance 1, 2, and 3 of the Open Telemark. The position of the 3rd step will be Forward and slightly to the R. in P.P., R. shoulder leading. Continue as follows—

1. L.F. forward in P.P. facing diag. to centre, turning to the L., and begin to walk round partner.
2. Small step forward with R.F., facing centre. (Now in front of man but still slightly in P.P.)
3. Small step forward with L.F., facing against the L.O.D., and outside the man on his L. side.
   Step back with R.F., with the man outside on the L., and go into any ending described in the notes on the man's steps.

*Contrary Body Movement.* The 1st and 3rd steps are taken in C.B.M.P. Slight C.B.M. is used on 1.

*Rise and Fall (Body).* Commence to rise at end of 1; continue to rise on 2; up on 3. Lower at end of 3.

*Body Sway.* Sway to L. on 2 and 3.

*Amount of Turn.* Up to a half turn to L. may be made.

*Footwork* 1. H. T. 2. T. 3. T. H.

*General Notes.* If the man ends facing diagonally to centre the lady will continue to turn another eighth to L. as she steps back with the R.F., but she should not actually swivel on her L.F. The head may be turned to the L. or R. during the Wing. If turned to the L. the position is more easily kept compact.

## THE OPEN IMPETUS TURN

### (With Cross Hesitation Finish)

### Man

This figure consists of the first half of the Natural Turn, followed by the Impetus Turn, but turning out to Promenade Position on the last step.

Commence the Natural Turn diagonally to the wall.

1 to 3. Dance 1, 2, and 3 of the Natural Turn. Finish with the back to L.O.D.

4. L.F. back, down L.O.D., turning body to the R.

5. Close R.F. to L.F. turning on the L. heel (Heel Turn). Finish with weight on R.F. ready to step diag. to centre, and beginning to turn the lady to P.P.

6. L.F. diag. forward in P.P., L. shoulder leading. (L.F. is pointing diag. to centre, body facing the L.O.D.)

Continue with the Cross Hesitation as follows—

1. R.F. forward, in P.P., diag. to centre.

2. Close L.F. to R.F. without weight, turning lady square.

3. Hesitate.

Continue by stepping back with L.F. (partner outside) diag. to wall against the L.O.D., and do 4, 5, and 6 of the Natural Turn, making a quarter turn to the R. to finish facing diag. to wall.

*Contrary Body Movement.* C.B.M. on 1 and 4. The 1st step of the Cross Hesitation is placed in C.B.M.P.

*Rise and Fall (Body).* Normal rise on 1, 2, 3 of Natural Turn. Rise at end of 5; up on 6. Lower at end of 6. Cross Hesitation: commence to rise at end of 1; continue to rise on 2 and 3. Lower at end of 3.

*Body Sway.* Sway to the R. on 2 and 3, to the L. on 5. No sway on the Cross Hesitation.

*Amount of Turn.* Make three-eighths on 1, 2, 3 of the Natural Turn. Three-eighths on steps 4, 5 and a slight body turn to R. on 6. There is a slight body turn only on the Cross Hesitation (to L.).

*Footwork.* 1. H. T. 2. T. 3. T. H. 4. T. H. 5. H. T. 6. T. H. Cross Hesitation: 1. H. T. 2. Toes (both feet). 3. T. H. (R.F.).

*General Notes.* After the Cross Hesitation the Outside Spin could be used, and followed by 1, 2, 3 of the Natural Turn, commenced diagonally to centre and ended backing centre. Follow with an Outside Change. The Wing or the Weave from P.P. could follow the Open Impetus Turn.

# THE OPEN IMPETUS TURN

## (With Cross Hesitation Finish)

### Lady

1 to 3. First three steps of the Natural Turn. Finish facing L.O.D.

4. R.F. forward, turning body to the R.

5. L.F. to side, slightly across the L.O.D.
6. Continue turning on ball of L.F. and step to side with R.F. diag. to centre, having first brushed R.F. to L.F. and turned to P.P. (R.F. should point towards centre).

Continue with the Cross Hesitation as follows—

1. L.F. forward, across the body in P.P., turning body to L., moving diag. to centre.
2. R.F. to side (small step), still turning to get square to partner. Body backing L.O.D.
3. Close L.F. to R.F. Now backing diag. to centre.

To continue, step forward with R.F. outside partner, diag. to wall against the L.O.D., and do 4, 5, and 6 of the Natural Turn, making a quarter turn to the R.

*Contrary Body Movement.* C.B.M. on 1 and 4. The 1st step of the Cross Hesitation is placed in C.M.B.P., and C.B.M. is also used to turn to the L.

*Rise and Fall (Body).* Normal rise on 1, 2, 3 of Natural Turn. Rise at end of 5; up on 6. Lower at end of 6. Cross Hesitation: commence to rise at end of 1; continue to rise on 2 and 3. Lower at end of 3.

*Body Sway.* Sway to L. on 2 and 3, to the R. on 5. Cross Hesitation: sway to L. on 2 and 3.

*Amount of Turn.* Make three-eighths of a turn on 1, 2, 3 of Natural Turn. Make three-quarters of a turn on steps 4, 5, 6, the body turning slightly less to keep the position compact. There will be three-eighths of a turn to L. on the Cross Hesitation.

*Footwork.* 1. T. H. 2. T. 3. T. H. 4. H. T. 5. T. 6. T. H. Cross Hesitation: 1. H. T. 2. T. 3. T. H.

*General Notes.* When the Wing follows the Open Impetus Turn the lady will make an eighth of a turn on each step of the Wing to end backing diag. to centre.

# THE WHISK

## Man

The Whisk is a delightful variation to dance, and it has the advantage that it is quite easy to lead. It introduces another position to ballroom dancing, a position that is now known as "Whisk Position."

It is usually danced after a complete Reverse Turn.

Commence and finish the Whisk facing diagonally to the wall.

1. L.F. forward, diag. to wall.
2. R.F. to the side and slightly forward, turning lady to P.P.
3. Cross L.F. behind and a few inches to the R. of R.F., now in P.P., facing diag. to wall.

Endings to this figure are given below.

*Contrary Body Movement.* Slight C.B.M. on 1.

*Rise and Fall (Body).* Commence to rise at end of 1; continue to rise on 2; up on 3. Lower at end of 3.

*Body Sway.* Sway to the L. on 2, 3.

*Amount of Turn.* There is no turn for the man.

*Footwork.* 1. H. T. 2. T. 3. T. H.

*General Notes.* As the 1st step is taken the man must apply pressure with his R. hand on the lady's L. side to turn her to P.P.

Care must be taken not to let the weight fall back on the 3rd step. When the 3rd step is in position the body should be inclined to the L., and it is this L. sway of the body while the foot is crossed behind that makes the figure so attractive. The L. heel will lower lightly as the R.F. moves forward into the following figure.

*Amalgamations.* (a) *The Chassé.* This is the original and most popular ending. It is similar to the Chassé in the Quickstep. After the 3rd step of the Whisk, continue as follows—

1. Move the R.F. slightly forward along the L.O.D. in P.P.
2. L.F. to the side and slightly forward along L.O.D. ($\frac{1}{2}$ beat).
3. Close R.F. to L.F. Lady square ($\frac{1}{2}$ beat).
4. L.F. to side and slightly forward, on the same L.O.D.

To continue, step forward R.F. outside partner, diag. to wall, into a Natural Turn.

*Notes.* The Chassé is counted 1, 2, "and" 3 denoting that there is only a half beat on each of the 2nd and 3rd steps.

Rise at the end of 1; continue to rise on 2 and 3; up on 4. Lower at end of 4. There is no sway.

(b) *The Wing.* This is a popular ending. See page 141.

(c) *The Weave from P.P.* (See page 158.) The Whisk may be used at a corner. If commenced facing diag. to wall near a corner the man will make a quarter turn to L. on the Whisk and the lady will make no turn. When danced in this way the man's 2nd step will be "R.F. diag. forward, R. shoulder leading" and the lady's 2nd step will be "L.F. back, L. shoulder leading." Man will be facing L.O.D. on 2 and facing diag. to wall of the new L.O.D. on 3.

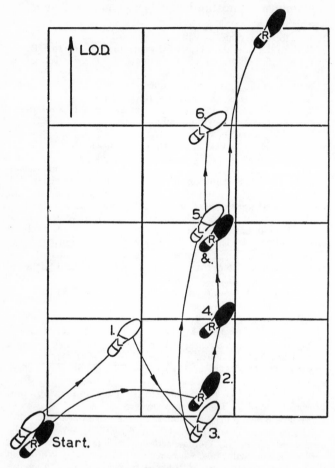

THE WHISK
(Man)
Steps 1, 2, 3 are The Whisk
Steps 4, 5, "and" 6 are The Chassé

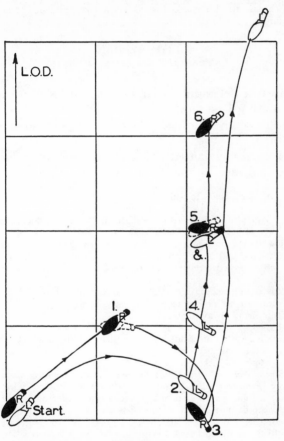

THE WHISK
(Lady)·
Steps 1, 2, 3, are The Whisk
Steps 4, 5, "and" 6 are The Chassé

149

The Whisk could be commenced backwards after the first 3 steps of a Reverse Corté or after steps 1, 2, 3 of a Natural Turn, in which case the Wing and Closed Telemark would be the easiest ending.

# THE WHISK

## Lady

This is a delightful variation and the lady can help to make it look most attractive. The notes below and also those given with the man's description should be studied.

It is usually danced after a complete Reverse Turn. Commence backing diagonally to the wall.

1. R.F. back, diag. to wall.
2. L.F. diagonally back, commencing to turn to P.P.
3. Turning into P.P., cross the R.F. behind and a few inches to the L. of L.F. Finish facing diag. to centre.

The two nicest endings to this figure are given in the man's description, and notes on these will be found below.

*Contrary Body Movement.* Lady has no C.B.M. as she is turning to the R.

*Rise and Fall (Body).* Commence to rise at end of 1 (N.F.R.); continue to rise on 2; up on 3. Lower at end of 3.

*Body Sway.* Sway to the R. on 2, 3.

*Amount of Turn.* The lady's feet will make a quarter turn between steps 1 and 2 but her body turns slightly less. Her body will complete the turn on 3.

*Footwork.* 1. T. H. 2. T. 3. T. H.

*General Notes.* As the lady takes her first step back the man will apply pressure on her L. side, to indicate the Whisk. This will result in her second step being placed diagonally back, but the body should not complete the turn into P.P. until the R.F. is crossing behind on 3. Care should be taken not to let the weight fall back on the 3rd step. When the 3rd step is in position the body should be inclined to the R. The R. heel will lower lightly as the L.F. moves forward into the following figure.

When the Chassé ending is used (see man's notes) the steps of the lady are the normal opposite and she must wait for the indication from the man before turning square to him, as in some advanced endings, the lady is kept in P.P. at the end of the Chassé. (Diagram on p. 149.)

The Weave from P.P. ending is attractive and a description of this will be found on page 158.

# THE DRAG HESITATION
## and
# THE BACKWARD LOCK
### Man

Although these are two distinct variations and can be used separately, they are frequently danced as a complete amalgamation, and they are described as such below.

The Drag Hesitation can be commenced diagonally to the centre after a Closed Change on the R.F., or down the L.O.D. after the Double Reverse Spin. It is described from the latter position.

Commence facing the L.O.D.

## Drag Hesitation

1. L.F. forward, down the L.O.D. turning body to L.
2. R.F. to side, on the same L.O.D. Body now facing centre.
3. Continue turning slightly to L. and drag L.F. slowly to R.F. without putting the weight on to it.
   Finish backing diag. to wall, preparing to pass partner outside.

## Backward Lock

1. L.F. back, diag. to wall, partner outside.            (1)
2. R.F. back. (½ beat).                                   (2)
3. Cross L.F. in front of R.F. (½ beat).                  (&)
4. R.F. diag. back.                                       (3)
   Continue by stepping back with L.F. diag. to wall and with partner outside, into 4, 5, 6 of a Natural Turn, or into an Impetus, an Open Impetus Turn, or a Back Whisk.
   *Contrary Body Movement.* C.B.M. on 1 of Drag Hesitation. C.B.M. on 1 of Backward Lock. It is also placed in C.B.M.P.

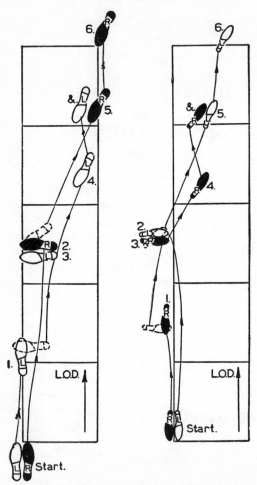

THE DRAG HESITATION AND BACKWARD LOCK
(Man and Lady)
Steps 1, 2, 3 are the Drag Hesitation
Steps 4, 5, "and" 6 are the Backward Lock

*Rise and Fall (Body)*. Drag Hesitation: rise at end of 2; up on 3. Lower at end of 3. Backward Lock: commence to rise at end of 1 (N.F.R.); continue to rise on 2 and 3; up on 4. Lower at end of 4.

*Body Sway*. There is no sway on either figure.

*Amount of Turn*. Make three-eighths of a turn on the Drag Hesitation, or a quarter if commenced diag. to centre. No turn on the Backward Lock.

*Footwork*. Drag Hesitation: 1. H. T. 2. T. 3. Toes (both feet) then T. H. (R.F.). Backward Lock: 1. T. H. 2. T. 3. T. 4. T. H.

*General Notes*. It should be noted that the man rises at the end of 2 in the Drag Hesitation. If the man remembers to keep this step fairly wide and with no rise (although it is taken on the ball of the foot) and also to drag the L.F. *slowly* to R.F., the lady will not mistake the lead for that of a Reverse Turn. It is easier to lead from a Double Reverse Spin than from a Closed Change.

After the Drag Hesitation, an underturned Outside Spin may be danced. Make three-quarters of a turn to the R. on the Outside Spin, and follow it with a step *back* on R.F., diag. to centre, into 4, 5, 6 of a Reverse Turn.

When 4, 5, 6 of the Natural Turn is used following the Backward Lock, make a quarter turn to R. to finish facing diag. to centre and follow with a Closed Change and a Reverse figure. If three-eighths of a turn is made, finish facing the L.O.D. and follow with 1, 2, 3 of a Natural Turn and an Outside Change.

# THE DRAG HESITATION
## and
# THE BACKWARD LOCK
### Lady

Although these are two distinct variations and can be used separately, they are frequently danced as a complete amalgamation, and they are described as such below.

The Drag Hesitation can be commenced backing diagonally to the centre after a Closed Change on the

L.F. or down the L.O.D. after the Double Reverse Spin. It is described from the latter position.

Commence backing the L.O.D.

## Drag Hesitation

1. R.F. back, down the L.O.D. turning body to L.
2. L.F. to side, on the same L.O.D.
3. Drag the R.F. slowly to L.F. without putting the weight on to it. Finish facing diag. to wall, preparing to step outside partner.

## Backward Lock

1. R.F. forward, diag. to wall, outside partner      (1)
2. L.F. diag. forward ($\frac{1}{2}$ beat).      (2)
3. Cross R.F. behind L.F. ($\frac{1}{2}$ beat).      (&)
4. L.F. diag. forward.      (3)

Continue by stepping forward with R.F., diag. to wall and outside partner into 4, 5, 6 of a Natural Turn, or into an Impetus, an Open Impetus Turn, or a Back Whisk.

*Contrary Body Movement.* C.B.M. on 1 of Drag Hesitation. C.B.M. on 1 of Backward Lock. It is also placed in C.B.M.P.

*Rise and Fall (Body).* Drag Hesitation: rise at end of 2; up on 3. Lower at end of 3. Backward Lock: commence to rise at end of 1; continue to rise on 2 and 3; up on 4. Lower at end of 4.

*Body Sway.* There is no sway on either figure.

*Amount of Turn.* Make three-eighths of a turn or less on the Drag Hesitation. No turn on the Backward Lock.

*Footwork.* Drag Hesitation: 1. T. H. 2. T. 3. Toes (both feet) then T. H. (L.F.). Backward Lock: 1. H. T. 2. T. 3. T. 4. T. H.

*General Notes.* The notes following the description of the man's steps should be studied.

# PROGRESSIVE CHASSÉ TO THE RIGHT

## Man

The Progressive Chassé to the Right is a more recent addition in the Waltz but is very popular with advanced dancers. The easiest entry is after a Hesitation Change which has ended diagonally to centre. More advanced entries are given in the General Notes.

Commence facing diagonally to centre.

count:

1. L.F. forward, turning body to L.        1
2. R.F. to side with body backing wall.        2
3. Close L.F. to R.F., turning slightly to L. to back diag. to wall. &
4. R:F. to side and slightly back.        3

    Now step back L.F., partner outside and continue with a Back Whisk or a Backward Lock Step, etc.

    *Contrary Body Movement.* C.B.M. on 1. The following step back on L.F. would be placed in C.B.M.P.

    *Rise and Fall (Body).* Commence to rise at end of 1; continue to rise on 2 and 3; up on 4; lower at end of 4.

    *Body Sway.* No sway is used on this figure.

    *Amount of Turn.* Make an eighth turn to L. between 1 and 2 and an eighth between 2 and 3. The body should turn slightly less than the feet between 2 and 3.

    *Footwork:* 1. H. T.   2. T.   3. T.   4. T. H.

    *General Notes.* The count of 1, 2, & 3 means that the 2nd and 3rd steps have a half beat only on each step. Other good entries are:

    (*a*) Open Impetus Turn or a Whisk followed by a Wing and ended facing diag. to centre. Now step forward L.F. outside lady on her L. side, and continue with the Progressive Chassé to R.

    (*b*) After the Wing, dance the Progressive Chassé to R. making a half turn to L. to end backing diag. to centre. Now step back L.F. with Lady outside, and continue with an Outside Change, lady getting in line on step 2. End facing diag. to wall and follow with a Natural figure.

## PROGRESSIVE CHASSÉ TO THE RIGHT
### Lady

Commence backing diagonally to centre.

1. R.F. back, turning body to L.        1
2. L.F. to side, along L.O.D., body facing wall.        2
3. Close R.F. to L.F.        &
4. L.F. to side and slightly forward.        3

    Now step forward R.F., outside partner, diag. to wall and continue into a Back Whisk or a forward Lock Step.

    *Contrary Body Movement.* C.B.M. on 1. The following step forward on R.F. will be placed in C.B.M.P.

*Rise and Fall (Body).* Commence to rise at end of 1 (N.F.R.); continue to rise on 2 and 3; up on 4; lower at end of 4.

*Body Sway.* No sway is used on this figure.

*Amount of Turn.* Make a quarter turn to L. between steps 1 and 3 but the body will turn slightly less.

*Footwork.* 1. T. H. 2. T. 3. T. 4. T. H. The following step forward on the R.F. will be H.

Please see the notes following the description of the man's steps.

## THE TURNING LOCK
### (after a Spin Turn)

### Man

The Spin and Turning Lock has rapidly become one of the most popular variations in the Waltz. It consists of a backward Lock Step on which a turn is made to the left on the third step, allowing the dancer to continue into another Natural Turn.

Dance a Natural Spin Turn and end backing diagonally to centre, with the L.F. to the side and slightly back in its normal position. Continue —

|  |  | Beats |
|---|---|---|
| 1. | R.F. back, diag. to centre, with the R. shoulder leading. | ½ |
| 2. | Cross L.F. in front of R.F. | ½ |
| 3. | R.F. back and slightly rightwards. | 1 |
| 4. | With a slight body turn to L. step to side and slightly forward L.F. | 1 |

The next step is taken forward with R.F., diag. to wall outside partner, into a Natural Turn.

*Contrary Body Movement.* Although turn is made on step 3 C.B.M. is not used.

*Rise and Fall (Body).* Commence to rise at end of 1; continue to rise on 2 and 3; up on 4. Lower at end of 4.

*Body Sway.* Sway to L. on steps 1 and 2.

*Amount of Turn.* A quarter turn to L. is made between 3 and 4.

*Footwork.* 1. T. 2. T. 3. T. 4. T. H.

*General Notes.* The R. shoulder lead and the sway to L. on steps 1 and 2 are most important and enhance the beauty of the figure. The R. shoulder lead is lost as the R.F. moves back and rightwards

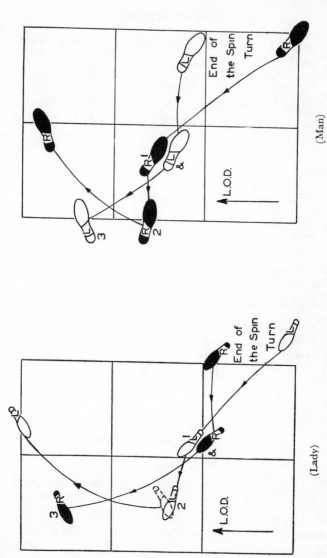

(Lady)

(Man)

THE TURNING LOCK STEP AFTER THE SPIN TURN

on step 3. The continuance of the rise on step 3 is also important.
Step 4 (L.F.) may be taken to the side in Promenade Position.

## Lady

Commence facing diagonally to centre after a Natural
Spin Turn. The weight will be on the R.F. which is
placed diagonally forward. Lower the R. heel lightly
before moving forward into the first step of the Turning
Lock.

|  |  | Beats |
|---|---|---|
| 1. | L.F. forward, diag. to centre, L. shoulder leading. | ½ |
| 2. | Cross R.F. behind L.F. | ½ |
| 3. | L.F. forward and slightly leftwards, in line with partner. | 1 |
| 4. | With a slight body turn to L. step to side and slightly back with R.F., backing diag. to wall. | 1 |

The next step is taken back with L.F., diag. to wall, with
partner outside, into a Natural Turn.

*Contrary Body Movement.* C.B.M. is not used when turning to L.
on step 3.

*Rise and Fall (Body).* Commence to rise at end of 1; continue to
rise on 2 and 3; up on 4; Lower at end of 4.

*Body Sway.* Sway to R. on steps 1 and 2.

*Amount of Turn.* A quarter turn to L. is made between 3 and 4.

*Footwork.* 1. T. 2. T. 3. T. 4. T. H.

*General Notes.* Step 1 is taken on the ball of foot, rising higher
throughout steps 2 and 3. Step 4 may be taken in P.P.


## THE WEAVE
### (from Promenade Position)

### Man

The Weave was originally a Foxtrot variation and is
described in the Foxtrot section of this book. The idea
of commencing the Weave in Promenade Position was
found to be so attractive that it is now used in both the
Waltz and Foxtrot.

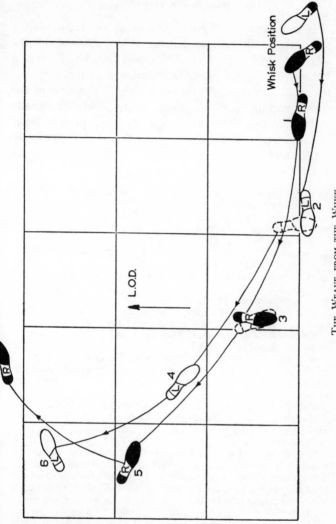

THE WEAVE FROM THE WHISK
(Man)

It is a beautiful figure with great rhythmic feeling and is not difficult to learn. When danced in the Waltz it can be taken after an Open Impetus Turn or a Whisk. In the following description it is assumed that the man has danced the Whisk along the side of the room, ending in P.P. with his body facing diagonally to the centre. Notes on other entries are given below.

Commence in P.P. with man facing diagonally to centre and lady facing diagonally to centre against the L.O.D.

1. R.F. forward, in P.P., moving towards centre and with R.F. pointing to centre.
2. Turning Lady square, step forward L.F., to centre.
3. Turning to L. step to side and slightly back with R.F., body backing the L.O.D.
4. Still turning slightly, step back L.F., diag. to centre with the Lady outside.
5. R.F. back, diag. to centre, with Lady in line, and turning to the L.
6. L.F. to side and slightly forward.

The following step on R.F. is taken diag. to wall, outside partner, and is the first step of a Natural Turn.

*Contrary Body Movement.* C.B.M. on 2 and 5. The 1st and 4th steps are placed in C.B.M.P.

*Rise and Fall (Body).* Commence to rise at end of 1; continue to rise on 2; up on 3; lower at end of 3. Commence to rise at end of 4 (N.F.R.); continue to rise on 5; up on 6; lower at end of 6.

*Body Sway.* No sway is used on this figure in the Waltz.

*Amount of Turn.* Make three-eighths of a turn to L. between 2 and 4 and a quarter turn to L. between 5 and 6.

*Footwork.* 1. H. T. 2. T. 3. T. H. 4. T. H. 5. T, 6. T. H.

*General Notes.* Do not attempt to turn the Lady square too abruptly at the end of step 1. The man should lead the lady to move more sideways on step 2 and she will then turn square gradually as the turn is continued on her R.F. It is attractive to hurry the timing a little on steps 1, 2, so that a hover effect can be made before placing the 3rd step in position. The continuance of the rise on steps 2 and 5 enhances the rhythmic feeling of the figure.

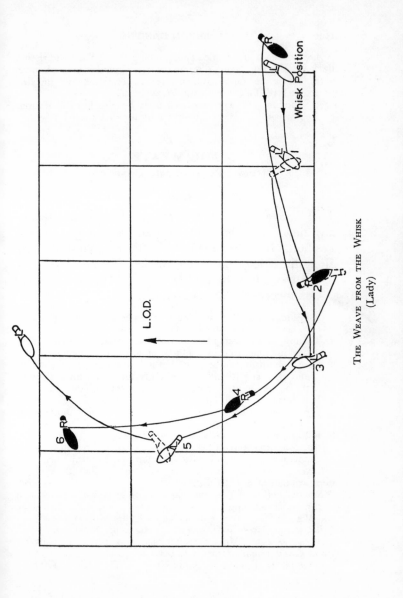

THE WEAVE FROM THE WHISK
(Lady)

*Amalgamations.* (*a*) Dance 1, 2, 3, of a Natural Turn and then a Back Whisk. End facing diag. to centre. Follow with the Weave.

(*b*) Dance an Open Impetus Turn, end moving towards centre in P.P. Follow with the Weave.

(*c*) The Spin and Turning Lock could be ended in P.P. on step 4. Follow with the Weave, overturning the first 4 steps.

# THE WEAVE
## (from Promenade Position)

### Lady

The Weave in the Waltz can be danced practically any time when the man and lady are in Promenade Position. It is described below after a Whisk danced along the side of the room, the lady facing diagonally to centre against the L.O.D.

Commence in P.P. as above, then—

1. L.F. forward in P.P., moving towards centre and facing diag. to centre against the L.O.D.
2. Turning to the L. step to side and slightly back with R.F., now backing diag. to centre and turning square to man.
3. Continue turning to L. on ball of R.F. until facing the L.O.D. and then step to side and slightly forward with L.F. with the L. toe pointing diag. to centre. Now square.
4. R.F. forward, outside partner, diag. to centre.
5. L.F. forward, diag. to centre, in line with partner and turning to the L.
6. R.F. to side and slightly back, now backing diag. to wall.

   The following step on L.F. is taken back diag. to wall with the partner outside, and is the first step of a Natural Turn.

*Contrary Body Movement.* C.B.M. on 1 and 5. The 1st and 4th steps are placed in C.B.M.P.

*Rise and Fall (Body).* Commence to rise at end of 1; continue to rise on 2; up on 3; lower at end of 3. Commence to rise at end of 4; continue to rise on 5; up on 6; lower at end of 6.

*Body Sway.* No sway is used on this figure in the Waltz.

*Amount of Turn.* Make three-quarters of a turn to L. between 1 and 4, and a quarter turn to L. between 5 and 6.

*Footwork.* 1. H. T.  2. T.  3. T. H.  4. H. T.  5. T.  6. T. H.

*General Notes.* Do not attempt to turn square too abruptly between steps 1 and 2. The 2nd step should move mainly to the side and the turn continue throughout steps 2 and 3.

It will be noted that the lady has much more turn to make than the man. The additional three-eighths of a turn is accounted for by the man making an eighth of a turn to L. (with his R.F.) as his 1st step is taken, and the lady has an additional quarter turn to make to get square to the man. The head should be kept to the R. on steps 1 and 2.

## SUGGESTED WALTZ AMALGAMATIONS

1. Natural Turn—Closed Change—Reverse Turn—Closed Change. Repeat.

2. Hesitation Change—1, 2, 3 of Reverse Turn—Reverse Corté—Natural Spin Turn.

3. 1, 2, 3 of Natural Turn—Outside Change—Natural Spin Turn—Reverse Corté—Back Whisk—Chassé.

4. Natural Spin Turn—4, 5, 6 of Reverse Turn, turning to L.O.D.—Double Reverse Spin—Drag Hesitation—Backward Lock. End with 4, 5, 6 of Natural Turn or: Open Impetus Turn—Cross Hesitation—Outside Spin—Closed Change—Reverse Turn—Whisk—Chassé.

5. Reverse Turn—Whisk and Chassé ending—Natural Spin Turn—Turning Lock.

6. Double Reverse Spin—Open Telemark—Wing—Closed Telemark.

7. Open Impetus Turn—Wing—Overturned Progressive Chassé to R.—Outside Change (Lady outside on the first step)—Natural Spin Turn.

8. Reverse Turn—Whisk, turning to Left to end facing the L.O.D. or diag. to centre—Weave from P.P.

## SECTION III

### THE FOXTROT

THE Slow Foxtrot is characterized by long, gliding, and perfectly smooth steps, demanding ease of movement and control in order to give the dance a lazy and unhurried appearance.

The construction of the Foxtrot is such that it is only possible to dance it in a large and uncrowded ballroom. The keen dancer, who will doubtless practise and dance at one of the many excellent dance studios or public dance halls throughout the country, will find it of great assistance in acquiring balance and control.

Whilst the Foxtrot is the most delightful dance and most typical of English ballroom dancing, it is unfortunate that it is of little direct use to the social dancer. The social dancers, whose dancing activities are likely to be restricted to club, hotel and restaurant dances, would be well advised to learn to adapt the simple basic figures of the Quickstep to the slower tempo. This type of dancing is called "Rhythm Dancing."

### General Notes

*Time.* 4/4. 4 beats in a bar. The 1st and 3rd beats are accented, but not so definitely as in the Quickstep.

*Tempo.* Music should be played at 30 bars a minute.

*Basic Rhythms.* Slow, Slow. Quick, Quick, Slow. Each "Slow" has 2 beats of music. The "Quicks" have 1 beat each.

*Figures.* Walk, Three-step, Feather-step, Natural

Turn, Reverse Turn, Reverse Wave, Change of Direction Step, Impetus Turn, Telemark, Open Telemark, Hover Telemark, Hover Feather, Natural Telemark, Natural Hover Telemark, Natural Twist Turn, Weave, Top Spin, Outside Swivel, Natural Weave, Weave from P.P.

The first thing for the beginner to appreciate is that, whereas in the Quickstep the change to a quicker rhythm is made with a Chassé, in the Foxtrot this change is made with a figure called the Three-step, a description of which is given on pages 167 and 168.

The correct interpretation of the Three-step is of utmost importance, and the beginner would be well advised to practise this, combined with the Walk, before attempting any other figure. Although the following amalgamation does not appear in the finished dance, it is by far the simplest method of acquiring the smooth and unhurried entry from the Walk to the Three-step which is the basis of the Foxtrot.

Face the Line of Dance

|  | Count |
|---|---|
| Walk forward with R.F. | S |
| Walk forward with L.F. | S |
| Three-step (Right, Left, Right) | Q Q S |
| Walk forward with L.F. | S |
| Walk forward with R.F. | S |
| Three-step (Left, Right, Left) | Q Q S |
| Repeat walk with R.F., L.F., etc. | |

This amalgamation should be practised with music, taking care that the entry to each Three-step is made without *obvious* effort. Careful attention to the foot-work and rise and fall will help the dancer to attain a smooth and flowing movement.

Before learning the basic figures which comprise the

Foxtrot, the novice should have some idea of its construction.

The Walk, as a separate figure, does not appear in the dance, all slow walking steps forming a part of a basic figure.

It should be noted that, in joining two figures such as the Three-step and the Natural Turn, the last step of the Three-step will also be the first step of the Natural Turn. Hints on amalgamation are given after the description of each figure, but, as a preliminary guide, the following amalgamation, which is the first to be attempted by the beginner, may be helpful.

### The Feather-step, Three-step and Natural Turn

Rhythm as separate figures—

| Feather-step | Three-step | Natural Turn |
|---|---|---|
| S Q Q S | Q Q S | S Q Q S S S |

Rhythm when amalgamated—

| Feather-step | Three-step | Natural Turn |
|---|---|---|
| S Q Q S | Q Q S | Q Q S S S |

Thus it will be noted that the last step of the Three-step (R.F.) has been used as the first of the Natural Turn.

## THE WALK—FORWARD AND BACKWARD

A full description of the Walk is given on pages 9-15, and unless this has been correctly mastered the pupil should not attempt the Foxtrot, which is the most difficult of all ballroom dances.

The Walk in the Foxtrot is practically the same as in the Quickstep, but the following special points should be noted.

1. The steps will be slightly longer than in the Quickstep owing to the slower music.

2. The slower music will result in the knees being slightly more relaxed than in the Quickstep.

This is especially noticeable when a slow step is to be followed by a quick step. As the weight is taken on to the slow step the knee will relax rather more than usual, and the gradual straightening of that knee will result in a "softer" entry into the following quick step.

## THE THREE-STEP

### Man

The Three-step is the basic movement of the Foxtrot. It can be danced forward and backward. As a basic figure it is always commenced with the R.F. when moving forward, and the L.F. when moving backward. When used as a part of another figure it is rhythmically the same, but the steps are altered in many cases. The description below is for moving forward, as when the figure is taken after a Feather-step.

Commence facing the L.O.D.

| | |
|---|---|
| 1. R.F. forward. | Q |
| 2. L.F. forward. | Q |
| 3. R.F. forward. | S |

*Contrary Body Movement.* If danced as a separate figure, no C.B.M. would be used. As an entry to the Natural Turn, C.B.M. would be used on 3.

*Rise and Fall (Body).* Rise at end of 1; up on 2. Lower at end of 2.

*Body Sway.* Sway to L. on 1 and 2.

*Amount of Turn.* Can be taken straight. Advanced dancers often curve this figure slightly to the L. when taken after a Reverse Turn. The turn comes from the preceding slow step.

*Footwork.* 1. H. T. 2. T. H. 3. H.

*General Notes.* Avoid any effect of hurrying the two quick steps. Interpretation of the rhythm is largely a matter of personal expression. A good general hint is to be a little late with the second "Quick". All the steps must be long. The second will be *very slightly* shorter owing to the rise, whilst the third step, being an entry into the following Natural Turn, will be slightly longer, but avoid a forceful action. Most advanced dancers use a slight R. shoulder lead on the first 2 steps.

## THE THREE-STEP

### Lady

As a basic figure the Three-step is always commenced with the L.F. when moving backward and the R.F. when moving forward. The description below is for moving backward, as when the figure is taken after a Feather-step.

Commence backing the L.O.D.

1. L.F. back.          Q
2. R.F. back.          Q
3. L.F. back.          S

*Contrary Body Movement.* If danced as a separate figure, no C.B.M. would be used. As an entry to the Natural Turn, C.B.M. would be used on 3.

*Rise and Fall (Body).* Rise at end of 1 (N.F.R.); up on 2 (N.F.R.). Lower at end of 2.

*Body Sway.* Sway to R. on 1 and 2.

*Amount of Turn.* The figure can be taken straight. Advanced dancers often turn this figure slightly to the L. after a Reverse Turn. The turn comes from the preceding slow step.

*Footwork.* 1. T. H. 2. T. H. 3. T.

*General Notes.* Most men dancers use a R. shoulder lead on steps 1 and 2 and the lady should respond to this with a L. shoulder lead. Although rise will be felt in the body it is most important that when each step commences to move back from a forward position the *heel* is in contact with the floor. If the foot moves back with the toe in contact with the floor the movement will be seriously restricted.

## THE FEATHER-STEP

### Man

The Feather-step consists of a slow step followed by a type of Three-step in which the man steps outside the lady on the second quick step. The rise is also taken earlier.

It can be taken along the L.O.D., diagonally to the centre, or diagonally to the wall. In the first basic amalgamation it is taken along the L.O.D.

Commence and finish facing the L.O.D.

1. R.F. forward, turning body slightly to R.                           S
2. L.F. forward, preparing to step outside partner, L. shoulder leading                                                     Q
3. R.F. forward, outside partner                                       Q
4. L.F. forward, in line with partner, body facing L.O.D.              S

*Contrary Body Movement.* C.B.M. on 1 and 4. C.B.M.P. on 3.

*Rise and Fall (Body).* Rise at end of 1; up on 2 and 3. Lower at end of 3.

*Body Sway.* Sway to R. on 2 and 3.

*Amount of Turn.* There is no turn, except for the L. shoulder lead on steps 2 and 3.

*Footwork.* 1. H. T.  2. T.  3. T. H.  4. H.

*General Notes.* The stepping outside the partner on the 3rd step needs great care, otherwise an ugly hip movement will result. The bodies must be kept square and together all the time. The L. shoulder lead on 2 will result in the man stepping forward in an "open" position, and this will enable him to step outside without losing contact with his partner. (Diagram on p. 170.)

*Amalgamations.* (a) Feather-step down the L.O.D. into the Three-step and Natural Turn.

(b) Feather-step diag. to centre, into any reverse figure.

(c) Feather-step down the L.O.D. into the Reverse Wave.

(d) Feather-step diag. to the wall or into a corner and followed by a Change of Direction step.

(e) A Three-step may follow a Feather-step that has been ended diag. to wall. It may be continued in a direction diag. to wall or curved to L. to finish down the L.O.D.

## THE FEATHER-STEP

### Lady

The Feather-step consists of a slow step followed by a type of Three-step in which the man steps outside the lady on the 2nd quick step. The positions in which it is used will be found in the notes on the man's steps.

Commence with the back to the L.O.D. Finish with the back to the L.O.D.

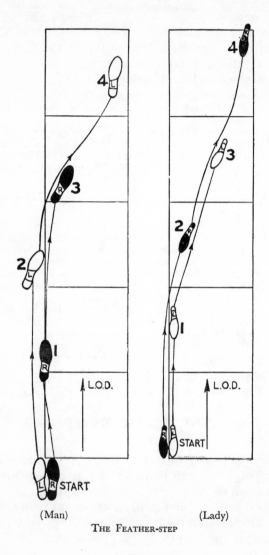

(Man)                              (Lady)

THE FEATHER-STEP

170

1. L.F. back, turning body slightly to R.                              S
2. R.F. back, R. shoulder leading.                                     Q
3. L.F. back, partner outside.                                         Q
4. R.F. back, partner in line.                                         S

*Contrary Body Movement.* C.B.M. on 1 and 4. C.B.M.P. on 3.

*Rise and Fall (Body).* Rise at end of 1 (N.F.R.); up on 2 and 3 (N.F.R.). Lower at end of 3.

*Body Sway.* Sway to L. on 2 and 3.

*Amount of Turn.* There is no actual turn.

*Footwork.* 1. T. H.  2. T. H.  3. T. H.  4. T.

*General Notes.* Although the technical position of the 2nd step is R.F. *back*, the R. shoulder lead will result in this step being in an "open" position. If it is placed straight back, contact with partner may be lost. It is most important to remember that each step should move back from a forward position with the *heel* in contact with the floor. If foot rise is used, the flow of the figure will be seriously restricted.

# THE NATURAL (OR RIGHT) TURN

## Man

The Natural Turn consists of an Open Turn and a type of Heel Turn called a Pull Step.

The Natural Turn can be used either at a corner or when progressing along the sides of the room. It can be commenced facing the L.O.D. or diagonally to the wall, the amount of turn on each part varying according to the commencing and finishing positions.

Commence facing the L.O.D. Finish facing diagonally to the centre or facing the new L.O.D.

1. R.F. forward, turning body to R.                                    S
2. L.F. to side, across the L.O.D.                                     Q
3. Continue turning on ball of L.F. and step R.F. back.                Q
4. L.F. back, down L.O.D. turning body to R.                           S
5. Pull R.F. back firmly, at the same time turning on
   L. heel. Finish with R.F. at the side of L.F., feet
   parallel and about 10 inches apart. Weight on R.F.                  S
6. L.F. forward, body turning to the L.                                S

*Contrary Body Movement.* C.B.M. on 1, 4 and 6.

*Rise and Fall* (*Body*). Rise at end of 1; up on 2 and 3. Lower at end of 3.

*Body Sway.* Sway to R. on 2 and 3. Sway to L. on 5.

*Footwork.* 1. H. T. 2. T. 3. T. H. 4. T. H. 5. H., I.E. of foot, whole foot, then I.E. of L.F. 6. H.

*Amount of Turn.* (*a*) When danced down the sides of the room. Make half a turn on 1, 2, 3; make three-eighths of a turn on 4, 5, 6 to finish facing diagonally to the centre and follow with a Feather-step and any Reverse figure.

When 4, 5, 6 are taken at a corner make a quarter turn to finish facing the *new* L.O.D. and follow with a Feather-step, Three-step and Natural Turn, or a Feather-step and Reverse Wave. Alternatively, make an eighth of a turn on 4, 5, 6 and finish facing diagonally to the centre of the *new* L.O.D. and follow with a Feather and any Reverse figure.

(*b*) When commenced very near a corner, make three-eighths of a turn on 1, 2, 3 so that steps 2, 3, 4 are taken moving across the corner. On 4, 5, 6 make a quarter turn to face diagonally to the new centre or three-eighths of a turn to face the new L.O.D.

*General Notes.* Try to get the effect of "cutting" the R.F. under the body on the 3rd step. This will help the dancer feel the sway. Attempt to make the R. toe just touch the L. heel in passing.

When the R.F. is in position on 5, the body will cease to turn to the R., and will immediately commence to turn to the L. as the L.F. brushes past the R.F. and steps forward. This gives a continuous and attractive movement of the body during a somewhat stationary part of the figure.

The first amalgamation to use is: Feather-step, Three-step, Natural Turn. Use the last step of the Three-step as the first of the Natural Turn.

An Impetus Turn may follow the 3rd step of the Natural Turn. The Hover Feather may follow the 5th step.

## THE NATURAL (OR RIGHT) TURN

### Lady

The Natural Turn is used either at a corner or when progressing along the sides of the room.

It includes a Heel Turn and a Brush Step.

Commence with the back to the L.O.D. Finish with

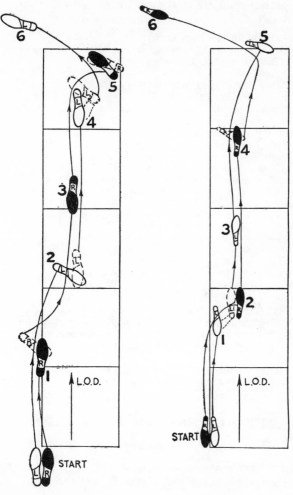

(Man)       (Lady)

THE NATURAL (OR RIGHT) TURN

173

the back diagonally to the centre, or with the back to the new L.O.D. (See notes on man's steps.)

1. L.F. back, turning body to R.                                          S
2. Close R.F. to L.F., turning on L. heel (Heel Turn).
   Finish facing L.O.D., weight on R.F.                             Q
3. L.F. forward.                                                          Q
4. R.F. forward, turning body to R.                                 S
5. L.F. to side, across the L.O.D.                                  S
6. Brush R.F. up to L.F., and then step back with R.F., body
   turning to the L.                                                      S

*Contrary Body Movement.* C.B.M. on 1, 4 and 6.

*Rise and Fall (Body).* Rise slightly at end of 1 (N.F.R.); continue to rise on 2; up on 3. Lower at end of 3.

*Body Sway.* Sway to L. on 2 and 3. Sway to R. on 5.

*Amount of Turn.* Make half a turn between 1 and 3. Make three-eighths of a turn between 4 and 5, to finish with the back diagonally to the centre, or a quarter turn to finish backing the new L.O.D. if taken into a corner. (See also man's notes on the amount of turn.)

*Footwork.* 1. T. H. 2. H. T. 3. T. H. 4. H. T. 5. T. H., then I.E. of T. of R.F. 6. T.

*General Notes.* Keep the hips well forward when taking the 3rd step. Relax the R. knee well when taking the weight on to the 4th step, and then let the L.F. swing to the side across the front of the partner quite *slowly on* 5.

When brushing the R.F. to L.F. on the 6th step keep the knees well relaxed, and brush with the R. toe about level with the L. instep. It is not necessary for the *toes* of both feet to touch when brushing. Note that the body turns to the L. as the R.F. moves back.

An Impetus Turn may follow the 3rd step of the Natural Turn. The Hover Feather may follow the 5th step.

## THE REVERSE (OR LEFT) TURN

### Man

The Reverse Turn consists of an Open Turn and a Feather finish. It is a progressive figure, and cannot be used to turn a corner

Commence facing diagonally to the centre and finish

facing diagonally to the wall. The Reverse Turn
should not be commenced from the L.O.D., except by
advanced dancers. The fact that the lady is always
held slightly towards the man's R. side makes it difficult
to get good alignment on the backward steps if half a
turn is attempted on the first part.

1. L.F. forward, turning body to L.                            S
2. R.F. to side, across the L.O.D.                             Q
3. Continue turning on ball of R.F. and step L.F. back.        Q
4. R.F. back, down L.O.D., turning body to L.                  S
5. L.F. to side and slightly forward, body facing wall.        Q
6. R.F. forward, diag. to wall, outside partner.               Q
7. L.F. forward, in line with partner.                         S

*Contrary Body Movement.* C.B.M. on 1, 4, and 7. The 6th step
is placed in C.B.M.P.

*Rise and Fall (Body).* Rise at end of 1; up on 2 and 3. Lower at
end of 3. Rise at end of 4; up on 5 and 6. Lower at end
of 6.

*Body Sway.* Sway to L. on 2 and 3. Sway to R. on 5
and 6.

*Amount of Turn.* Make three-eighths of a turn between 1 and 3,
and three-eighths of a turn between 4 and 7.

*Footwork.* 1. H. T. 2. T. 3. T. H. 4. T. H. T. 5. T. 6. T. H.
7. H.

*General Notes.* Do not let the 3rd step swing outwards. Keep
it well behind the body. The 6th step should be placed slightly
across the body in order to keep hip contact during the outside
movement. The body should face the wall on 5, with the L.
shoulder slightly forward.

Note that although the man is on the inside of the turn on the
last part of the figure, he will get a *foot rise* on step 4. This exception to the usual rule is to enable him to get a good forward swing
into the following Feather finish.

The Reverse Turn should be preceded by a Feather-step taken
diagonally to the centre, the last step of the Feather-step being
used as the first of the Reverse Turn.

Follow with a Three-step, taken either diagonally to wall or
curved to L. to end down the L.O.D. Follow with the Natural
Turn.

A Change of Direction step or a Reverse Wave can also follow
the Reverse Turn. (Diagram on p. 176.)

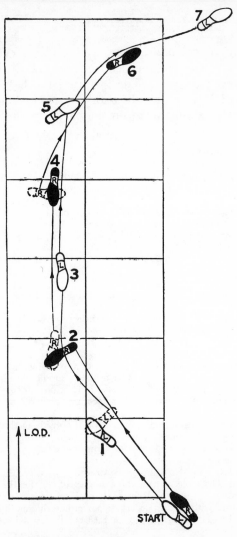

THE REVERSE (OR LEFT) TURN
(Man)

176

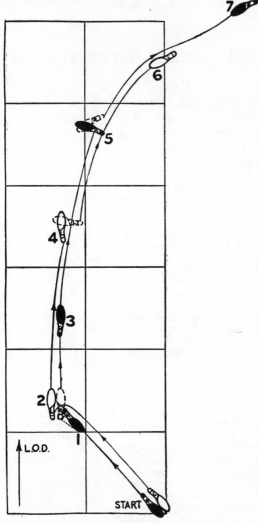

THE REVERSE (OR LEFT) TURN
(Lady)

# THE REVERSE (OR LEFT) TURN

## Lady

The Reverse Turn consists of a Heel Turn and a Feather finish. It is preceded by a Feather-step.

Commence the Reverse Turn with the back diagonally to the centre. Finish with the back diagonally to the wall.

| | |
|---|---|
| 1. R.F. back, turning body to L. | S |
| 2. Close L.F. to R.F., turning on R. heel (Heel Turn). Finish facing L.O.D., weight on L.F. | Q |
| 3. R.F. forward. | Q |
| 4. L.F. forward, turning body to L. | S |
| 5. R.F. to side, body backing the wall. | Q |
| 6. Continue turning slightly, and step back with L.F. diag. to wall, partner outside. | Q |
| 7. R.F. back, partner in line. | S |

*Contrary Body Movement.* C.B.M. on 1, 4, and 7. The 6th step is placed in C.B.M.P.

*Rise and Fall (Body).* Rise slightly at end of 1 (N.F.R.); continue to rise on 2; up on 3. Lower at end of 3. Rise at end of 4, up on 5; up on 6 (N.F.R.). Lower at end of 6.

*Body Sway.* Sway to R. on 2 and 3. Sway to L. on 5 and 6.

*Amount of Turn.* Make three-eighths of a turn between 1 and 3, and three-eighths of a turn between 4 and 7.

*Footwork.* 1. T. H. 2. H. T. 3. T. H. 4. H. T. 5. T. H. 6. T. H. 7. T.

*General Notes.* Keep the hips well forward when taking the 3rd step. Relax the L. knee well on 4. The 5th step (R.F.) should be placed to the side with the toe slightly turned out. This will ensure that the turn is gradual and prevent overturning. The body should be backing towards the wall on 5 and the 6th step will move slightly across the back of the body in a direction diagonally to the wall. Note that there is no foot rise on 6. When the R.F. commences to move back for the 7th step the *heel* must be in contact with the floor. (Diagram on p. 177.)

## THE REVERSE WAVE

### Man

The Reverse Wave has a variety of uses. A list of the positions from which it can be taken is given in the general notes.

It consists of the first four steps of the Reverse Turn (taken in a different direction), a Three-step, and then a Pull Step (5 and 6 of the Natural Turn). It is preceded by a Feather-step.

The most popular position in which to use the Wave is described.

Commence facing the L.O.D. Finish facing diagonally to the centre.

1. L.F. forward, turning body to L.                                         S
2. R.F. to side, on same L.O.D.                                            Q
3. L.F. back, diag. to wall.                                               Q
4. R.F. back, diag. to wall, body turning to L.                           S
5. L.F. back, curving towards the L.O.D.                                   Q
6. R.F. back, down L.O.D.                                                  Q
7. L.F. back, down L.O.D., body turning to R.                             S
8. Pull R.F. back firmly, at the same time turning on L. heel. Finish with R.F. at the side of L.F., feet parallel and about ten inches apart. Weight on R.F.      S
9. L.F. forward, body turning to the L.                                    S

*Contrary Body Movement.* C.B.M. on 1, 4, 7, and 9.

*Rise and Fall (Body).* Rise at end of 1; up on 2 and 3. Lower at end of 3. Rise at end of 5; up on 6. Lower at end of 6.

*Body Sway.* Sway to L. on 2 and 3. Sway to R. on 5 and 6. Sway to L. on 8.

*Amount of Turn.* The amount of turn on each part of the Wave is given in the notes below.

*Footwork.* 1. H. T. 2. T. 3. T. H. 4. T. H. 5. T. 6. T. H. 7. T. H. 8. H., I.E. of foot, whole foot, then I.E. of L.F. 9. H.

*General Notes.* When moving backwards the man must not let his poise or weight fall back. Note that the rise is taken from the ball of L.F. on 5. The L. heel does not lower.

*Possible Alignments for the Reverse Wave*

(*a*) Along side of room. Commence facing L.O.D. Turn

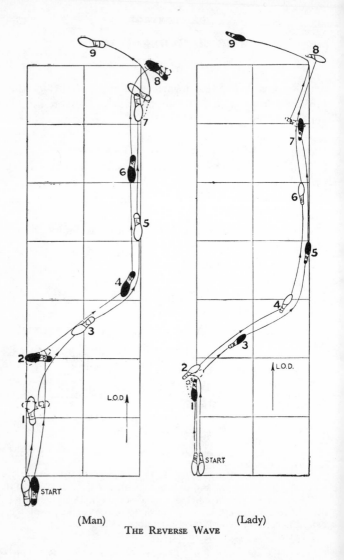

(Man)     (Lady)

THE REVERSE WAVE

three-eighths between 1 and 3 and take 4th step diagonally to wall. Make an eighth turn on 4, 5, 6 to back the L.O.D.

On steps 7, 8 turn three-eighths to face diagonally to centre. If at a corner, turn a quarter to face the new L.O.D. or an eighth to face diagonally to centre of the new L.O.D.

(b) Round a corner. Commence facing L.O.D. Turn three-eighths between 1 and 3 and take 4th step diagonally to wall. Make a quarter turn on 4, 5, 6 to back diagonally to wall of the new L.O.D.

On steps 7, 8 turn a quarter to face diagonally to centre of the new L.O.D.

(c) Along side of room. Commence facing diagonally to wall. Make a half turn between 1 and 3 and take 4th step back diagonally to wall. Continue as in alignment (a) above.

(d) Round a corner. Commence facing diagonally to wall. Make a half turn between 1 and 3 and take 4th step back diagonally to wall. Continue as in alignment (b) above.

(e) Round a corner. Commence facing diagonally to centre. Make three-eighths turn between 1 and 3 and take 4th step down the L.O.D. near a corner. Make a quarter turn on steps 4, 5, 6 to back the new L.O.D. and then three-eighths on steps 7, 8 to face diagonally to centre of the new L.O.D.

Although the above are the accepted alignments for the Reverse Wave, the figure may be danced from practically any position. Main point to remember is that the turn must be gradual, and not abrupt between steps 4 and 6.

The Wave may be danced directly after a Reverse Turn or any Feather finish ended diagonally to wall.

A Hover Feather may follow the 8th step. An Impetus Turn may be used after the 6th step and a Weave is used after checking on the 4th step.

## THE REVERSE WAVE

### Lady

The Reverse Wave consists of the first four steps of the Reverse Turn (taken in a different direction), a Three-step and then a Brush Step (5 and 6 of the Natural Turn). A chart appears on page 180.

The Wave can be taken from many positions. A list of these is given at the end of the notes on the man's steps. The most popular position from which to use the Wave is described. It is preceded by a Feather-step, the last step of the Feather being the first of the Wave.

Commence with the back to the L.O.D. Finish with the back diagonally to the centre or to the *new* L.O.D.

1. R.F. back, turning body to L.                                    S
2. Close L.F. to R.F. turning on R. heel (Heel Turn).
   Finish facing diag. to wall, weight on L.F.                     Q
3. R.F. forward, diag. to wall.                                    Q
4. L.F. forward, diag. to wall, body turning to L.                 S
5. R.F. forward, curving towards the L.O.D.                        Q
6. L.F. forward, down L.O.D.                                       Q
7. R.F. forward, down L.O.D., turning body to R.                   S
8. L.F. to side, across the L.O.D.                                 S
9. Brush R.F. up to L.F., and then step back with R.F.,
   body turning to L.                                              S

*Contrary Body Movement.* C.B.M. on 1, 4, 7, and 9.

*Rise and Fall (Body).* Rise slightly at end of 1 (N.F.R.); continue to rise on 2; up on 3. Lower at end of 3. Rise at end of 5; up on 6. Lower at end of 6.

*Body Sway.* Sway to R. on 2 and 3. Sway to L. on 5 and 6. Sway to R. on 8.

*Amount of Turn.* The amount of turn on each part together with possible uses of the Wave is given at the end of the notes on the man's steps.

*Footwork.* 1. T. H. 2. H. T. 3. T. H. 4. H. 5. H. T. 6. T. H. 7. H. T. 8. T. H., then I.E. of T. of R.F. 9. T.

*General Notes.* The lady can materially assist the man's backward movement by keeping the hips well forward and rather "pressing" forward towards him from steps 4 to 7. The poise, however, must still be kept slightly back from the hips.

## THE CHANGE OF DIRECTION

### Man

The Change of Direction actually consists of three steps only and is counted "Slow, Slow, Slow." In the description below the second step is divided into beats of the music to make it more easily understood.

It is preceded by a Feather-step or a Reverse Turn.

1. L.F. forward, turning body to L.                                                    S
2. R.F. diagonally forward, R. shoulder leading, &#125;
   sliding it along the floor on the inside edge
   of the toe.                                          1st beat
   With the knees well relaxed, brush the L.F.
   sharply to R.F., at the same time turning
   up to a half turn to L. Turn on ball of                                         S
   R.F. but keep the R. heel down.                      2nd beat
3. L.F. forward, across the body.                                                      S

*Contrary Body Movement.* C.B.M. on 1 and 3. The 3rd step is placed in C.B.M.P.

*Rise and Fall.* None.

*Body Sway.* Sway to L. on 2.

*Amount of Turn.* The turn is governed by the following figure. Half a turn is the most effective. See notes below.

*Footwork.* 1. H. 2. I.E. of T., H., then I.E. of T. of L.F. 3. H.

*General Notes.* Although the 2nd step is termed diagonally forward, it must follow the line of the preceding step on the L.F. The fact that the R. shoulder is leading slightly on this step accounts for it being diagonally forward. The turn must be sharp. Keep pressure on the inside edge of the toe of the L.F. as it closes, and close the L. toe slightly in advance of the R. toe.

*Amalgamations.* (a) Along the sides of the room. Dance a Reverse Turn and then a Change of Direction, make a quarter turn on the Change of Direction and follow with a Feather-step diagonally to centre, and any Reverse figure.

(b) At a corner, after a Reverse Turn. Make three-eighths of a turn to finish facing the new L.O.D. or a half turn to finish facing diagonally to centre of the new L.O.D.

*Note.* Step 2 may be held for an additional "Slow".


# THE CHANGE OF DIRECTION

## Lady

The Change of Direction actually consists of three steps only and is counted "Slow, Slow, Slow." In the description below the second step is divided into beats of the music to make it more easily understood.

It is usually preceded by a Feather-step or a Reverse Turn.

1. R.F. back, turning body to the L.                        S
2. L.F. diagonally back—not a long step.     1st beat
   With the knees well relaxed, brush R.F. to            S
   L.F., at the same time turning up to half
   a turn to L. Turn on ball of L.F.       2nd beat
3. R.F. back, across the body.                           S

*Contrary Body Movement.* C.B.M. on 1 and 3. The 3rd step is placed in C.B.M.P.

*Rise and Fall.* None.

*Body Sway.* Sway to R. on 2.

*Amount of Turn.* The turn is governed by the following figure. Half a turn is the most effective.

*Footwork.* 1. T. H. 2. T., I.E. of T., H., then I.E. of T. of R.F. 3. T.

*General Notes.* Although the 2nd step is termed diagonally back, it must follow the line of the preceding step on the R.F. The fact that the L. shoulder is leading slightly on this step accounts for it being diagonally back.

The lady's 2nd step must not be quite as long as the man's, otherwise she will finish at his R. side when the turn is completed.

When the R.F. brushes up to the L.F. the R. toe will be level with the L. instep, not toe to toe.

## THE IMPETUS TURN

### Man

This figure is very popular in the Foxtrot and is also used in other dances. It can be danced either at a corner or as a progressive figure along the sides of the room.

It is usually danced after the first three steps of the Natural Turn and is followed by the last part of the Reverse Turn. It can be used after the 6th step of the Reverse Wave. A diagram appears on page 186.

Dance 1, 2, and 3 of the Natural Turn. SQQ. Finish with the back to the L.O.D. Continue—

1. L.F. back, turning body to the R.               S
2. Close R.F. to L.F. turning on L. heel. Finish with weight on R.F. facing diag. to centre. (Heel Turn.)     Q
3. Continue turning on ball of R.F. and step to side and slightly back with L.F.           Q
4. R.F. back, diag. to centre against the L.O.D., turning to the L.              S

     Follow with 5, 6, 7 of a Reverse Turn ending this diag. to centre, or, if at a corner, diag. to wall of the new L.O.D.         QQS

*Contrary Body Movement.* C.B.M. on 1 and 4.

*Rise and Fall (Body).* Rise at end of 2; up on 3. Lower at end of 3.

*Body Sway.* Sway to L. on 2.

*Amount of Turn.* Make three-eighths of a turn on steps 1 and 2 and a quarter between 2 and 3. A quarter turn to the L. is made between steps 4 and 7.

*Footwork.* 1. T. H. 2. H. T. 3. T. H. 4. T.

*Leading.* As the L.F. is taken back on the 1st step, the man should begin to incline his body to the L., so that the lady's forward impetus is received on his R. side. He must lead the lady firmly with his R. hand as she steps forward with her R.F. to assist her forward swing. If this is done it will be found that the lady's impetus will create the turn with no further effort from the man.

*General Notes.* Advanced dancers tend to hurry the 1st step and thus get a "Hover" effect between steps 2 and 3. It could be counted QSQS by experienced dancers. Although steps 1, 2 are a Heel Turn, there is no rise. The knees should be relaxed on 2 and the rise taken at the end of 2.

# THE IMPETUS TURN

## Lady

This figure may be danced either at a corner or along the sides of the room.

It is usually danced after the first three steps of the Natural Turn, and is followed by the last part of the Reverse Turn. It can be used after the 6th step of the Reverse Wave. A diagram appears on page 186.

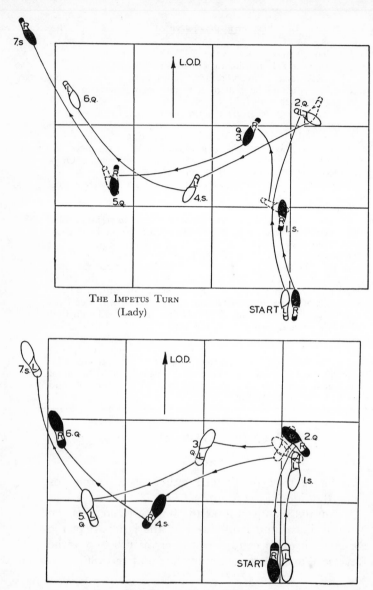

THE IMPETUS TURN
(Lady)

THE IMPETUS TURN (Man)

Dance 1, 2, and 3 of the Natural Turn (SQQ). Finish facing the L.O.D. Continue as follows—

1. R.F. forward, turning body to the R.    S
2. L.F. to side, across the L.O.D.    Q
3. Continue turning on ball of L.F. and take a small
    step diag. forward with R.F.    Q
4. L.F. forward, diag. to centre against the L.O.D.,
    turning to L.    S
    Follow with 5, 6, and 7 of the Reverse Turn    QQS

*Contrary Body Movement.* C.B.M on 1 and 4.

*Rise and Fall (Body).* Rise at end of 2; up on 3. Lower at end of 3.

*Body Sway.* Sway to R. on 2.

*Amount of Turn.* Make three-eighths turn on the first 2 steps and a quarter between 2 and 3. Make a quarter turn to L. between steps 4 and 7.

*Footwork.* 1. H. T. 2. T. 3. T. H. 4. H.

*General Notes.* On the 3rd step, the R.F. should lightly brush up to the L.F. before going diagonally forward. The body must swing well forward on the 1st step, in order to assist the man's turn. Although the 2nd step is taken on the ball of the L.F. there is no rise until the end of this step.


## THE TELEMARK

### Man

The Telemark is a very useful figure when space is limited, and can be used instead of a Reverse Turn.

It is usually preceded and followed by a Feather-step, the last Feather being commenced outside the partner.

Commence facing diagonally to the centre. Finish facing diagonally to the wall.

1. L.F. forward, turning body to the L.    S
2. R.F. to side, across the L.O.D.    Q
3. Continue turning on ball of R.F., step to side and slightly
    forward with L.F. Finish with body facing wall.    Q
4. R.F. forward, diag. to wall, outside partner.    S
    Follow with 2, 3, and 4 of Feather-step. End facing
    diag. to wall. (QQS.)

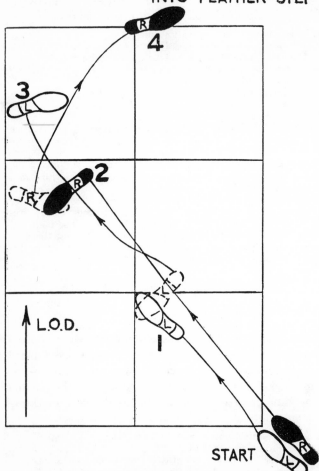

INTO FEATHER-STEP

THE TELEMARK
(Man)

188

*Contrary Body Movement.* C.B.M. on 1 and 4. The 4th step is placed in C.B.M.P.

*Rise and Fall (Body).* Rise at end of 1; up on 2 and 3. Lower at end of 3.

*Body Sway.* Sway to L. on 2.

*Amount of Turn.* Make three-quarters of a turn between 1 and 4, the body turning slightly less.

*Footwork.* 1. H. T. 2. T. 3. T. H. 4. H.

*General Notes.* Care should be taken not to get the feet too close together on the 3rd step, otherwise the body will overturn. The Telemark could be followed by a Natural Turn, the last step of the Telemark becoming the first of a Natural Turn. This is not to be generally recommended; as the man is commencing from an outside position. the lady would have difficulty in executing her heel turn.

Standard technique demands just over a quarter turn between steps 1 and 2, but this is unnecessary and likely to result in a forced movement on step 1. The normal quarter turn, as shown in the diagram, will give the figure a more even turn.

## THE TELEMARK

### Lady

The Telemark is usually preceded by a Feather-step taken diagonally to the centre, and also followed by a Feather-step. The second Feather-step is commenced with the man outside the lady.

The last step of the preceding Feather will be the first of the Telemark, and the last step of the Telemark becomes the first of the following Feather-step.

Commence with the back to the centre diagonally. Finish with the back diagonally to the wall.

1. R.F. back, turning body to L.                  S
2. Close L.F. to R.F., turning on R. heel. Finish facing L.O.D., weight on L.F.           Q
3. Continue turning on ball of L.F. and step to side and slightly back with R.F. Finish with back to wall.    Q
4. L.F. back, diag. to wall, partner outside.        S
   Follow with 2, 3, and 4 of Feather-step, finishing with back diag. to wall. (QQS.)

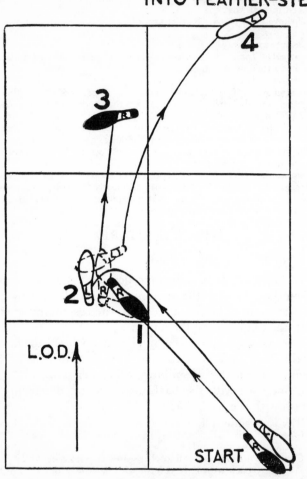

INTO FEATHER–STEP

3

4

2

1

L.O.D.

START

THE TELEMARK
(Lady)

190

*Contrary Body Movement.* C.B.M. on 1 and 4. The 4th step is placed in C.B.M.P.

*Rise and Fall (Body).* Rise slightly at end of 1 (N.F.R.); continue to rise on 2; up on 3. Lower at end of 3.

*Body Sway.* Sway to R. on 2.

*Amount of Turn.* Make three-quarters of a turn between 1 and 4, the body turning slightly less.

*General Notes.* The 3rd step should be quite long, otherwise the lady will get left too much at the side of the man when the 4th step is taken.

# THE OPEN TELEMARK
## (With a Feather Ending)
### Man

The Open Telemark is a variation of the Telemark in which the 3rd and 4th steps are taken in Promenade Position. It can be used in any position which is appropriate for the ordinary Telemark. It is usually preceded by a Feather-step taken diagonally to the centre, and ended with a Feather-step diagonally to the wall on which the lady turns square on the second step.

Commence facing diagonally to the centre.

1. L.F. forward, turning body to L. — S
2. R.F. to side, across the L.O.D. — Q
3. Continue turning on ball of R.F. until body is facing towards outside wall, and step to side and slightly forward with L.F. (Now in P.P. See note below.) — Q
4. R.F. forward, in P.P., diag. to wall. — S
5. Turning lady square, step diagonally forward L.F. — Q
6. R.F. forward, outside partner. — Q
7. L.F. forward, in line with partner (diag. to wall). — S

*Contrary Body Movement.* C.B.M. on 1, 4, and 7. The 4th and 6th steps are placed in C.B.M.P.

*Rise and Fall (Body).* Rise at end of 1; up on 2 and 3. Lower at end of 3. Rise at end of 4; up on 5 and 6. Lower at end of 6.

*Body Sway.* Sway to L. on 2. Sway to R. on 5 and 6.

*Amount of Turn.* The turn of man and lady differs in this figure. Open Telemark: man makes three-quarters of a turn, the body turning slightly less. Slight body turn to L. in the Feather finish.

*Footwork.*  1. H. T.  2. T   3. T. H.  4. H. T.  5. T.  6. T. H. 7. H.

*General Notes.* As the man continues to turn on his 2nd step he must guide the lady by applying pressure with the *base* of his R. hand on her *L.* side. He must endeavour to indicate that *he* is turning to the Promenade Position and that she is not to continue the turn with him. As he leads her into the 5th step the pressure will be transferred to the fingers, to indicate that the lady must turn to face him again.

A Natural Turn may follow the Open Telemark. Please see page 214.

# THE OPEN TELEMARK
## (With a Feather Ending)
### Lady

The Open Telemark is a variation of the Telemark in which the 3rd and 4th steps are taken in Promenade Position. It is preceded by a Feather-step taken diagonally to the centre, and ended with a Feather-step taken back diagonally to the wall on which the lady turns square to partner on the 2nd step.

Commence with the back to the centre diagonally.

1. R.F. back, turning body to L.                                    S
2. Close L.F. to R.F., turning on R. heel.  (Heel Turn.) Finish facing the L.O.D.                                        Q
3. R.F. diag. forward in P.P., R. shoulder leading.  The R. toe should be pointing to L.O.D.                          Q
4. L.F. forward, across the body, in P.P. Begin to turn to L.   S
5. Turning to the L. until body is square to man, step to side and slightly back with R.F.                              Q
6. L.F. back, partner outside (diag. to wall).                    Q
7. R.F. back.                                                       S

*Contrary Body Movement.* C.B.M. on 1, 4, and 7. The 4th and 6th steps are placed in C.B.M.P.

*Rise and Fall (Body).* Rise slightly at end of 1 (N.F.R.); continue to rise on 2; up on 3. Lower at end of 3. Rise at end of 4; up on 5; up on 6 (N.F.R.). Lower at end of 6.

*Body Sway.* Sway to R. on 2. Sway to L. on 5 and 6.

*Amount of Turn.* Make three-eighths turn on steps 1 and 2 and a slight body turn to L. on 3. To regain normal position turn three-eighths to L. on steps 4 to 7.

*Footwork.* 1. T. H. 2. H. T. 3. T. H. 4. H. T. 5. T. H. 6. T. H. 7. T.

*General Notes.* When the lady turns to P.P. it is more effective if she turns her head to face the direction of her 3rd step. Some ladies prefer to keep the head turned to the L. Either is correct. It is a matter of personal taste. The direction of steps 3 and 4 is diagonally to wall, although the feet are pointing to L.O.D.

## THE HOVER TELEMARK

### Man

The Hover Telemark is a most attractive type of variation. It is so named because instead of turning on the second step of a Telemark, the dancer "hovers" and replaces the 3rd step in approximately the same position as it started.

It is danced when the man is stepping forward with his L.F. The last step of a Reverse Turn or any Feather finish is a good entry.

Dance six steps of a Reverse Turn. Finish facing diagonally to wall and continue as follows—

1. L.F. forward, diag. to wall, turning body to the L.    S
2. R.F. to side and let the L.F. close slightly towards the R.F. Now facing the L.O.D.    Q
3. L.F. to side and slightly forward, L.F. pointing diag. to centre but body still facing the L.O.D.    Q
4. R.F. forward, outside partner, diag. to centre.    S
   Continue by doing 2, 3, 4 of a Feather-step. (QQS.)

*Contrary Body Movement.* C.B.M. on 1 and 4. The 4th step is placed in C.B.M.P.

*Rise and Fall (Body).* Commence to rise at end of 1; continue to rise on 2; up on 3. Lower at end of 3.

*Body Sway.* Sway to the L. on 2.

*Amount of Turn.* A quarter turn to the L., the body turning slightly less.

*Footwork.* 1. H. T. 2. T. (R.F.), then I.E. of T. of L.F. 3. T. H. 4. H.

*General Notes.* Care should be taken to rise very gradually between steps 1 and 2, reaching the greatest height when the L.F. has brushed towards the R.F. The L. knee should be relaxed and veering inwards at this point. Although the position of 3 is "side and slightly forward" the L.F. should tend to move more sideways. The man may turn lady to P.P. at the end of 2 and take steps 3 and 4 in P.P.

# THE HOVER TELEMARK

## Lady

1. R.F. back, turning body to L.                                                  S
2. Step to side with L.F., letting R.F. close slightly towards the L.F. Body backing the L.O.D.                                   Q
3. R.F. to side and slightly back, body still backing the L.O.D.                                                                Q
4. L.F. back diag. to centre, partner outside.                          S

Continue with 2, 3 and 4 of the Feather-step. (QQS.)

*Contrary Body Movement.* C.B.M. on 1 and 4. The 4th step is placed in C.B.M.P.

*Rise and Fall (Body).* Commence to rise at end of 1 (N.F.R.); continue to rise on 2; up on 3. Lower at end of 3.

*Body Sway.* Sway to R. on 2.

*Amount of Turn.* A quarter turn to the L. is made, the body turning slightly less.

*Footwork.* 1. T. H. 2. T. (L.F.), then I.E. of T. of R.F. 3. T. H. 4. T.

# THE HOVER FEATHER

## Man

The Hover Feather consists of three steps, and is danced after the man has done a Pull Step. The best positions in which to use it are given in the notes below. It is described from the most popular position which is after the 5th step of a Natural Turn.

Dance steps 1 to 5 of the Natural Turn. Finish facing diagonally to the centre and continue as follows—

1. At the end of the Pull Step (5th step of Natural Turn),
     rise to toes and place the L.F. diag. forward, with the
     L. shoulder leading and preparing to step outside
     partner                                                    Q
2. R.F. forward, outside partner.                               Q
3. L.F. forward, diag. to centre.                               S
     Follow with any Reverse figure.
   *Contrary Body Movement.* C.B.M. on 3. The 2nd step is placed
in C.B.M.P.
   *Rise and Fall (Body).* Rise at the end of the preceding step   Up
on 1 and 2. Lower at end of 2.
   *Body Sway.* The body is swaying to the L. on the Pull Step.
Sway to the L. on 1 of Hover Feather.
   *Amount of Turn.* There is no turn.
   *Footwork.* 1. T. 2. T. H. 3. H.
   *General Notes.* When dancing the Pull Step preceding a Hover
Feather the body should be allowed to overturn slightly to the
R. as the rise is made. The L. knee will then veer inwards towards
the R. knee without the L. toe leaving the floor. Pressure is kept
on the inside edge of the toe of L.F. to assist the balance.
   The Hover Feather can be used after the 8th step of the
Reverse Wave. It is also included as a part of the Natural Hover
Telemark, the Natural Twist Turn, and the Natural Telemark.

## Lady

Dance steps 1 to 5 of the Natural Turn. Finish
backing diagonally to the centre. Continue as follows—

1. As the 5th step of the Natural Turn is taken, the R.F.
     should brush to the L.F. At the same time rise to the
     toes. Place the R.F. diag. back, with the R. shoulder
     leading.                                                   Q
2. L.F. back, partner outside.                                  Q
3. R.F. back, diag. to centre.                                  S
     Follow with any Reverse figure.
   *Contrary Body Movement.* C.B.M. on 3. The 2nd step is placed in
C.B.M.P.
   *Rise and Fall (Body).* Rise at the end of the preceding step; up
on 1; up on 2 (N.F.R.). Lower at end of 2.
   *Body Sway.* The body is swaying to the R. on the Brush Step
(5th step of Natural Turn). Sway to the R. on 1 of Hover Feather.
   *Amount of Turn.* There is no turn.
   *Footwork.* 1. T H. 2. T. H. 3. T.

*General Notes.* As the R.F. brushes to the L.F. on the preceding step the body should overturn slightly to the R. The rise is taken from the ball of the L.F. The L. heel does not touch the floor.

## THE NATURAL TELEMARK

### Man

The Natural Telemark is a comparatively easy and most useful figure, which can be used instead of a Natural Turn.

The easiest position to introduce it is at the corner of the room, but it is possible to use it along the side of the room. It is described as it would be used in the latter position.

Commence facing diagonally to the wall. Finish facing diagonally to the centre. ·

1. R.F. forward, turning body to the R.                                        S
2. L.F. to side, across the L.O.D.                                             Q
3. Continue turning on the ball of L.F. and take a small step
   to side with R.F., on the toes. Now facing diag. to centre.   Q
4. L.F. diag. forward, preparing to step outside partner, L.
   shoulder leading.                                                          Q
5. R.F. forward, outside partner.                                             Q
6. L.F. forward, diag. to centre.                                             S
   Follow with any Reverse figure.

*Contrary Body Movement.* C.B.M. on 1 and 6. The 5th step is placed in C.B.M.P.

*Rise and Fall (Body).* Rise at end of 1; up on steps 2, 3, 4, and 5. Lower at end of 5.

*Body Sway.* Sway to the R. on 2 and to the L. on 4.

*Amount of Turn.* Make a quarter turn on the first 2 steps and a half turn between steps 2 and 3. At a corner make only a quarter turn on the last part to end facing diagonally to centre of the new L.O.D. or three-eighths to face the new L.O.D.

*Footwork.* 1. H. T. 2. T. 3. T. 4. T. 5. T. H. 6. H.

*General Notes.* Do not hurry between steps 2 and 3 otherwise the lady will be "pulled off" her Heel Turn. Dance the figure quietly and without the Hover effect used with the more difficult Natural Hover Telemark described on page 199.

*Amalgamations.* (*a*) Reverse Turn, followed by a Three-step continued in a direction diagonally to wall; Natural Telemark ending diagonally to centre. Follow with any Reverse figure.

(*b*) Feather-step, Three-step taken down the L.O.D. and ending near a corner; Natural Telemark making five-eighths of a turn to end diagonally to centre of the new L.O.D. Follow with any Reverse figure.

# THE NATURAL TELEMARK

## Lady

A simple and most useful figure which can be used instead of a Natural Turn. Commence backing diagonally to the wall.

1. L.F. back, turning body to the R.                                    S
2. Close R.F. to L.F. making a Heel Turn to face the L.O.D.    Q
3. Continue turning to the R. on the ball of R.F. and step to side L.F. Now backing diag. to centre. The R.F. will now brush slightly towards L.F.    Q
4. R.F. diag. back, R. shoulder leading.                           Q
5. L.F. back, partner outside.                                           Q
6. R.F. back, diag. to centre.                                           S

Follow with any Reverse figure.

*Contrary Body Movement.* C.B.M. on 1 and 6. The 5th step is placed in C.B.M.P.

*Rise and Fall (Body).* Rise slightly at end of 1 (N.F.R.); continue to rise on 2; up on 3 and 4; up on 5 (N.F.R.). Lower at end of 5.

*Body Sway.* Sway to L. on 2 and to R. on 4.

*Amount of Turn.* Make three-eighths of a turn to R. on 1 and 2 and three-eighths between 2 and 3. When danced at a corner, making only a half a turn on the complete figure, make three-eighths of a turn between 1 and 2 and an eighth between 2 and 3.

*Footwork.* 1. T. H.  2. H. T.  3. T.  4. T. H.  5. T. H.  6. T.

*General Notes.* Do not attempt to brush the R.F. up to L.F. on step 3 otherwise the continuity of the movement will be lost. The R.F. should brush slightly towards L.F. but there is not sufficient time for it to brush completely to L.F.

A HOVER MOVEMENT
Demonstrated by Bill and Bobbie Irvine

# THE NATURAL HOVER TELEMARK

## Man

This is a most attractive and difficult figure which requires firm control on the part of the man. It resembles the Natural Telemark but the turn is made with a Heel Pull, and it has an additional step on which a Hover is made.

It is for advanced dancers only.

Commence facing diagonally to the wall.

1. R.F. forward, turning body to the R.      S
2. L.F. to side, across the L.O.D.      Q
3. Continue turning, first on the ball and then on the heel of L.F. and pull the R.F. to the side of the L.F. (as in a Pull Step). Finish facing diag. to centre.      Q
4. Rise to the toes, and let L. knee veer inwards as body overturns slightly to the R.      S
5. L.F. diag. forward, preparing to step outside partner, L. shoulder leading.      Q
6. R.F. forward, outside partner.      Q
7. L.F. forward, diag. to centre.      S

*Contrary Body Movement.* C.B.M. on 1 and 7. The 6th step is placed in C.B.M.P.

*Rise and Fall (Body).* Rise at end of 1; up on 2. Lower at end of 2. Rise at end of 3; up on 4, 5, and 6. Lower at end of 6.

*Body Sway.* Sway to R. on 2 and to the L. on 3, 4, and 5.

*Amount of Turn.* Make a quarter turn on the first 2 steps and a half turn between steps 2 and 3, the body turning slightly more as the Hover is made on step 4. If the figure is used at a corner, less turn is made between steps 2 and 3 (quarter or three-eighths).

*Footwork.* 1. H. T. 2. T. H. 3. H., I.E. of foot, whole foot. 4. T. (R.F.), and pressure on I.E. of T. of L.F. 5. T. 6. T. H. 7. H.

*General Notes.* Keep well down on the Pull Step (step 3) and take this step slightly wider than in a normal Pull Step. Do not rise abruptly to the toes on 4. The speed of the lady will create the rise for the man and although the body will overturn slightly to the R. the inside edge of the toe of the L.F. must be pressed firmly into the floor in order to retain control. The veering inwards of the L. knee and a *very slight* breaking of the body line from the hips upwards will give the Hover an attractive appearance.

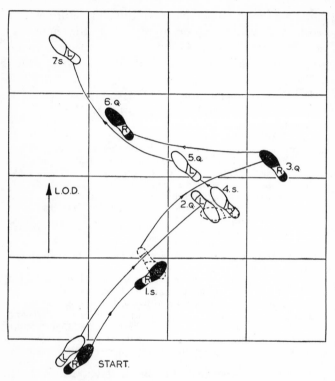

7 s.

6. Q.
R

5. Q.

3. Q.
R

4. s.

2. Q.

L.O.D.

1. s.
R

R    START.

THE NATURAL HOVER TELEMARK
(Man)

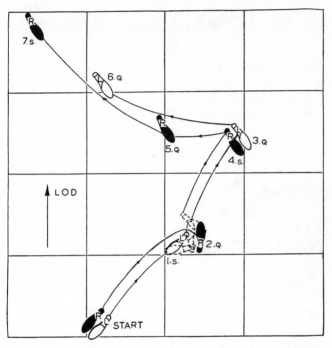

THE NATURAL HOVER TELEMARK
(Lady)

The change of Sway from R. to L. between steps 2 and 3 should not be abrupt.

The amalgamations given in the general notes following the Natural Telemark will also apply to this figure.

# THE NATURAL HOVER TELEMARK

## Lady

This is a difficult figure but looks most attractive when danced well.  It resembles the Natural Telemark but has an additional step on which a Hover is made.

Commence backing diagonally to the wall.

1. L.F. back, turning body to the R.                                    S
2. Close R.F. to L.F. making a Heel Turn to face the L.O.D.   Q
3. Continue turning to the R. on the ball of R.F. and step
      to side L.F., well across the front of the man.  Now
      backing diag. to centre.                                           Q
4. Brush R.F. to L.F. rising to the toes and allow the body to
      overturn slightly to the R.                                       S
5. R.F. diag. back, R. shoulder leading.                            Q
6. L.F. back, partner outside.                                         Q
7. R.F. back, diag. to centre.                                         S

*Contrary Body Movement.*  C.B.M. on 1 and 7.  The 6th step is placed in C.B.M.P.

*Rise and Fall (Body).*  Rise slightly at end of 1 (N.F.R.); continue to rise on 2 (N.F.R.).  Down on 3.  Rise at end of 3; up on 4 and 5; up on 6 (N.F.R.).  Lower at end of 6.

*Body Sway.*  Sway to L. on 2 and to the R. on 3, 4, and 5.

*Amount of Turn.*  Make three-eighths of a turn to R. on 1 and 2 and three-eighths between 2 and 3, the body turning slightly more to the R. on 4.  When danced at a corner, making only a half turn on the complete figure, make three-eighths of a turn between 1 and 2 and an eighth between 2 and 3.

*Footwork.*  1. T. H.  2. H. T.  3. T.  4. T. (L.F.), and I.E. of T. of R.F.  5. T. H.  6. T. H.  7. T.

*General Notes.*  The rise on steps 1 and 2 is Body stretch only and there is no rise in the feet.  The 3rd step is taken on the ball of L.F. and the rise is then taken without lowering the L. heel on 3.  Although standard technique gives the turn on 4 as only a turn of the body, it will be found that the L.F. will also turn slightly almost to back the L.O.D. (Diagram on p. 201.)

# THE NATURAL TWIST TURN

## Man

The Natural Twist Turn can be used instead of a Natural Turn. Although it can be danced by quite average dancers, it looks most effective when danced with the speed and polish that the more experienced dancer can give to a variation of this type.

It could be used at a corner but is better when used along the sides of the room. The latter method of dancing is described below.

Commence facing the L.O.D. Finish facing diagonally to the centre.

1. R.F. forward, turning body to the R.                                    S
2. L.F. to side, across the L.O.D.                                        Q
3. Continue turning slightly to R. and take a small step back with the R.F. on the ball of the foot, crossing it well behind the L.F. Now backing the L.O.D.   "and"
4, 5. Keeping the feet as flat as possible, twist on both feet for three-eighths of a turn to the R. Finish facing diag. to centre with feet apart as in a Pull Step and slowly rise to the toes.                        QS
6, 7, 8. L.F. diag. forward and go into a Hover Feather.      QQS

*Contrary Body Movement.* C.B.M. on 1 and 8. The 7th step is placed in C.B.M.P.

*Rise and Fall (Body).* There is no rise on the first part. Rise on 5; up on 6 and 7. Lower at end of 7.

*Body Sway.* Sway to R. on 2, 3. Sway to L. on 5, 6.

*Amount of Turn.* Make seven-eighths of a turn to R. between steps 1 and 5. When danced at a corner, it is better to end facing the new L.O.D. or facing diagonally to the wall of the new L.O.D. The body will overturn slightly to the R. on 5.

*Footwork.* 1. H. T. 2. T. H. 3. T. 4. Twist on T. of R.F., and H. of L.F., with feet flat. End with weight on whole of R.F. 5. T. (R.F.) with pressure on I.E. of T. of L.F. 6. T. 7. T. H. 8. H.

*General Notes.* After the man has taken his 2nd step he must lead the lady slightly to his R. side so that she takes steps 3, 4, 5 moving round and outside him on his R. She will get square to him again at the end of her 5th step. The rise at the end of 5 must not be abrupt, and the L. knee should veer inwards as the body overturns to the R. It should be noted that steps 2 and 3 have only a half beat each, and it is this quickening of the turn, followed by a slow rise and Hover, that makes the figure so attractive. The man should remember to move the R.F. quickly on 3, and not try to get speed by rushing the 2nd step.

Some men dancers take the 2nd step to the side on the heel first, and find this gives them more control, whilst others dance it by stepping first on the ball of the foot. The latter method is to be preferred. There is no rise on the first 2 steps, these being taken without the swing used in the Natural Hover Telemark.

The normal entry to this figure is a Three-step down the L.O.D.

## THE NATURAL TWIST TURN

### Lady

This variation is commenced backing the L.O.D.

1. L.F. back, turning body to the R.      S
2. Close R.F. to L.F., turning on the L. heel (Heel Turn).      Q
3. Small step forward with L.F., preparing to step outside partner, L. shoulder leading.      "and"
4. Small step forward with R.F., outside partner and moving diag. to wall.      Q
5. L.F. to side, with body backing diag. to centre. Rise to toes and allow R.F. to brush to L.F., body overturning slightly to the R.      S
6, 7, 8. R.F. diag. back and go into a Hover Feather.      QQS

*Contrary Body Movement.* C.B.M. on 1, 4 and 8. The 4th and 7th steps are placed in C.B.M.P.

*Rise and Fall (Body).* There is no rise on the first 4 steps. Rise on 5; up on 6; up on 7 (N.F.R.). Lower at end of 7. Steps 3, 4, and 5 are taken on the balls of the feet.

*Body Sway.* Sway to the L. on 2, 3. Sway to R. on 5, 6.

*Amount of Turn.* Make seven-eighths of a turn to R. between steps 1 and 5. Less turn will be made when danced at a corner.

*Footwork.* 1. T. H. 2. H. T. 3. T. 4. T. 5. T. and I.E. of T. of R.F. 6. T. H. 7. T. H. 8. T.

*General Notes.* If the man leads the figure properly the lady will feel his increased speed at the end of the second step and she must then move away from her Heel Turn very quickly. It should be noted that steps 2 and 3 have only a half beat each.

# THE WEAVE

## Man

The Weave is a very popular variation. Normally it is used as a progressive figure, although it can be adapted for use at a corner. It is described as it would be used along the sides of the room.

Commence facing the L.O.D. and dance steps 1 to 4 of the Reverse Wave. Finish backing diagonally to the wall, and commence the Weave from this position.

1. Step forward on to L.F., turning body to the L.     Q
2. R.F. to side, body backing the L.O.D.     Q
3. L.F. back, diag. to centre, partner outside.     Q
4. R.F. back, diag. to centre, partner in line. Body turning to the L.     Q
    (The next 3 steps are the same as steps 5, 6, 7 of the Reverse Turn.)
5. L.F. to side and slightly forward, body facing wall.     Q
6. R.F. forward, outside partner.     Q
7. L.F. forward, diag. to wall.     S

*Contrary Body Movement.* C.B.M. on 1, 4, and 7. The 3rd and 6th steps are placed in C.B.M.P.

*Rise and Fall (Body).* Rise at end of 1; up on steps 2, 3, 4, 5, and 6. Lower at end of 6.

*Body Sway.* Sway to the L. on 2, 3. Sway to the R. on 5, 6.

*Amount of Turn.* Make a quarter turn between 1 and 3 and a quarter turn between 4 and 7.

*Footwork.* 1. H. T. 2. T. 3. T. 4. T. 5. T. 6. T. H. 7. H. (See note below.)

*General Notes.* Care should be taken not to let the weight drop back too much on the 4th step of the preceding Wave, otherwise the entry to Weave will be forced. If this step is taken well across the body in C.B.M. Position an attractive body line will result, and the subsequent entry to the Weave will be easier.

On step 3 (L.F.) it is permissible to use the Footwork of T. H. and this will often result in a more soft and flowing movement.

The Weave can be danced at a corner. Dance 1 to 4 of the Reverse *Turn*, finishing backing the L.O.D. near a corner. Now turn a quarter turn to L. on steps 1 to 3 of the Weave; take the

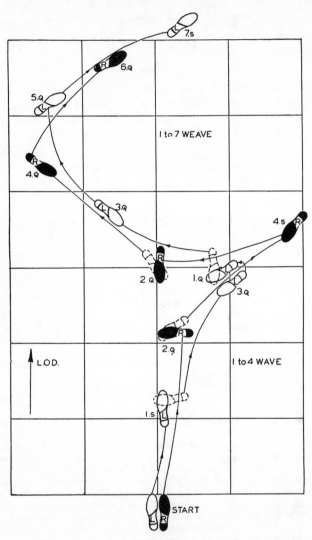

THE WEAVE
(Man)
206

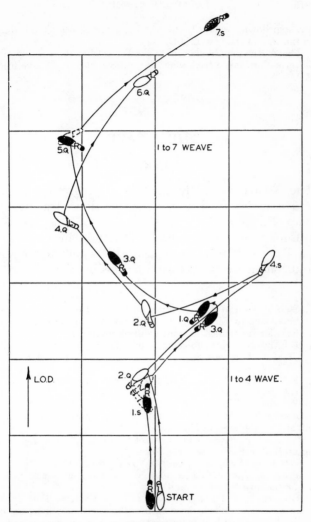

THE WEAVE
(Lady)
207

4th step down the *new* L.O.D. and end the Feather finish diag. to the wall of the new L.O.D.

The Weave may be danced in the Waltz after the 4th step of a Reverse Turn taken back diag. to wall. See also the Weave from P.P.

# THE WEAVE

## Lady

The Weave is mostly used as a progressive figure and it is described as it would be danced along the sides of the room.

Commence backing the L.O.D. and dance 1 to 4 of the Reverse Wave. Finish facing diagonally to the wall and commence the Weave from this position.

1. Step back on to R.F., turning the body to the L.      Q
2. Small step to side with L.F. Body now facing the L.O.D.      Q
3. R.F. forward, diag. to centre, outside partner.      Q
4. L.F. forward, diag. to centre, body turning to L.      Q
     (The next 3 steps are the same as steps 5, 6, 7 of the Reverse Turn.)
5. R.F. to side. Body backing towards the wall.      Q
6. L.F. back, partner outside.      Q
7. R.F. back, diag. to wall.      S

*Contrary Body Movement.* C.B.M. on 1, 4, and 7. The 3rd and 6th steps are placed in C.B.M.P.

*Rise and Fall (Body).* Rise at end of 1 (N.F.R.); up on 2, 3, 4, 5; up on 6 (N.F.R.). Lower at end of 6.

*Body Sway.* Sway to R. on 2, 3. Sway to L. on 5, 6.

*Amount of Turn.* Make a quarter turn between 1 and 3 and a quarter turn between 4 and 7.

*Footwork.* 1. T. H. 2. T. 3. T. 4. T. 5. T. H. 6. T. H. 7. T.

*General Notes.* When the man uses the alternative footwork on 3, the lady will still step forward on the toes on steps 3 and 4, although the rise will not be so pronounced. (Diagram on p. 207.)

# THE TOP SPIN
## Man

This variation is not only attractive to dance, but it is a very useful figure in a crowded room, and an experienced dancer will use it instinctively to change his direction when a collision is imminent. The Top Spin consists of two backward turning steps which are used after checking forward on the R.F., these two steps being followed by 5, 6, 7 of a Reverse Turn.

It is possible to dance the Top Spin along the sides of the room, and a diagram of this is given. The following description is of a Top Spin danced at a corner.

Commence when near a corner.
Dance steps 1 to 6 of the Reverse Turn. Finish
    with the R.F. forward, outside partner.
    Remain up on toes, body facing diag. to wall.    SQQSQQ

1. Turning the body to the L., move the L.F. slightly to
   the R., behind the R.F. and directly against the
   L.O.D. Partner outside.    Q
2. R.F. back, diag. to wall against the L.O.D Partner in
   line. Body still turning to the L.    Q
   (The next 3 steps are the same as steps 5, 6, 7 of the
   Reverse Turn.)
3. L.F. to side and slightly forward, body facing the *new*
   L.O.D.    Q
4. R.F. forward, diag. to centre of the new L.O.D., outside
   partner.    Q
5. L.F. forward, in line with lady, diag. to centre of new
   L.O.D.    S

*Contrary Body Movement.* C.B.M. on 2 and 5. The 1st and 4th steps are placed in C.B.M.P.

*Rise and Fall (Body).* Up on steps 1 to 4. Lower at end of 4.

*Body Sway.* Sway to the R. on 3, 4.

*Amount of Turn.* Make an eighth of a turn between the preceding step and step 1; an eighth between 1 and 2 and a quarter between 2 and 5.

*Footwork.* 1. T. 2. T. 3. T. 4. T. H. 5. H. Note: on step 1 the footwork of T. H. may be used and this will often result in a more soft and flowing movement.

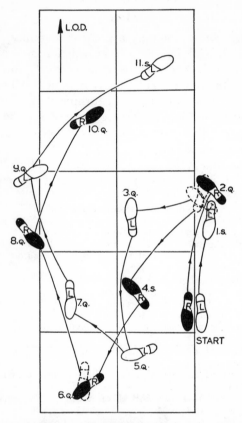

THE TOP SPIN

(Man)

*Note.* Steps 1, 2, 3 are an Impetus Turn
Steps 4, 5, 6 are 4, 5, 6 of a Reverse Turn
Steps 7 to 11 are the Top Spin

*General Notes.* It should be noted that when the Top Spin follows the 6th step of a Reverse Turn, this step should be taken with the feet *and body* facing diagonally to wall. Normally on the 6th step of a Reverse Turn the R.F. is diagonally to wall, but the body has turned slightly less.

*Amalgamations.* (*a*) At a corner. The description above shows the entry into Top Spin at a corner. It should be followed by any Reverse figure. The Top Spin could be underturned to end down the new L.O.D., when a Three-step and Natural Turn would follow.

(*b*) Along the sides of the room. Dance 1, 2, 3 of a Natural Turn, followed by an Impetus Turn (SQQSQQS). Make a half turn on the Impetus Turn so that the last step is taken back on R.F. in a direction against the L.O.D. Now dance steps 5, 6 of the Reverse Turn (QQ) finishing with the R.F. forward outside partner. The R.F. is taken in a direction diagonally to the centre against the L.O.D. Check on this step and continue with the Top Spin. The body will be backing the L.O.D. on 1 of the Top Spin, backing diagonally to centre on 2, and facing diagonally to wall on 5. A diagram of this amalgamation is on page 210.

There are numerous other amalgamations, but these two are the most important. Any time that the R.F. has stepped forward outside partner in a Feather-step or a Feather finish to any figure, the movement may be checked and followed by a Top Spin. The amount of turn would vary according to the position in the room. Remember that a half turn is the most comfortable amount of turn to make on the complete figure. If the dancer will visualize the Top Spin as two steps back, turning to the L. and followed by 5, 6, 7 of the Reverse Turn, its introduction into the dance will be very much simplified.

# THE TOP SPIN

## Lady

The notes at the beginning of the man's steps and the general notes and amalgamations should be studied very carefully. The description that follows is of the Top Spin as danced at a corner. A diagram showing the use of the Top Spin along the sides of the room is given on page 212.

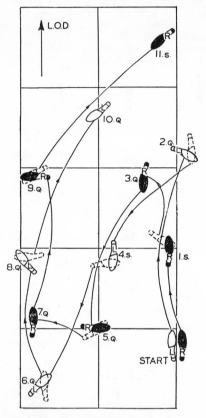

THE TOP SPIN

(Lady)

*Note.* Steps 1, 2, 3 are an Impetus Turn

Steps 4, 5, 6 are 4, 5, 6 of a Reverse Turn

Steps 7 to 11 are the Top Spin

Commence near a corner.

Dance steps 1 to 6 of a Reverse Turn. Finish
with the L.F. back, partner outside. Remain
up on toes, body backing diag. to wall.          SQQSQQ

1. Turning the body to the L. move the R.F. to the L.
across the front of the L.F. Outside partner.          Q

2. L.F. forward, diag. to wall against the L.O.D., still
turning to L.          Q

(The next 3 steps are just the same as steps 5, 6, 7 of
the Reverse Turn.)

3. R.F. to side, body backing the *new* L.O.D.          Q

4. L.F. back, diag. to centre of the *new* L.O.D., partner
outside.          Q

5. R.F. back, partner now in line. Diag. to centre of the
new L.O.D.          S

*Contrary Body Movement.* C.B.M. on 2 and 5. The 1st and 4th
steps are placed in C.B.M.P.

*Rise and Fall (Body).* Up on steps 1, 2, 3; up on 4 (N.F.R.).
Lower at end of 4.

*Body Sway.* Sway to the L. on 3, 4.

*Amount of Turn.* Up to a half turn may be made on the complete
figure. Make an eighth between the preceding step and 1, an
eighth between 1 and 2, an eighth between 2 and 3, and an
eighth between 3 and 4.

*Footwork.* 1. T. 2. T. 3. T. H. 4. T. H. 5. T.

*General Notes.* When checking on 6 of a Reverse Turn to follow
with a Top Spin the lady will not lower her R. heel on the 5th
step of the Reverse. She should remain on her toes for steps 5 and
6 otherwise her weight will move too far back.

For other amalgamations of the Top Spin please see the man's
notes.

# THE OUTSIDE SWIVEL

## (From the Open Telemark and Natural Turn)

### Man

The Outside Swivel consists of two steps only. It
can be used from several positions, but it was in the
amalgamation described overleaf that the figure first
gained popularity.

Commence facing diagonally to the centre and dance 1, 2, 3 of a Feather-step. Continue as follows—

## Open Telemark

1. L.F. forward, turning body to L.     S
2. R.F. to side, across the L.O.D.     Q
3. Continue turning on ball of R.F. until body is *backing diag. to centre* and step sideways with L.F.     Q
   Now in P.P.

## Natural Turn

1. R.F. forward, across the body in P.P., moving towards the wall, and begin to turn to R.     S
2. L.F. to side, body now backing the L.O.D. and having turned square to partner.     Q
3. Still turning slightly, step back R.F., R. shoulder leading, now backing diag. to wall.     Q

## Outside Swivel

1. L.F. back, diag. to wall, with the toe turned inwards, partner outside. As this step is taken, let the *body* continue to turn to the R. as the R.F. is drawn back across the front of L.F. without weight on it. (See notes below.) Both man and lady are now in P.P. (The lady having swivelled to P.P.) The man is facing diag. to centre.     S
2. R.F. forward, across the body in P.P. towards centre.     S

## Feather Ending

Follow with steps 2, 3, 4 of a Feather-step, taken diag. to centre, and turning lady square on 2 of Feather-step.     QQS

*Contrary Body Movement.* Open Telemark: C.B.M. on 1. Natural Turn: C.B.M. on 1. This step is also placed in C.B.M.P. Outside Swivel: C.B.M. on 1 and 2. Both steps are placed in C.B.M.P.

*Rise and Fall (Body).* Open Telemark: ,rise at end of 1; up on 2 and 3. Lower at end of 3. Natural Turn: rise at end of 1; up on 2 and 3. Lower at end of 3. No rise on the Outside Swivel.

*Body Sway.* Open Telemark: sway to L. on 2. There is no sway on a Natural Turn commenced in Promenade Position and no sway on the Outside Swivel.

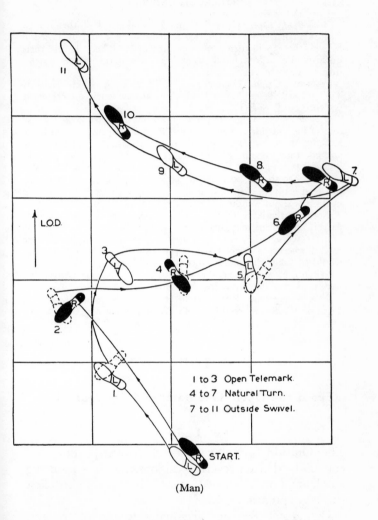

1 to 3  Open Telemark.
4 to 7  Natural Turn.
7 to 11  Outside Swivel.

LOD.

11
10
9
8
7
6
5
4
3
2
1
START.

(Man)

215

*Amount of Turn.* Open Telemark: make a half turn to L. Natural Turn: make a quarter turn between 1 and 3. Outside Swivel: body will turn a quarter turn to R. The L.F. will turn inwards to point diagonally to centre as the step is taken, but the turn of the body is gradual.

*Footwork.* Open Telemark: 1. H. T. 2. T. 3. T. H. Natural Turn: 1. H. T. 2. T. 3. T. H. Outside Swivel: 1. T. H. with pressure on T. of R.F. 2. H.

*General Notes.* When the man takes his L.F. back on the 1st step of the Outside Swivel, he must keep a firm pressure with his R. hand on the lady's L. side. He must check her forward impetus and continue pressure on her L. side to lead her into the Outside Swivel. It is essential that his body should turn gradually as she turns. Care should be taken to avoid dropping the R. elbow as this lead is given. Pressure on the floor with the R.F. as it crosses in front without weight will help the man to retain good balance.

Note particularly that the Open Telemark is underturned. Advanced dancers may turn more, but the position described is the best for average dancers. Less turn may be made on the Outside Swivel when it is danced at a corner, and the following Feather would be taken diagonally to centre of the new L.O.D.

When dancing the Feather-step after the Outside Swivel the L.F. is placed diagonally forward on 2.

The Weave from P.P. is an excellent figure to follow step 7. Turn on the Swivel could be adjusted if at a corner.

# THE OUTSIDE SWIVEL

## (From the Open Telemark and Natural Turn)

### Lady

The Outside Swivel consists of two steps only. It can be used from several positions, but it was in the amalgamation described below that the figure first gained popularity.

Commence backing diagonally to the centre and dance 1, 2, 3 of a Feather-step. Continue as follows—

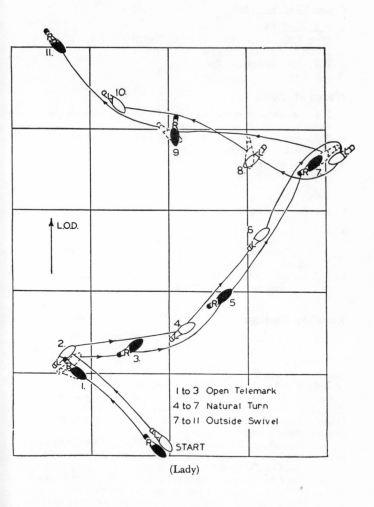

I to 3  Open Telemark
4 to 7  Natural Turn
7 to II  Outside Swivel

(Lady)

## Open Telemark

1. R.F. back, turning body to L.                                   S
2. Close L.F. to R.F., turning on R. heel (Heel Turn).   Q
   Finish facing diag. to wall.
3. R.F. diag. forward in P.P.                                    Q

## Natural Turn

1. L.F. forward, across the body in P.P., moving towards the
   wall, with L.F. pointing diag. to wall.                      S
2. R.F. forward, between the man's feet, body square to
   man and facing diag. to wall.                             Q
3. L.F. forward, preparing to step outside partner, L.
   shoulder leading.                                          Q

## Outside Swivel

1. R.F. forward, diag. to wall, outside partner. Swivel
   on the ball of the R.F. for a half turn to the R. and
   at the same time close the L.F. to R.F., slightly back,
   without weight on it. Finish in P.P.                S
2. L.F. forward, across the body in P.P. and turning body
   to L., moving towards centre.                       S

## Feather Ending

Turn square to partner and follow with steps 2, 3,
4 of a Feather-step, taken back diag. to centre.    QQS

*Contrary Body Movement.* Open Telemark: C.B.M. on 1.
Natural Turn: the 1st step is placed in C.B.M.P. Outside
Swivel: C.B.M. on 1 and 2. Both steps are placed in C.B.M.P.

*Rise and Fall (Body).* Open Telemark: rise slightly at end of 1
(N.F.R.); continue to rise on 2; up on 3. Lower at end of 3.
Natural Turn: rise at end of 1; up on 2 and 3. Lower at end of 3.
Outside Swivel: there is no rise.

*Body Sway.* Open Telemark: sway to R. on 2. There is no sway
on a Natural Turn commenced in Promenade Position, and no
sway on the Outside Swivel.

*Amount of Turn.* Open Telemark: make a quarter turn between
1 and 2. Natural Turn: there is no turn on this part of the
figure. Outside Swivel: make a half turn to R. Less turn may be
made at a corner.

*Footwork.* Open Telemark: 1. T. H. 2. H. T. 3. T. H. Natural Turn: 1. H. T. 2. T. 3. T. H. Outside Swivel: 1. H. T. H. and pressure on I.E. of T. of L.F. 2. H.

*General Notes.* Although the turn is made on the ball of R.F. in the Outside Swivel the foot must be kept quite flat. The knees should be relaxed. The pressure on the inside edge of the toe of the L.F. will materially assist the balance.

When turning square to partner to take the Feather-step ending to the Outside Swivel the R.F. should be placed to the side and slightly back for the 2nd step of the Feather.

*Special Note.* The Weave from P.P., described on pages 223 to 226 of the Waltz section, can be danced in the Foxtrot after the Outside Swivel. It is better to underturn the Outside Swivel and to move to centre or diag. to centre against the L.O.D. for the first step of the Weave. Rhythm in the Foxtrot will be QQQQQQS.

# THE NATURAL WEAVE

## Man

The Natural Weave is a delightful free moving figure which can be used as an alternative to the Natural Turn. Normally it is danced after a Three-step. Other entries are noted below.

Commence facing the L.O.D.

1. R.F. forward, turning to R.                                    S
2. L.F. to side, almost backing diag. to centre.                 Q
3. Still turning slightly to R. step back R.F. diag. to centre, with R. shoulder leading.                                     Q
4. L.F. back, diag. to centre, partner outside.                  Q
5. R.F. back, partner in line and turning to L.                  Q
6. L.F. to side and slightly forward, body facing wall.          Q
7. R.F. forward, diag. to wall, outside partner.                 Q
8. L.F. forward, diag. to wall.                                  S

*Contrary Body Movement.* C.B.M. on 1, 5, and 8. The 4th and 7th steps are placed in C.B.M.P.

*Rise and Fall (Body).* Rise at end of 1; up on steps 2, 3, 4, 5, 6, 7; lower at end of 7.

*Body Sway.* Sway to R. on 2; to L. on 4; to R. on 6 and 7.

*Amount of Turn.* Make three-eighths of a turn to R. between 1 and 3 and a quarter turn to L. between 5 and 8.

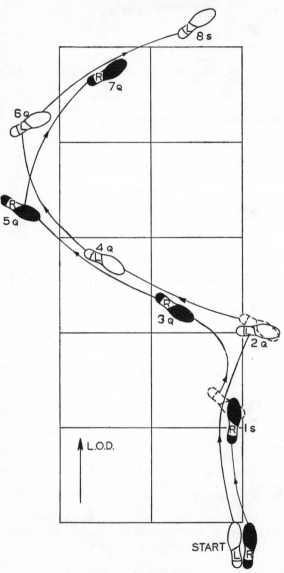

THE NATURAL WEAVE
(Man)

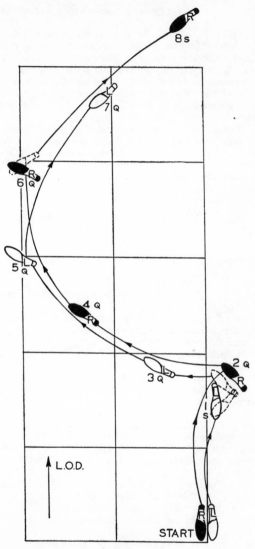

THE NATURAL WEAVE
(Lady)

*Footwork.*  1. H. T.  2. T.  3. T.  4. T.  5. T.  6. T.  7. T.H.  8. H.

*General Notes.* Note the slight continuance of the turn between steps 2 and 3 and also the quick change of sway on steps 2 and 4. When taking the 3rd step it is advisable to feel that it moves slightly rightwards. If it is taken back under the body, a common fault, an ugly body line will result. On step 4 it is permissible to use the Footwork of T. H. on L.F. This often results in a softer movement.

The Natural Weave can be danced after any Three-step and can also be commenced in Promenade Position, when the man will turn square to lady as the 2nd step is danced. When commenced in P.P. the lady's 1st step will be forward and her 2nd step danced diagonally forward (making no Heel Turn). The Open Telemark is a good entry.

# THE NATURAL WEAVE

## Lady.

Commence backing the L.O.D.

1. L.F. back, turning to the R.  S
2. Close R.F. to L.F. turning on the L. heel (Heel Turn). End facing diag. to centre.  Q
3. L.F. forward, diag. to centre, with L. shoulder leading and preparing to step outside partner.  Q
4. R.F. forward, outside partner.  Q
5. L.F. forward, diag. to centre, in line with partner, and turning to L.  Q
6. R.F. to side, backing towards wall.  Q
7. Still turning slightly to L. step back L.F., diag. to wall, partner outside.  Q
8. R.F. back, diag. to wall.  S

*Contrary Body Movement.* C.B.M. on 1, 5, and 8. The 4th and 7th steps are placed in C.B.M.P.

*Rise and Fall (Body).* Rise slightly at end of 1 (N.F.R.) continue to rise on 2; up on steps 3, 4, 5, 6, up on 7 with N.F.R.; Lower at end of 7.

*Body Sway.* Sway to L. on 2; to R. on 4; to L. on 6 and 7.

*Amount of Turn.* Make three-eighths of a turn to R. on steps 1 and 2 and a quarter turn to L. between 5 and 8.

*Footwork.*  1. T. H.  2. H. T.  3. T.  4. T.  5. T.  6. T. H. 7. T. H.  8. T.

*General Notes.* See notes following the man's steps.

# THE WEAVE
## (From Promenade Position)
## Man

This beautiful variation is also described in the Waltz section but with a different alignment. The alignments are interchangeable and suggested entries are the Open Impetus Turn (shown in the diagram) or the Hover Telemark ended in Promenade Position.

Dance steps 1, 2, 3 of a Natural Turn and then 4, 5, 6 of an Open Impetus Turn. Count SQQSQQ and end in Promenade, moving diagonally to centre as shown in the diagram. Continue—

1. R.F. forward in P.P. moving diag. to centre.                    S
2. Turning Lady square, step forward L.F., diag. to centre.      Q
3. Turning to L. step to side and slightly back with R.F. body
   backing diag. to wall.                                         Q
4. Still turning slightly, step back L.F., down the L.O.D. with
   partner outside.                                               Q
5. R.F. back, down the L.O.D. with Lady in line and turning
   to the L.                                                      Q
6. L.F. to side and slightly forward, body facing wall.           Q
7. R.F. forward, diag. to wall, outside partner.                  Q
8. L.F. forward, in line with partner.                            S

*Contrary Body Movement.* C.B.M. on 2, 5, and 8. Steps 1, 4, and 7 are placed in C.B.M.P.

*Rise and Fall (Body).* Rise at end of 1; up on steps 2 to 7; lower at end of 7.

*Body Sway.* Sway to L. on 3 and 4. Sway to R. on 6 and 7.

*Amount of Turn.* Make a quarter turn to L. between 2 and 3 and an eighth between 3 and 4. Make three-eighths to L. between 5 and 8.

*Footwork.* 1. H. T. 2. T. 3. T. 4. T. 5. T. 6. T. 7. T. H. 8. H.

*General Notes.* Some dancers find it easier to get a softer movement by lowering the L. heel on step 4, but avoid completely lowering the body and getting an ugly "dipping" movement on step 5. Please also read the General Notes on this figure in the Waltz section.

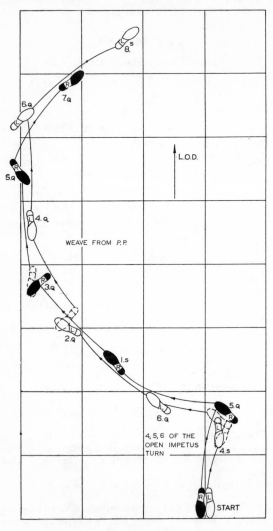

L.O.D.

8.s

7.q

6.q

5.q

4.q

WEAVE FROM P.P.

3.q

2.q

1.s

5.q

6.q

4.s

4, 5, 6 OF THE
OPEN IMPETUS
TURN

START

THE WEAVE
(From Promenade Position)

(Man)

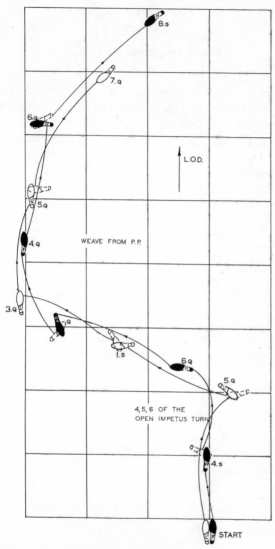

L.O.D.

WEAVE FROM P.P.

4, 5, 6 OF THE
OPEN IMPETUS TURN

START

THE WEAVE
(From Promenade Position)
(Lady)

# THE WEAVE
## (From Promenade Position)
### Lady

Although this delightful variation is described from an entry of the Open Impetus Turn it can be used from any Promenade Position with similar alignment.

Dance steps 1, 2, 3 of a Natural Turn and then 4, 5, 6 of an Open Impetus Turn. Count SQQSQQ and end in Promenade, moving diagonally to centre but with the R.F. pointing to centre, as shown in the diagram. Continue—

1. L.F. forward and across R.F., in P.P., moving diag. to centre and with L.F. pointing to centre.　　　　　　　S
2. Turning to the L., step to side and slightly back with R.F. with body backing diag. to centre and turning square to man.　　　　　　　Q
3. Continue turning to L. on ball of R.F. until almost facing the L.O.D. and then step to side and slightly forward with L.F. with L. toe pointing to L.O.D.　　　　Q
4. R.F. forward, outside partner, down the L.O.D.　　　Q
5. L.F. forward, in line with partner and turning to L.　Q
6. R.F. to side, body backing towards wall.　　　　　Q
7. Continue turning slightly and step back L.F., diag. to wall, partner outside.　　　　　　　　　　　Q
8. R.F. back, partner in line.　　　　　　　　　　　S

*Contrary Body Movement.* C.B.M. on 1, 5, and 8. Steps 1, 4, and 7 are placed in C.B.M.P.

*Rise and Fall (Body).* Rise at end of 1; up on steps 2 to 7 (with N.F.R. on 7) lower at end of 7.

*Body Sway.* Sway to R. on 3 and 4. Sway to L. on 6 and 7.

*Amount of Turn.* Make three-eighths to L. between 1 and 2 and three-eighths between 2 and 3. Make a quarter to L. between 5 and 6 and an eighth between 6 and 8.

*Footwork.* 1. H. T. 2. T. 3. T. 4. T. 5. T. 6. T. H. 7. T. H. 8. T.

*General Notes.* Advanced lady dancers often keep the head turned to the R. on steps 1 to 5, turning it back to its normal position as the Feather Finish is danced. Please also read the General Notes on this figure in the Waltz section.

# SUGGESTED FOXTROT AMALGAMATIONS

1. Feather-step—Three-step—Natural Turn.

2. Feather-step diagonally to centre—Reverse Turn
—Three-step—Natural Turn into a corner—Finish
facing the new L.O.D.

3. Feather-step—4 steps of Reverse Wave—Weave—
Change of Direction.

4. Feather-step—Three-step—Natural Turn ending
with an Impetus Turn followed by 5, 6, 7 of a Reverse
Turn, ending diagonally to the centre. Follow with
any Reverse figure.

5. Feather-step diagonally to the centre—Reverse
Turn—Straight into a Reverse Wave, ending with a
Hover Feather taken diagonally to the centre—Open
Telemark, Natural Turn and Outside Swivel—Weave
from P.P.

6. Feather-step — Three-step — Natural Weave —
Change of Direction.

7. Feather-step—Three-step—Natural Turn—End-
ing with an Impetus Turn. Underturn the Impetus
Turn and follow with 4, 5, 6 of a Reverse Turn—Top
Spin.

8. Feather-step—Reverse Turn—Hover Telemark
ending in P.P.—Weave from P.P.—Three-step—
Natural Turn.

9. Feather-step down L.O.D.—First four steps of
Reverse Wave—Weave—Three-step—Natural Twist
Turn, Natural Telemark, or Natural Weave.

## SECTION IV

## THE TANGO

THE average Englishman looks upon the Tango as a dance full of eccentricities, and probably regards it as extremely difficult to acquire. Actually, the steps can be acquired much more easily than those of the Quick-step and Foxtrot, but the "style" and "character" of the Tango is very elusive—Tango "atmosphere" it is usually termed.

Until recent years English dancers have endeavoured to capture this "atmosphere" by the introduction of an unnatural and rather cramped type of hold to-gether with the use of a very relaxed movement, the resultant dance being both "creepy" and ungainly. The introduction of a more staccato action has con-siderably enlivened the dance, and, although the tendency to exaggerate this action brought forth a certain amount of criticism, its influence remains.

Tango music is so attractive that the moderate dancer will be well repaid for the time spent in learning a few of the simple basic figures. The keen dancer who takes the trouble to acquire that elusive Tango atmo-sphere will find full compensation from the correct interpretation of what is undoubtedly one of the most fascinating dance rhythms.

### General Notes

*Time.* 2/4. Two beats in a bar. Both the 1st and 2nd beats are accented.

228

THE TANGO HOLD
Shown by Bill and Bobbie Irvine

229

*Tempo.* Music played at about 33 bars a minute.

*Basic Rhythms.* Slow, Slow. Quick, Quick, Slow. As Tango music is in 2/4 time, each "Slow" has only one beat of music, and each "Quick" has a ½ beat.

*Figures.* Walk, Progressive Side Step, The Rock Turn, Closed Promenade, Open Promenade, Back Corté, The Rocks, Open Reverse Turns, Basic Reverse Turn, Progressive Side Step Reverse Turn, Natural Twist Turn, Natural Promenade Turn, Progressive Link, Promenade Link, The Four Step, Fallaway Promenade, Outside Swivel and Brush Tap, Outside Swivel turning to L.

The Tango being an entirely different type of dance from the other standard dances, a detailed description of its chief characteristics is given in the following pages. The manner of approach depends very much upon the ability of the dancer, but it is advisable for all dancers to read the instructions on the Hold, the Placing of the Feet, and the characteristics of the Walk.

The construction of the Tango is comparatively simple owing to the fact that more walking steps are used, thus giving the dancer time to think which figure to use next. The following suggestions regarding the order in which to learn the basic figures should prove useful to the beginner.

*The Walk.* Learn this first. Approach it by means of a perfectly natural movement, afterwards trying to introduce points 1, 2 and 3 referred to in the notes on the Walk.

*Progressive Side Step.* Learn this figure, and then practise it, using three walking steps between each Progressive Side Step.

*Rock Turn.* Usually a Reverse Turn is introduced

next, but the Rock Turn will be found easier and more useful.

*Closed Promenade, Open Promenade.* These figures will follow quite easily from the Rock Turn.

*Reverse Turn.* The Open Reverse Turn, with the closed or open finish is probably the most popular and should be learned next. As an alternative the Basic Reverse Turn could be used.

Notes on the general construction are given in the descriptions of the separate figures.

## The Hold

The hold in the Tango is rather more compact than in the moving dances. The lady is held slightly more on the man's R. side, but this must not be exaggerated. The man's R. arm will be slightly farther round the lady. To obtain the correct hold for the extended arms, stand in position and with the L. arm held in the normal Foxtrot hold. The man should now bring his L. hand slightly in towards him, and also lower it a little. These movements must be made from the elbow, the forearm only moving. To correspond with this alteration the lady should drop her elbow slightly as well as moving her hand. The man, however, should endeavour to keep his elbow in the normal position.

Owing to the position of her body in the Tango (slightly more to the man's R.), the lady will find it more comfortable to place her L. hand rather more at the back of the man's R. arm or with the hand actually resting on the man's back, just under his arm-pit.

## Position in the Walk

Walking movements in the Tango are not taken with

the man facing square to the L.O.D. When a step is taken down the L.O.D. his feet and body will be facing almost diagonally to the centre, with his R. hip and shoulder in advance of his L. In backward movements the reverse will apply. This positioning of the body at the commencement of the dance will affect the Walk in the following ways—

Each step taken forward with the L.F. will give the effect of moving across the body (called "Contrary Body Movement Position") and the legs will be "locked" together above the knees.

As a step is taken with the R.F. the legs will "unlock"; and the term *Right shoulder leading* is used to describe this position in the following descriptions.

This action will result in the Walk taking the line of a wide curve to the man's L.

In backward movements the man's L. shoulder will lead, and the legs will lock and unlock in a similar manner.

*Further Characteristics of the Walk.* Although the balance and distribution of weight are similar to those in other dances, there are one or two important characteristics in the Tango Walk that should be noted.

1. *Knees.* The knees are kept slightly flexed throughout the dance. To realize the full meaning of this, the dancer must remember that in the other dances, when the leg is at the full extent of its stride, the knee is comparatively straight. In the Tango the feet are lifted slightly from the floor in the Walk (see Note No. 2 below), and when the foot meets the floor at the full extent of the stride, it does so with the knee slightly more flexed than in the moving dances, although the muscles of the leg are tensed to avoid any

suggestion of "drop" or softness as the weight is taken on to the step. Naturally, the *moving* leg will flex even more as it is passing through to its forward position, but care must be taken not to relax the knee of the supporting leg further, otherwise a "lilting" or "up and down" movement will result.

2. *Placing of Feet.* All walking steps in the Tango are picked up from the floor slightly and placed into position. This, of course, is in direct opposition to the gliding movement of other dances. Care must be taken not to exaggerate this action. It is preferable to keep the ball of the foot of the moving leg skimming over the floor until it nearly reaches the supporting foot, before lifting it slightly from the floor and placing it in position with a crisp action. The keen dancer will also observe that the curving of the Walk to the L. will result in the weight being taken on the L. edge of both feet in all forward movements and on the R. edge in backward movements.

3. *Sharpness.* The crisp action of the Walk is obtained by delaying the movement of the foot that is not supporting the weight of the body. If a step forward has been taken with the R.F., the moving of the L.F. should be delayed slightly, so that when it does move forward it must move quickly in order to be in position on the next beat of the music. Do not delay the back foot too long, as this would result in a loss of continuity in the movement of the body.

Whilst these three points apply also to the backward Walk, it must be admitted that it is much more difficult when doing a backward movement to "feel" the action referred to in Notes 2 and 3. This is owing to the fact that the toe will meet the floor first. One can get more

character into a movement that is led with the heel
first. No attempt must be made to lift the foot upwards
at the full extent of the stride and then force it down to
the floor in an effort to achieve sharpness of action in
the backward walk.

All steps should be of medium length, not short.
They will not be as long as in moving dances. The
action of the step comes from the hip, not from the knee
only, but the swinging action of the other dances is
not used.

## The Turns

*Contrary Body Movement.* Although Contrary Body
Movement is often used in turning figures in the
Tango, the "swing" into the turns, to which I have
referred in the moving dances, is almost completely
absent. The turns in the Tango are less acute, and
the R. shoulder lead adopted in this dance (referred to
under "Position in the Walk") makes the entry into
L. turns much easier. Right-hand turns are often
taken from Promenade Position or are so constructed
that a conscious swing of the body is unnecessary.

*Contrary Body Movement Position.* This is referred to
frequently in the descriptions of the Tango figures, and
is the position achieved when the body is not turned
but the leg placed across the body, so giving the
appearance of Contrary Body Movement. Every normal step forward with the L.F. and back with the R.F.
by both man and lady will be in Contrary Body Movement Position. It frequently happens that Contrary
Body Movement is used on a Contrary Body Movement
Position step. This is noted in the descriptions. The

2nd step of every Promenade figure automatically results in Contrary Body Movement Position.

*Rise and Fall.* There is no Rise in the Tango. The absence of "swing" on the turns, and the fact that the feet are placed rather than swung into position, account for this difference from the moving dances. In one or two figures, steps are taken and swivels made on the ball of the foot, but there is no pronounced Rise, and the heel is kept close to the floor.

In the accompanying charts a few swivels of the feet have been shown but it is important to remember that in practically every case this swivel of the foot is made *after* the next step is in position.

## Body Sways

The reasons for the absence of Rise and Fall in the Tango also account for the lack of Body Sways. The shoulders should be kept as level as possible.

## Footwork

In the Tango, the word *Ball* instead of *Toe* is used in describing Footwork. Other terms used are *Inside edge of foot, Inside edge of Ball of foot,* and *Whole foot.* The correct footwork on each step is given following the descriptions of the figures, but some helpful rules to remember are—

1. All forward steps, whether taken in C.B.M.P. or with a shoulder lead are described as *Heel.* It is not necessary to say *Heel, then Flat.* The first two steps of promenade figures are also *Heel.*

2. All backward steps taken in C.B.M.P. are *Ball, Heel,* indicating that the step is taken on to the Ball, then lowering to the whole foot.

3. All backward steps taken with a L. or R. shoulder lead are *Inside edge of Ball, Heel.* The reason for this is quite obvious.

4. The footwork of side steps varies. Some are *Inside edge of foot* and others are *Inside edge of Ball, Heel*, or just *Ball, Heel*. A few are *Whole Foot*. The use of these terms will be found consistent in all figures, and it will help the student to get a truer interpretation of the dance if the correct footwork is used.

5. The footwork of Closing steps also varies. The majority are *Whole Foot*, but in some more advanced figures it will be found that a foot closes with the footwork of *Ball, Heel*.

## Alignment

It is important to remember that the alignment on forward and backward steps in the Tango descriptions is a *directional* term, and that the Right shoulder lead used by the man in a forward walk, and the Left shoulder lead used in a backward walk will result in the feet and body having a different alignment from the actual direction of the step.

The following examples will assist students to understand this point—

1. *Step back L.F., down the L.O.D.* The direction of the step will be down the L.O.D. but the L. shoulder lead will result in the feet and body backing *diagonally to the centre*.

2. *Step forward R.F., diag. to centre.* The direction of the step will be diagonally to the centre, but the R. shoulder lead will result in the feet and body facing the *centre*.

## Closing of the Feet

The feet are closed very frequently in the Tango, and much more character can be given to the dance if the feet are closed correctly.

The feet are usually closed after a step to the side, an example being: "L.F. to side; close R.F. to L.F." The following details should be studied—

1. When stepping to the side with L.F. take the step on the inside edge of the L.F., with the L. knee veering inwards. The whole foot will be on the floor as the complete weight moves on to the foot.

2. Delay moving the R.F. and feel that the pressure is left on the inside edge of the ball of the R.F. with the R. heel almost touching the floor. The R. knee will tend to move towards the L. knee.

3. Pick the R.F. very slightly off the floor and then close it *deliberately*, but not very sharply, to the L.F.

4. Advanced dancers never close the feet tightly together. The R. toe should be level with the L. instep and about an inch away from it, but the knees must be touching, with the R. knee tucked slightly behind the L. knee. The R.F. should tend to turn *very slightly* inwards.

Anything in the nature of a "solid" closing of the feet, with an upright stance should be avoided. The closing of the foot slightly back instead of completely level with the L.F. will result in the body assuming the same position as is used in a forward walk.

A similar movement is used by the lady when closing her L.F. to her R.F. Differences are that her R.F. will be placed to the side with the inside edge of the *ball* of the foot making the first contact with the floor, and her L.F. will close, or rather nearly close, with the Left heel near the Right instep.

## Promenade Figures

Promenade figures are danced with the man's R. side and the lady's L. side in close contact, and with the opposite sides of the body "open" or apart, so that the bodies form a "V" shape.

Normally, if a Promenade is taken along the L.O.D. the man will be facing diagonally to the wall, and the lady will face diagonally to the centre. It is, however, advisable to keep the position slightly more compact than this, with the lady facing between diagonally to the centre and the centre.

The position of the lady's head in Promenade

figures is a matter of personal taste. The normal position is for the lady to turn her head to the Right so that she is facing the direction of the Promenade. Some ladies prefer to keep the head in the usual position or even turn it more to the Left.

It is advisable to use the position which feels most comfortable.

## THE WALK FORWARD

Notes on the characteristics of the Walk are given on the preceding pages. It should be noted that each Walk occupies only one beat of music, but it is easiest to count it "Slow" as the slow tempo of the music makes the step of the same duration as a "Slow" in the Foxtrot. The actual movement of the feet is as follows—

Take a natural-length step forward with the R.F., placing the foot heel first and going immediately on to the flat foot. Bring the rear foot forward with the toe skimming the floor. Lift this foot slightly from the floor just before it reaches the supporting foot, and then continue forward to repeat the Walk on the L.F.

Note that the heel of the supporting foot is always released just after the moving foot passes the supporting foot.

As the R.F. commences to move forward the weight is on the supporting (L.) foot. When the R.F. is placed, the weight is central for a moment, and then taken forward on to the R.F. The body must be kept moving all the time, and any tendency to "sit back" on the supporting foot must be avoided.

## THE WALK BACKWARD

Take a natural-length step backward with the L.F., placing the toe first and lowering to the ball of the foot. Draw the front foot back with the heel skimming the floor, and lower the heel of the supporting (L.) foot as the moving foot passes to continue with another Walk.

It should be noted that in actual practice the heel of the supporting foot tends to lower slightly earlier than it does in the Walk used in the Quickstep and Foxtrot.

As the L.F. commences to move back the weight is on the supporting (R.) foot. When the L.F. is placed back the weight is central for a moment, and then taken on to the back foot.

# THE PROGRESSIVE SIDE STEP

## Man

The Progressive Side Step might be termed a quickening of the Walk in which the second step is taken sideways. This figure can be taken in any forward direction, and should tend to curve slightly to the L.

1. L.F. forward, across the body.                                        Q
2. R.F. to the side and slightly back.*                                  Q
   (The ball of the R.F. should be level with the L. instep.)
3. L.F. forward, across the body.                                        S
   *Contrary Body Movement Position.* Steps 1 and 3 are in C.B.M.P.
   *Footwork.* 1. H. 2. I.E. of foot. 3. H.
   *General Notes.* Although the man's 2nd step is to the side and *slightly back* in relation to the body, it will progress further along the L.O.D. than the L.F. if the figure is turned. This step should be placed sharply, using the inside edge of the foot.
   One or three walking steps should be used before the Progressive Side Step is repeated. Diagram overleaf.

## Lady

1. R.F. back, across the body.                                           Q
2. L.F. to the side and slightly forward.*                               Q
   (The ball of the R.F. should be level with the L. instep.)
3. R.F. back, across the body.                                           S
   *Contrary Body Movement Position.* Steps 1 and 3 are in C.B.M.P.
   *Footwork.* 1. B. H. 2. I.E. of B., H. 3. B.
   *General Notes.* When the 2nd step is placed on the inside edge of the Ball of the L.F., the L. Heel should be quite close to the floor. If the L. Heel is raised too much a "bouncing" movement will result.

   * Although in the charts the 1st and 2nd steps appear to toe the same line, the position described above is correct in relation to the body, as indicated by the dotted line.

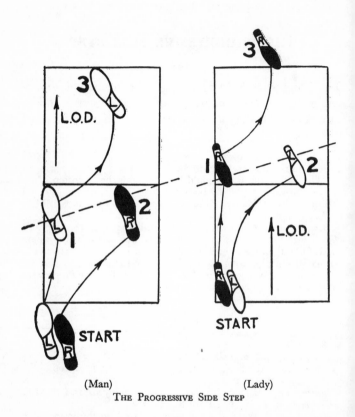

(Man)    (Lady)

THE PROGRESSIVE SIDE STEP

# THE ROCK TURN

## Man

A simple and useful figure comprising the Rock and the last three steps of a closed Reverse Turn.

This figure can be commenced when the man is travelling down the L.O.D. or diagonally to the wall. Finish facing diagonally to the wall.

1. R.F. forward, turning body to the R.                              S
2. L.F. to side and slightly back.  Backing centre.                  Q
3. Still turning body to the R., rock forward on to R.F..
     R. shoulder leading.                                            Q
4. Rock back on to L.F., lengthening the step by a few
     inches, moving diag. to centre with the L. shoulder
     leading.                                                        S
5. R.F. back (to centre) turning body to L.                          Q
6. L.F. to side, and slightly forward.                               Q
7. Close R.F. to L.F., slightly back.  Face diag. to wall.           S

*Contrary Body Movement and Position.*  C.B.M. on 1 and 5.  5 is also taken in C.B.M.P.

*Footwork.*  1. H.  2. I.E. of B. H.  3. I.E. of B. H.  4. I.E. of B. H. 5. B.H.  6. I.E. of foot.  7. Whole foot.

*Amount of Turn.*  Make a quarter turn to the R. between 1 and 3, and a quarter turn to L. between 3 and 6.

*General Notes.*  On the first step no swivel is made on R.F. As the L.F. moves sideways for the 2nd step, the R. Heel will be released from the floor.  Pressure is then felt on the I.E. of the ball of the R.F. before the heel is replaced on the 3rd step.  Alternatively the R.F. may be picked up slightly and then replaced on the heel and then the flat foot.  The knees must be kept well relaxed in the Rock.

*Amalgamation.*  A good elementary amalgamation is—
   Commence facing diag. to wall.
   Walk—R.F., L.F., R.F.                                          SSS
   Progressive Side Step.                                         QQS
   Rock Turn.                                                   SQQSQQS
   Finish diag. to wall to continue with Walk.

The Rock Turn may follow the Natural Promenade Turn.  The man will not turn the lady to P.P. on the 4th step of the Promenade Turn.

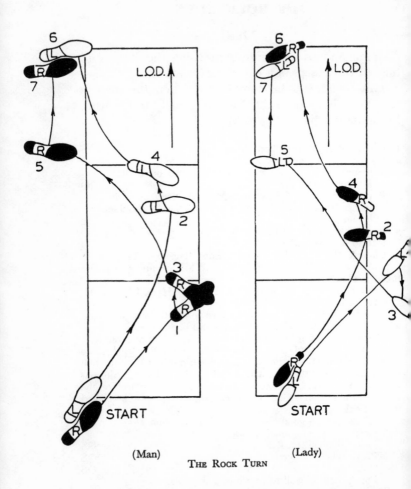

(Man)      THE ROCK TURN      (Lady)

# THE ROCK TURN

## Lady

This figure can be commenced when backing the L.O.D., or when backing the wall diagonally. It is usually ended with the lady backing the wall diagonally.

1. L.F. back, turning body to the R.                                          S
2. Move R.F. sideways to the R., leaving it forward, slightly
    between man's feet.                                     Q
3. Still turning to R., rock back on to the L.F. moving it slightly
    leftwards, L. shoulder leading                          Q
4. Rock forward on to R.F., lengthening the step by a few
    inches. Moving diag. to centre, R. shoulder leading.   S
5. L.F. forward (to centre), turning body to L.                               Q
6. R.F. to side and slightly back.                                           Q
7. Close L.F. to R.F., slightly forward.                                      S

*Contrary Body Movement and Position.* C.B.M. on 1 and 5. 5 is also taken in C.B.M.P.

*Amount of Turn.* Make a quarter turn to the R. between 1 and 3, and a quarter turn to the L. between 3 and 6.

*Footwork.* 1. B. H. 2. H. 3. I.E. of B. H. 4. H. 5. H. 6. I.E. of B. H. 7. Whole foot.

*General Notes.* On the actual Rock Turn (steps 1 to 4) the lady is on the inside of the turn. As the R.F. is moving sideways, it is kept between the man's feet as he, being on the outside of the turn, steps round her with his L.F. Finish in normal alignment.

The knees must be kept well relaxed in the Rock.

*Amalgamations.* A useful amalgamation is given in the notes on the man's steps.

# FROM THE WALK INTO PROMENADE

The descriptions of the Closed and Open Promenades are given in the following pages. Methods of turning to commence these figures from a Walk should be studied.

The normal position to dance a Promenade is sideways along the L.O.D. Assuming the dancer has just completed a figure such as the Rock Turn, or a Reverse

Turn with a closed finish, he would be facing diagonally to the wall with the feet closed. After a step forward with the L.F. the procedure would be—

(1) Step forward with the R.F. more in line with the L.F. than a normal R.F. walk, and at the same time turn the lady to Promenade Position by applying pressure with the base of the R. hand on the L. side of her back. The man will have practically no turn to make as he is already in a diagonal position.

On the latter part of the "Slow" count on which this step is made, the man should close, or nearly close (either is correct and depends on individual style), the L.F. to the R.F., without weight, before stepping to the side for the 1st step of the Promenade.

It is not good style to "brush" the L.F. past the R.F. and go straight into a Promenade. The L.F. should make a slight pause before moving sideways for the first step of the Promenade, and the inside edge of the ball of the L.F. should be in contact with the floor at this point.

The lady should close, or nearly close, her R.F. to her L.F., without weight, before stepping to the side. The notes in the preceding paragraph also apply to the lady's R.F.

(2) If a Promenade figure is taken following a Walk when moving along the L.O.D. it is better to dance the entire Promenade in a direction diagonally to the centre. The step following the Promenade is taken forward with the L.F. down the L.O.D.

(3) A more advanced entry to the Promenade is the Progressive Link. This is described on page 274.

## THE CLOSED PROMENADE

### Man

The Closed Promenade can be danced moving sideways along the L.O.D., or in a direction diagonally to the centre. Methods of entry from the Walk are given on the previous page.

As previously mentioned, in Promenade figures the man's R. side and the lady's L. side are kept close together, whilst the opposite hips and shoulders are apart, the two bodies thus forming a "V." When moving along the L.O.D. in this way, the man's body

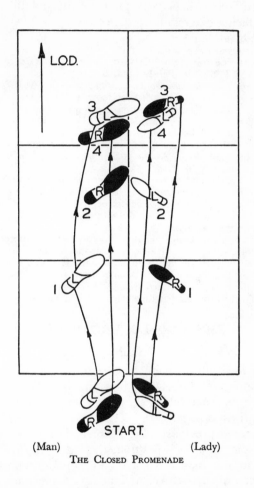

THE CLOSED PROMENADE

(Man)                    (Lady)

will be facing diagonally to the wall, and the lady's
body facing diagonally to the centre.

1. L.F. to side in P.P.                                         S
2. R.F. forward and across in P.P.                             Q
3. L.F. to side and slightly forward.                         Q
4. Close R.F. to L.F. slightly back.                          S

*Contrary Body Movement Position.* Step 2 is in C.B.M.P.

*Footwork.* 1. H. 2. H. 3. I.E. of foot. 4. Whole foot.

*General Notes.* Note that the first step is quite long and with the
toe turned slightly more towards the L.O.D. than in steps 2, 3, and
4. The 3rd step should be placed crisply on the inside edge of
L.F. and with the L. knee veering inwards before taking the weight
on to the whole foot. As the R.F. closes, the L. shoulder will
tend to move slightly back.

Although the bodies lose contact on one side, the Promenade
Position must be kept compact. This will be found easier if the
lady is held with her L. hip slightly behind the man's R. hip.

The man must lead the lady with his R. hand to turn her
square on the 3rd step.

Whilst beginners will find it useful to practise a succession of
Promenades, the more advanced dancer should never dance more
than one Promenade figure in succession. It is also better style
to take the Promenade from a Walk or a Progressive Link, and not
after a figure that has ended with the feet closed.

Follow the Promenade with a Walk taken diagonally to the wall.

## THE CLOSED PROMENADE

### Lady

The Closed Promenade can be danced moving sideways along the L.O.D., or in a direction diagonally to
the centre. Methods of entry from the Walk are given
on a previous page.

As stated previously, the Promenade is danced with
the bodies in a "V" position, the lady's L. side being
close to the man's R. side, and opposite hips and
shoulders are apart. When dancing a Promenade along
the L.O.D. the lady will be facing diagonally to the
centre.

1. R.F. to side in P.P.                                 S
2. L.F. forward and across in P.P.                   Q
3. R.F. to side and slightly back, and at the same time turning square to partner.          Q
4. Close L.F. to R.F., slightly forward.           S
    Finish with back diagonally to the wall.
    *Contrary Body Movement and Position.* C.B.M. and C.B.M.P. on 2.
    *Footwork.* 1. H. 2. H. 3. I.E. of B. H. 4. Whole foot.
    *General Notes.* The 1st step should be quite long, and the toe turned out, pointing almost down the L.O.D. This, and the fact that the man has taken his first step slightly back from the L.O.D. will enable the 2nd step to be taken with ease. The bodies should not turn more outwards as the 2nd step moves across.

    The modern method of dancing the Promenade is for the lady to turn square to man as she takes her 3rd step. This step is placed on the inside edge of the ball of R.F. before lowering the heel, but there must be no rise. The R. knee should veer inwards as this step is taken.

    When dancing a Promenade the lady may turn her head to the R. to face along the L.O.D. or leave it in the normal position. Both methods are correct and it is a matter of personal taste.

## THE OPEN PROMENADE

### Man

The Open Promenade is similar to the Closed Promenade, but the 4th step is taken forward outside the partner. It is usually danced sideways along the L.O.D.

Commence in Promenade Position, after a Walk forward on the R.F. or a Progressive Link. Finish facing almost diagonally to the wall.

1. L.F. to side in P.P.                               S
2. R.F. forward and across in P.P., and commence to turn to R.                         Q
3. Short step to side and slightly forward with L.F., turning partner square.          Q
4. R.F. forward, outside partner.               S
    *Contrary Body Movement and Position.* Steps 2 and 4 are in C.B.M.P. and slight C.B.M. is used on 2.

*Footwork.* 1. H. 2. H. 3. I.E. of foot. 4. H.

*General Notes.* As the 3rd step is taken to the side, it is advisable to turn very slightly to the right so that the body is almost square to the wall, otherwise an ugly hip movement is likely to result when the 4th step is taken forward across the body.

The weight is slightly more forward on the 3rd step of an Open Promenade than on the 3rd step of a Closed Promenade, and this will give a clear indication to the lady as to which Promenade is being danced. The direction of the 4th step will be between the wall and diagonally to wall.

*Amalgamations.* Follow with—

(1) Progressive Side Step. Step immediately forward with L.F. rather across the front of the body to get into line with the partner, and dance the Progressive Side Step.

(2) Open Finish. After stepping forward with the R.F. transfer the weight back to the L.F. with the partner outside (S). Step back with the R.F., the partner being in line (S), and then go forward with the L.F. into a Progressive Side Step.

(3) Rock Turn. After stepping forward with the R.F., transfer the weight back to the L.F., and dance steps 2 to 7 of the Rock Turn. The Rock will be taken outside the partner and about a quarter turn made to the R., so that the 4th step of the Rock Turn is taken with the back diagonally to the centre. Get the lady in line on the 5th step of the Rock Turn. (Rhythm QQ SQQ S.)

(4) Back Corté (see page 249). After stepping forward with the R.F. transfer the weight back to the L.F., turning the body slightly to the R. (S); then dance 2, 3, and 4 of the Back Corté, making very little turn to the L. (QQ S). The lady gets into line on the 2nd step of the Corté.

(5) Four Step (see page 276).

(6) The Outside Swivel.

Note that the first 3 steps of the Rock (3) and the 1st step of the Back Corté (4) will be in C.B.M.P.

# THE OPEN PROMENADE

## Lady

The Open Promenade is similar to the Closed Promenade, but the lady takes the 4th step back with the partner outside instead of closing it to R.F.

It is usually danced along the L.O.D.

Commence in Promenade Position, after a Walk

backward on the L.F. or a Progressive Link. Finish backing almost diagonally to the wall.

1. R.F. to side in P.P                                              S
2. L.F. forward and across in P.P., and commence to turn
   to L.                                                            Q
3. R.F. to side and slightly back, having turned square to the
   man.                                                            Q
4. L.F. back, partner outside.                                     S

*Contrary Body Movement and Position.* Steps 2 and 4 are placed in C.B.M.P. Slight C.B.M. will be used on 2 to turn square to the partner.

*Footwork.* 1. H. 2. H. 3. I.E. of B. H. 4. B.

*General Notes.* The 3rd step should not be too short, otherwise the lady will be left too much at the R. side of the man on the outside step. The 4th step is taken in a direction between the wall and diagonally to wall.

*Amalgamations.* Particulars of appropriate figures to follow the Open Promenade are given at the foot of the description of the man's steps.

## THE BACK CORTÉ

### Man

The Back Corté is used chiefly when the man is moving backwards to the L.O.D. and wishes to turn to a forward direction.

It consists of a step back with L.F. followed by the second half of the Reverse Turn.

Commence backing diagonally to the centre. Finish facing diagonally to the wall.

1. L.F. back down the L.O.D., L. shoulder leading.                 S
2. R.F. back, turning body to L.                                   Q
3. L.F. to side and slightly forward.                             Q
4. Close R.F. to L.F., slightly back. Finish diag. to wall.        S

*Contrary Body Movement and Position.* Step 2 is placed in C.B.M.P. Slight C.B.M. is also used.

*Amount of Turn.* A quarter turn to L. may be made.

*Footwork.* 1. I.E. of B. H. 2. B. H. 3. I.E. of foot. 4. Whole foot.

*General Notes.* It is important to remember the normal L. shoulder lead on the 1st step, otherwise the turn to the L. will

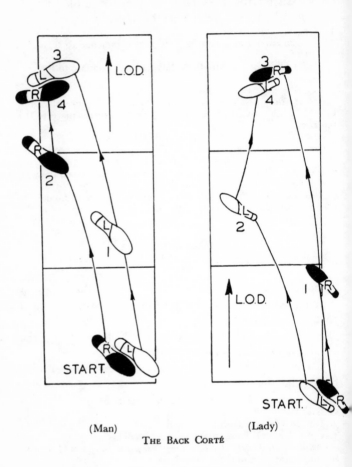

(Man)                    (Lady)

THE BACK CORTÉ

be abrupt. If the 1st step is taken down the L.O.D. with the body backing diagonally to centre, the direction of the 2nd step will be diagonally to centre and the 3rd step will point diagonally to wall with the body facing wall. The L. shoulder will move back as the R.F. closes. Follow with a Walk forward diagonally to the wall with the L.F.

*Amalgamations.* The Back Corté can be used in the following positions—

(1) After the 2nd half of any Reverse Turn that has been ended with the feet together and the man's back to the L.O.D. or diagonally to the centre.

(2) After the Open Promenade. When taken from this position the 1st step will be in C.B.M.P. and slight C.B.M. will be used.

(3) After the Natural (Twist) Turn (see page 266). Finish the twist with the feet together and the back diagonally to the centre, having turned square to partner, and follow with the Back Corté.

(4) After the Progressive Side Step Reverse Turn. When the first 4 steps of this Reverse Turn are not followed by a Rock, the Corté is the appropriate figure to use.

(5) After a Rock backwards on the R.F.

(6) After a Closed Promenade ended near a corner. Use the Corté to turn to face diagonally to wall of the *new* L.O.D.

## THE BACK CORTÉ

### Lady

The Back Corté is used when the man is moving backwards to the L.O.D. and wishes to turn to a forward direction.

It consists of a step forward with the R.F., followed by the second half of the Reverse Turn.

Commence facing diagonally to the centre. Finish backing diagonally to the wall.

1. R.F. forward down the L.O.D., R. shoulder leading.     S
2. L.F. forward, turning the body to L.     Q
3. R.F. to side and slightly back.     Q
4. Close L.F. to R.F., slightly forward.     S

*Contrary Body Movement and Position.* Step 2 is placed in C.B.M.P. Slight C.B.M. is also used.

*Amount of Turn.* A quarter turn to L. may be made.

*Footwork.* 1. H. 2. H. 3. I.E. of B. H. 4. Whole foot.

*General Notes.* Keep the R. hip well towards the partner as the 3rd step is taken.

If the direction of the 1st step is down the L.O.D. with the body facing diagonally to centre, the direction of the 2nd step will be diagonally to centre. The R.F. will be backing diagonally to wall on 3, but the body will complete the turn as the L.F. closes on 4.

# THE ROCK (BACKWARDS ON THE LEFT FOOT)

## Man

The Rock is used frequently in the Tango, and danced mainly with the L.F. leading first. The most popular way of introducing this figure is when the man is moving backwards down the L.O.D. The standard positions from which to use the Rock are given below. Commence with the back diagonally to centre. Finish in the same direction or having made a slight turn to the L.

1. L.F. back down the L.O.D., L. shoulder leading.     Q
2. Rock forward on to R.F., R. shoulder leading.     Q
3. Rock back to L.F., lengthening the step slightly, L. shoulder leading.     S

There is no C.B.M.P. Normally there is no turn, but a slight turn to the L. may be made.

*Footwork.* 1. I.E. of B. H. 2. H. 3. I.E. of B. H.

*General Notes.* The important points to remember are—

The first step must not be too long, and the foot must be placed on the inside edge of the ball of foot before lowering the heel.

When rocking forward to the R.F. it is absolutely necessary that this foot be moved slightly, or the body will tend to lurch forward. A slight foot-twist, or the replacing of the foot either slightly forward or preferably slightly towards the L.F., will meet the purpose. It is entirely a matter of individual style. The knees should be relaxed and the body taken well into this step.

When rocking back on to the L.F. on step 3 this step must always be lengthened slightly. A good rule to remember is—always move the 3rd step of a Rock towards the direction in which you intend to move afterwards.

*Amalgamations.* The following are some of the positions from which the Rock on the L.F. is danced.

(1) Progressive Side Step Reverse Turn. The L.F. Rock is used after the 4th step of this figure (see page 263).

(2) Any position where the man has feet together and his back towards the L.O.D. or diagonally to centre.

(3) After the Natural (Twist) Turn (see page 266). Finish the twist with the back diagonally to the centre having turned square to partner and follow with the Rock and the Closed Finish.

# THE ROCK (FORWARDS ON THE RIGHT FOOT)

## Lady

The Rock is a very popular figure in the Tango and is mostly danced by the lady with her R.F. leading first, and facing diagonally to the centre.

1. R.F. forward down the L.O.D., R. shoulder leading     Q
2. Rock back on to L.F., L. shoulder leading.     Q
3. Rock forward on to R.F., lengthening the step slightly, R. shoulder leading.     S

There is no Contrary Body Movement Position. Normally, there is no turn, but a slight turn to the L. may be made.

*Footwork.* 1. H. 2. I.E. of B. H. 3. H.

*General Notes.* The lady should read carefully the notes at the foot of the description of the man's steps, as the same remarks apply to the lady's steps. A list of the positions from which to introduce the Rock is also given.

## The Rock (Other Positions)

*Right Foot Rock (Backwards).* The Rock is also danced with the man leading on the R.F. back. The description is the same, but it should be remembered that, as the man usually adopts a L. shoulder lead when moving backward, all steps will be in C.B.M.P. This applies to both man and lady.

The R.F. Rock is often used directly following a L.F. Rock. It could be used as follows—

(1) After any of the positions given for the L.F. Rock, substituting a R.F. Rock instead of the Open or Closed Reverse Finish (see amalgamations at top of this page).

(2) After the 4th step of the Rock Turn.
Follow the R.F. Rock with a Back Corté.
*Footwork.* Man: 1. B. H. 2. H. 3. B. (H.). Lady: 1. H. 2.
B. H. 3. H.
*Side Rocks.* The 1st step of a Closed Promenade could be used
as the 1st step of a Side Rock, the Promenade then being con-
tinued. The rhythm would be QQS, QQS.

# THE OPEN REVERSE TURN
## (Lady in Line—Closed Finish)
### Man

The Open Reverse Turn is probably the easiest
Reverse Turn for the beginner to learn first, the steps
being somewhat similar to the first three steps of the
Foxtrot Reverse Turn. The figure is preceded by a
Walk forward on the R.F.

Commence facing diagonally to the centre. Finish
facing diagonally to the wall.

| | |
|---|---|
| 1. L.F. forward, across the body, turning to L. | Q |
| 2. R.F. to side and slightly back, body backing the L.O.D. | Q |
| 3. L.F. back down the L.O.D., L. shoulder leading. | S |

*Closed Finish*

| | |
|---|---|
| 4. R.F. back, diag. to centre, turning to L. | Q |
| 5. L.F. to side and slightly forward. | Q |
| 6. Close R.F. to L.F., slightly back. Facing diag. to wall. | S |

*Contrary Body Movement and Position.* C.B.M. on 1 and 4. Both
of these steps are placed in C.B.M.P.
*Amount of Turn.* Three-quarters of a turn on the complete
figure.
*Footwork.* 1. H. 2. B. H. 3. I.E. of B. H. 4. B. H. 5. I.E. of
foot. 6. Whole foot.
*General Notes.* The turn must be made without the "Body
swing" that is used in the moving dances.
The Open Finish (see page 258) may be used after the first
3 steps.
The Closed Finish could be underturned and followed by the
Back Corté or a L.F. Rock.

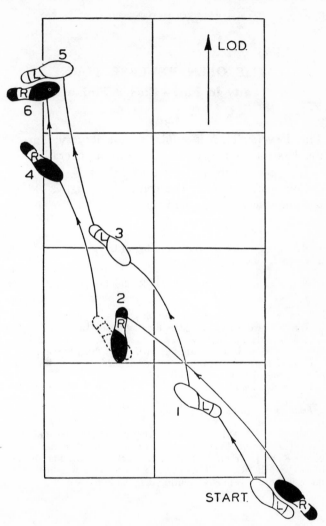

THE OPEN REVERSE TURN (LADY IN LINE)
(Man)

## THE OPEN REVERSE TURN
### (Lady in Line—Closed Finish)

### Lady

This Reverse Turn is similar to the Reverse Turn of the Foxtrot, and is, perhaps, the most generally used.

It is preceded by a step back on the L.F.

Commence backing the centre diagonally. Finish backing diagonally to the wall.

1. R.F. back, across the body, turning to L.                                              Q
2. Close L. heel to R. heel with the toe pointing to the L.O.D.                            Q
3. R.F. forward, down the L.O.D., R. shoulder leading.                                     S

*Closed Finish*

4. L.F. forward, diag. to centre, turning to the L.                                        Q
5. R.F. to side and slightly back.                                                        Q
6. Close L.F. to R.F. slightly forward. Back diag. to wall.                                S

*Contrary Body Movement and Position.* C.B.M. on 1 and 4. Both of these steps are placed in C.B.M.P.

*Amount of Turn.* Three-quarters of a turn on the complete figure.

*Footwork.* 1. B. H. 2. Whole foot. 3. H. 4. H. 5. I.E. of B. H. 6. Whole foot.

*General Notes.* Although the position of the 2nd step might be termed an "untidy" Heel Turn, no attempt must be made to turn on the R. heel. When the R.F. moves back it is placed on the ball of foot and the R.F. will then turn inwards as the weight is taken on to it, until it is finally pointing diagonally to wall.

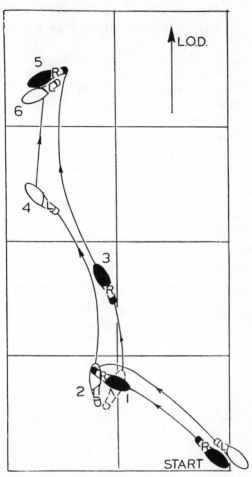

THE OPEN REVERSE TURN (LADY IN LINE)
(Lady)

# THE OPEN REVERSE TURN
## (Lady Outside—Open Finish)

### Man

This method of dancing the Open Reverse Turn is to lead the lady outside on the third step. The normal ending is the Open Finish, in which the man steps forward with the R.F. outside the lady, instead of closing his feet on the last step.

It is preceded by a step forward on R.F.

Commence facing diagonally to the centre. Finish facing almost diagonally to the wall.

1. L.F. forward, across the body, turning to the L.     Q
2. R.F. to side, body backing diag. to wall.     Q
3. L.F. back down the L.O.D., with partner outside.     S

*Open Finish*

4. R.F. back down the L.O.D., turning to the L., lady in line.     Q
5. L.F. to side and slightly forward.     Q
6. R.F. forward, outside partner, in a direction between the wall and diag. to wall.     S

*Contrary Body Movement and Position.* C.B.M. on 1 and 4. The 1st, 3rd, and 6th steps are placed in C.B.M.P.

*Amount of Turn.* Just under three-quarters of a turn on the complete figure.

*Footwork.* 1. H. 2. B. H. 3. B. H. 4. B. H. 5. I.E. of foot. 6. H.

*General Notes.* Note that less turn is made between the first 2 steps when the partner is to step outside on 3. Also note that the turn between steps 4 and 5 is slightly less than in a Closed Finish. This will help to keep contact with lady on the outside step and give a better body line. The 3rd step is taken straight back down the L.O.D. in C.B.M.P., and not with the usual L. shoulder lead. Because of this the 4th step will move down the L.O.D. instead of diagonally to centre.

The Open Finish could be followed by any of the endings used after the Open Promenade and given on page 248.

It is quite permissible to use the Closed Finish instead of the Open Finish when the lady is stepping outside on the 3rd step.

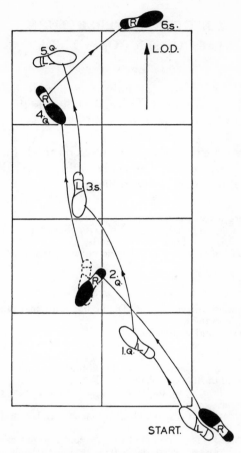

THE OPEN REVERSE TURN (LADY OUTSIDE)
(Man)

# THE OPEN REVERSE TURN
## (Lady Outside—Open Finish)
### Lady

In this Reverse Turn, the lady steps outside the man on the 3rd step and the normal ending is the Open Finish, in which the man steps outside the lady on the last step.

It is preceded by a step backward on the L.F.

Commence backing diagonally to the centre. Finish backing almost diagonally to the wall.

1. R.F. back across the body, turning to the L.                    Q
2. L.F. to side and slightly forward, with the toe pointing
   to L.O.D., but body turning slightly less.                     Q
3. R.F. forward down the L.O.D. and outside partner.              S

*Open Finish*

4. L.F. forward down the L.O.D., in line with man and
   turning to the L.                                              Q
5. R.F. to side and slightly back.                                Q
6. L.F. back, partner outside, in a direction between wall and
   diag. to wall.                                                 S

*Contrary Body Movement and Position.* C.B.M. on 1 and 4. The 1st, 3rd, and 6th steps are placed in C.B.M.P.

*Amount of Turn.* Just under three-quarters of a turn on the complete figure.

*Footwork.* 1. B. H. 2. Whole foot. 3. H. 4. H. 5. I.E. of B. H. 6. B.

*General Notes.* It will be noted that the 2nd step moves to side and slightly forward when the lady is stepping outside on the 3rd step.

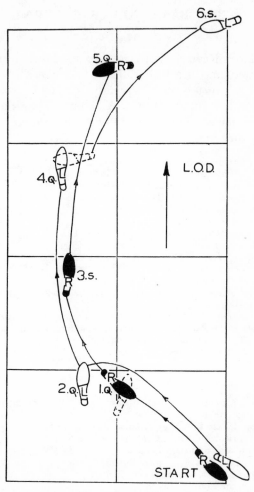

THE OPEN REVERSE TURN (LADY OUTSIDE)
(Lady)

# THE BASIC REVERSE TURN

## Man

The Basic Reverse Turn is easy to dance although beginners find it a little difficult to lead. The second half of this turn is used frequently as an ending to other figures. It is preceded by a Walk forward on the R.F.

Commence facing diagonally to the centre. Finish facing diagonally to the wall.

1. L.F. forward across the body, turning to L.     Q
2. R.F. to side and slightly back, a little across L.O.D.     Q
3. Cross L.F. in front of R.F. Backing the L.O.D.     S
4. R.F. back, down L.O.D., turning body to L.     Q
5. L.F. to side and slightly forward.     Q
6. Close R.F. to L.F., slightly back.     S

*Contrary Body Movement and Position.* C.B.M. on 1 and 4. C.B.M.P. on 1 only.

*Amount of Turn.* Three-quarters of a turn to L.

*Footwork.* 1. H. 2. B. H. 3. Whole foot. 4. B. H. 5. I.E. of foot. 6. Whole foot.

*General Notes.* The 2nd step should be placed with the toe turning inwards.

The second half of the turn may be danced with little or no turn, when the Back Corté or any suitable figure should follow.

If the figure is finished facing diagonally to the wall follow with the Walk or Progressive Side Step.

## Lady

1. R.F. back across the body, turning to L. Diag. to centre.     Q
2. L.F. to side and slightly forward.     Q
3. Close R.F. to L.F., slightly back. Facing the L.O.D.     S
4. L.F. forward, down L.O.D., turning body to L.     Q
5. R.F. to side and slightly back.     Q
6. Close L.F. to R.F., slightly forward.     S

*Contrary Body Movement and Position.* C.B.M. on 1 and 4. C.B.M.P. on 1 only.

*Amount of Turn.* Three-quarters of a turn to L.

*Footwork.* 1. B. H. 2. Whole foot. 3. Whole foot. 4. H. 5. I.E. of B. H. 6. Whole foot.

*General Notes.* The 2nd step must be placed with the toe pointing down the L.O.D. There is no swivel as the 3rd step is closed. Keep the R. hip well towards the partner as the 5th step is taken.

# THE PROGRESSIVE SIDE STEP REVERSE TURN

## Man

This figure consists of the Progressive Side Step danced with a strong turn to the left, a Walk on R.F. taken against the L.O.D., a Left foot Rock and the Closed Finish.

It is preceded by a Walk on the R.F.

Commence facing diagonally to the centre. Finish facing diagonally to the wall.

1. L.F. forward across the body, turning to the L.                    Q
2. R.F. to side and slightly back, across the L.O.D.                  Q
3. L.F. forward across the body, almost against the L.O.D.           S
4. R.F. forward against the L.O.D., R. shoulder leading.             S
   Now continue with the L.F. Rock as follows—
5. Transfer weight back to L.F., L. shoulder leading.                 Q
6. Rock forward on to R.F., R. shoulder leading.                      Q
7. Rock back to L.F. lengthening the step slightly with
     L. shoulder leading. Moving down the L.O.D.                      S
8. R.F. back, diag. to centre, turning to the L.                      Q
9. L.F. to side and slightly forward.                                 Q
10. Close R.F. to L.F., slightly back. Facing diag. to wall.          S

*Contrary Body Movement and Position.* C.B.M. on 1, 3, and 8. These steps are also placed in C.B.M.P.

*Amount of Turn.* Three-quarters of a turn to L. on the complete figure.

*Footwork.* 1. H.  2. I.E. of foot.  3. H.  4. H.  5. I.E. of B. H. 6. H.  7. I.E. of B. H.  8. B. H.  9. I.E. of foot.  10. Whole foot.

*General Notes.* When the 4th step is taken against the L.O.D. the body will be backing diagonally to centre and will remain in that position until the Rock is completed.

After dancing the first 4 steps the following alternative endings may be used—

(1) Back Corté. Transfer the weight back to L.F., moving it

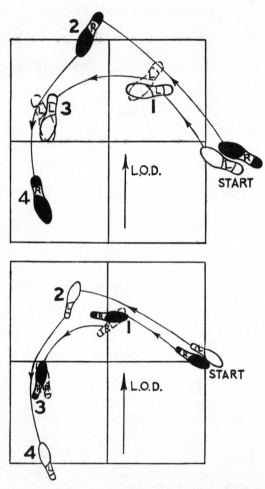

THE FIRST 4 STEPS OF THE PROGRESSIVE SIDE STEP REVERSE TURN
(*Top*, Man; *Bottom*, Lady)

slightly and dance the Back Corté (SQQS). Finish facing diagonally to wall.

(2) Rock and Progressive Open Finish. Transfer weight back to L.F. and Rock (QQS). Step back with R.F., diagonally to centre and turning to L. (S). Step forward, L.F. towards wall, and dance a Progressive Side Step (QQS), turning to finish facing diagonally to wall.

(3) Double Rock. Transfer weight back to L.F. and dance a L.F. Rock (QQS). Step back R.F. well under the body and down the L.O.D. to dance a R.F. Rock (QQS). Follow with the Back Corté (SQQS).

*Special Note.* After dancing the first 3 steps, a step *back*, down the L.O.D., may be taken with the R.F. This is preferred by some advanced dancers.

# THE PROGRESSIVE SIDE STEP REVERSE TURN

## Lady

This is an attractive Reverse Turn, consisting of a Progressive Side Step danced with a strong turn to the Left, a Walk on L.F., a Rock and the Closed Finish.

It is preceded by a Walk backwards on the L.F.

Commence backing diagonally to the centre. Finish backing diagonally to the wall.

1. R.F. back, across the body, turning to the L.       Q
2. L.F. to side and slightly forward, across the L.O.D.       Q
3. R.F. back, across the body. Almost against the L.O.D.     S
4. L.F. back, against the L.O.D., L. shoulder leading.     S
5. Transfer weight forward to R.F., R. shoulder leading.    Q
6. Rock back on to L.F., L. shoulder leading.       Q
7. Rock forward to R.F., lengthening the step slightly, with R. shoulder leading, moving down the L.O.D.    S
8. L.F. forward, diag. to centre, turning to the L.     Q
9. R.F. to side and slightly back.       Q
10. Close L.F. to R.F. slightly forward. Backing diag. to wall.    S

*Contrary Body Movement and Position.* C.B.M. on 1, 3, and 8. These steps are also placed in C.B.M.P.

*Amount of Turn.* Three-quarters of a turn to L. on the complete figure.

*Footwork.* 1. B. H. 2. I.E. of foot. 3. B. H. 4. I.E. of B. H. 5. H. 6. I.E. of B. H. 7. H. 8. H. 9. I.E. of B. H. 10. Whole foot.

*General Notes,* Care should be taken to place the 2nd step to the side and *slightly forward*, with the L. hip pressed firmly towards the man otherwise the character of the figure will be lost.

*Amalgamations.* Particulars of alternative endings to the first 4 steps of this figure are given in the notes on the man's steps.

## THE NATURAL (TWIST) TURN

### Man

This is a more advanced figure, but very attractive to dance. It commences in Promenade Position and is danced along the L.O.D. It can be finished along the L.O.D. or diagonally to the centre. (See notes below.)

1. L.F. to side in P.P. along L.O.D.    S
2. R.F. forward and across in P.P., turning to R.    Q
3. L.F. to side, across L.O.D., backing diag. to centre.    Q
4. Cross R.F. behind, and a few inches away from L.F.    S
   (Now backing the L.O.D.)
5. ) Turning on the ball of the R.F. and heel of the L.F.,
6. )    twist just over a half turn to the R. Finish in the
      normal P.P. with the feet nearly together and the
      weight on the R.F. Now facing diag. to wall.    QQ
   Continue along the L.O.D. into a Closed Promenade
   with L.F. (SQQS).

*Contrary Body Movement and Position.* The 2nd step is placed in C.B.M.P., and C.B.M. is also used.

*Amount of Turn.* Make a complete turn to the R. on the whole figure. The amount of turn on the twist (steps 5 and 6) depends on the following figure. (See General Notes.)

*Footwork.* 1. H. 2. H. 3. B. H. 4. B. 5, 6. Commence to twist on B. of R.F. and H. of L.F. End on whole of R.F. and I.E. of B. of L.F.

*General Notes.* Keep the feet flat during the twist. It is better to finish the twist with the feet slightly apart and with the L. knee veering inwards towards the R. knee.

Alternative endings are—

(1) Make a half turn only on the Twist and finish facing the L.O.D. Take the following Promenade diagonally to centre.

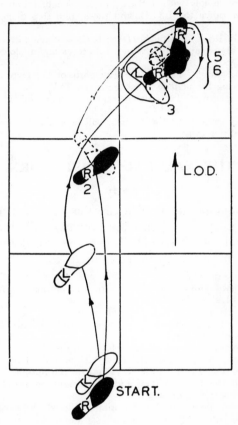

THE NATURAL (TWIST) TURN
(Man)

(2) Back Corté. Turn just over three-quarters of a turn on the Twist, and follow with a Back Corté. The first step of Corté will move down the L.O.D. and the second step diagonally to centre.

(3) L.F. Rock. Finish the Twist backing diagonally to centre as in (2) above, and follow with a L.F. Rock and a Closed Finish (QQSQQS).

(4) At a corner. Turn only three-eighths on the Twist and take the following Promenade along the new L.O.D.

(5) At a corner. Turn just over a half turn and follow with the Back Corté or Rock and Closed Finish.

On endings 2, 3, and 5 the man will be square to the lady at the end of the Twist.

# THE NATURAL (TWIST) TURN

## Lady

This is a more advanced figure that is very attractive to dance. It is commenced in Promenade Position and danced along the L.O.D. It can be finished along the L.O.D. or diagonally to the centre.

1. R.F. to side in P.P.                                                      S
2. L.F. forward and across in P.P. with foot pointing down the L.O.D.                                                                    Q
3. Small step forward R.F. between partner's feet.                            Q
4. L.F. forward, preparing to step outside partner, L. shoulder leading.                                                       S
5. R.F. forward, outside partner, towards wall.                               Q
6. Turning on the ball of R.F. close L.F. to R.F. Turn just over a half turn to the R. Finish in the normal P.P., with the feet together and the weight on the L.F. Facing diag. to centre.                                             Q

Continue along the L.O.D. into a Closed Promenade with R.F. (SQQS).

*Contrary Body Movement and Position.* The 2nd and 5th steps are placed in C.B.M.P. C.B.M. is used on 3 and 5.

*Amount of Turn.* Make a complete turn on the whole figure. The amount of turn on the twist depends on the following figure.

*Footwork.* 1. H. 2. H. 3. H. 4. H. 5. H. B. 6. B. H.

*General Notes.* The lady should note that she has very little turn to make on the first part, most of the turn being made by the man,

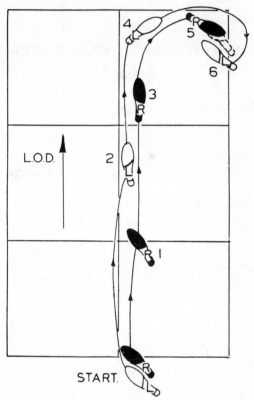

L.O.D.

START.

THE NATURAL (TWIST) TURN
(Lady)

who is on the outside of the turn. On the Twist the lady is on the outside, and her 5th step (R.F.) should be well round the man.

Several alternative endings to this figure are given in the notes on the man's steps. They are all basic figures, and the lady should have no difficulty in following them.

## THE NATURAL PROMENADE TURN

### Man

This is a simple Natural Turn taken from Promenade Position and should be used at a corner. It could be used when moving along the L.O.D., when it should be ended in a direction diagonally to the centre.

Commence in Promenade Position, moving towards a corner. Finish in Promenade Position along the *new* L.O.D.

1. L.F. to side in P.P. along L.O.D.      S
2. R.F. forward in P.P., moving diag. to wall and turning to R.      Q
3. L.F. to side and slightly back, body backing the L.O.D.      Q
4. Continue turning on the ball of L.F. for three-eighths of a turn to R., keeping the R.F. extended in front of L.F. and then step forward with R.F. diag. to wall of the new L.O.D.      S

    Man then turns the lady to P.P. as he places the L.F. to the side of R.F., without weight, ready to continue along the new L.O.D. into a Closed Promenade (SQQS).

*Contrary Body Movement and Position.* Steps 2 and 4 are placed in C.B.M.P. C.B.M. is used on both steps but the C.B.M. on 4 is slight.

*Amount of Turn.* Three-quarters of a turn to R. is made on the complete figure.

*Footwork.* 1. H. 2. H. 3. B. H. B. 4. H., then I.E. of B. of L.F.

*General Notes.* If the Promenade Turn is danced along the side of the room, make three-quarters of a turn to R., and then turn body slightly to R. as L.F. is placed to the side of R.F. on 4, to allow the following Promenade to be taken diagonally to centre.

An attractive ending to the Promenade Turn is to make the 4th step the 1st step of a Rock Turn (see page 241), omitting the placing of the L.F. to the side of the R.F. This can be danced

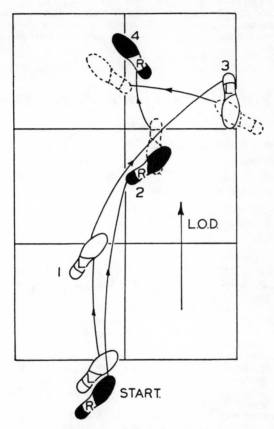

THE NATURAL PROMENADE TURN
(Man)

either at a corner or along the side of the room, when more turn would be made on the first part of the Rock Turn.

Note that the 2nd step of the Promenade Turn is *forward*, in a direction diagonally to wall. It is not taken across the body in a direction along the L.O.D. as is the case with most promenade figures.

# THE NATURAL PROMENADE TURN

## Lady

This is a simple Natural Turn taken from Promenade Position, and should be used at a corner. When used along the L.O.D., it should be ended in a direction diagonally to the centre.

Commence in Promenade Position, moving towards a corner. Finish in Promenade Position along the *new* L.O.D.

1. R.F. to side in P.P. along L.O.D.                                    S
2. L.F. forward and across in P.P. with foot pointing down the L.O.D.                                                              Q
3. R.F. forward, between partner's feet.                               Q
4. Still turning to R., step to side and slightly back with the L.F., with body backing diag. to wall of the new L.O.D.                                                                 S

   Lady will then continue to turn on the ball of L.F. until facing diag. to centre of new L.O.D. in P.P., and will place the R.F. to the side of L.F., without weight, ready to continue along the new L.O.D. into a Closed Promenade (SQQS).

*Contrary Body Movement and Position.* C.B.M. is used on step 3. The 2nd step is placed in C.B.M.P.

*Amount of Turn.* Three-quarters of a turn is made on the complete figure.

*Footwork.* 1. H. 2. H. 3. H. 4. B. H., then I.E. of B. of R.F.

*General Notes.* When the Rock Turn follows the 4th step of the Promenade Turn (see man's notes) the placing of the R.F. to the side of L.F. will be omitted.

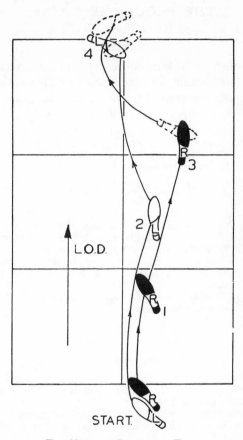

L.O.D.

START.

THE NATURAL PROMENADE TURN
(Lady)

# THE PROGRESSIVE LINK

## Man

This figure is a form of entry into a Promenade figure and became popular when a sharper action was introduced into the Tango. It can be commenced diagonally to the wall or facing the L.O.D.

1. L.F. forward, across the body.                                        Q
2. R.F. to side and slightly back. (See note below.)                    Q
    With L.F. continue by stepping sideways into a Promenade figure.

*Contrary Body Movement Position.* The 1st step is placed in C.B.M.P.

*Footwork.* 1. H. 2. I.E. of foot and I.E. edge of B. of L.F.

*General Notes.* As the 2nd step is taken, the man should bring the R. side of the body slightly back, and at the same time turn the lady to P.P. If the Progressive Link is commenced facing the L.O.D. the following Promenade should be taken diagonally to centre. If it is commenced facing diagonally to wall, the Promenade will be taken along the L.O.D. The 2nd step is short.

The Progressive Link can be danced following a Walk on the R.F. or after any Closed Finish or Promenade. It is also used directly following a Promenade Link.

## Lady

1. R.F. back, across the body.                                          Q
2. As the man turns lady to P.P. she will step to the side and slightly back with L.F. (short step).                        Q
    Finish in P.P. and follow with a Promenade figure.

*Contrary Body Movement Position.* The 1st step is placed in C.B.M.P.

*Amount of Turn.* Make a quarter turn to R.

*Footwork.* 1. B. H. 2. I.E. of B. H. and I.E. of B. of R.F.

*General Notes.* Although the 2nd step is termed "to side and slightly back" it should be noted that this refers to its position in relation to the body and the R.F. It is actually placed on the same line of dance as the 1st step.

# THE PROMENADE LINK

## Man

This figure is used to change from a Promenade figure to a forward figure. It is frequently used as an entry to the Four Step. Commence in Promenade Position moving along the L.O.D.

1. L.F. to side in P.P.                                                    S
2. R.F. forward and across in P.P. and commence to turn to R.    Q
3. Turning to R. to face wall, place the L.F. to the side of
    R.F. without weight. At the same time turn lady
    square.                                                               Q
   Continue by stepping forward L.F. towards wall into
    a Four Step, Progressive Side Step or a Walk.

*Contrary Body Movement and Position.* The 2nd step is placed in C.B.M.P. and slight C.B.M. is also used.

*Amount of Turn.* Turn an eighth to the R.

*Footwork.* 1. H. 2. H. B. (foot flat). 3. I.E. of B.

*General Notes.* Two other useful alignments are—

(1) Commence along L.O.D. and make no turn. Lady will then make a quarter turn to L. to get square to man. Follow with any of the endings given above. but commencing diagonally to wall. The Brush Tap could follow.

(2) Commence facing the L.O.D. and take the first 2 steps in a direction diagonally to centre. Man will then make an eighth of a turn to the *Left*, and lady will turn three-eighths to the L. Finish facing diagonally to centre and follow immediately with any Reverse figure. When this alignment is used the R.F. will point diagonally to centre on the 2nd step. The body only will turn on the 3rd step.

## Lady

Commence in Promenade Position moving along the L.O.D.

1. R.F. to side in P.P.                                                   S
2. L.F. forward and across in P.P. and commence to turn to L.   Q
3. Turning to L. to back the wall, place the R.F. to the side of
    L.F. without weight. Now square to man.                         Q
   Continue by stepping back on R.F. into a Four Step, a Pro-
    gressive Side Step or a Progressive Link.

*Contrary Body Movement and Position.* The 2nd step is placed in C.B.M.P. and slight C.B.M. is used.

*Amount of Turn.* Turn an eighth to the L.

*Footwork.* 1. H. 2. H. B. (foot flat). 3. I.E. of B.

*General Notes.* Other alignments are given in the man's notes. When alignment (2) is used, the R.F. will point towards centre on 1 and the L.F. will point diagonally to centre against the L.O.D. on 2. Three-eighths of a turn to the L. will be made.

# THE FOUR STEP

## Man

This figure is very popular and is often danced after the Promenade Link.

Commence facing the wall, with weight on R.F.

1. L.F. forward, slightly across the body.     Q
2. R.F. to side and slightly back. Now facing diag. to wall.   Q
3. L.F. back, partner outside and moving back diag. to centre against the L.O.D.     Q
4. Close R.F. to L.F., slightly back, and at the same time turn the lady to P.P.     Q

Continue by stepping to side with L.F., along the L.O.D. into a Promenade figure.

*Contrary Body Movement and Position.* The 1st and 3rd steps are placed in C.B.M.P. Slight C.B.M. on 1.

*Amount of Turn.* In the alignment above an eighth of a turn to L. is used. Up to a quarter or no turn may be used.

*Footwork.* 1. H. 2. B. H. 3. B. H. 4. B. H.

*General Notes.* Although the 2nd step is placed on the ball of the foot the R.F. should be almost flat. Beginners may find a tendency to jump or rise between steps 1 and 2.

A very good amalgamation is: dance the Progressive Link, the Promenade Link, then the Four Step. Follow the Four Step with the Fallaway Promenade. The Four Step can also follow any Closed Finish, Closed Promenade or Open Promenade.

## Lady

This figure is often danced after the Promenade Link.

Commence backing towards wall, with the weight on L.F.

1. R.F. back, slightly across the body.                                    Q
2. L.F. to side and slightly forward, with the foot pointing
    diag. to centre against the L.O.D.                                    Q
3. R.F. forward, outside partner.                                         Q
4. Close L.F. to R.F., slightly back, and at the same time
    turn to R. on ball of R.F. to end in P.P., body facing
    diag. to centre.                                                      Q
   Continue by stepping to side with R.F. along the L.O.D.
    into any Promenade figure.

*Contrary Body Movement and Position.* The 1st and 3rd steps are
placed in C.B.M.P. and C.B.M. is also used on these steps.

*Amount of Turn.* Make an eighth turn to L. between 1 and 2
and a quarter turn to R. between 3 and 4.

*Footwork.* 1. B.H. 2. Whole foot. 3. H.B. (Foot flat). 4. B.H.

*General Notes.* Although the L.F. is pointing diagonally to
centre against the L.O.D. on 2, the body should be facing centre.
Any attempt to turn the body too much to the L. will result in
loss of contact and a bad body line on the 3rd step.


# THE FALLAWAY PROMENADE

## Man

The Fallaway Promenade is a most attractive and
not very difficult Standard Variation. It should be
noted that both the man and lady remain in Promenade
Position throughout.

Commence in Promenade Position, along the L.O.D.

1. L.F. to side in P.P.                                                   S
2. R.F. forward and across in P.P., turning slightly to R.               Q
3. L.F. to side in P.P., now backing almost diag. centre.               Q
4. R.F. back, towards centre in Fallaway. R. shoulder leading
    and body backing diag. to centre.                                    S
5. L.F. back, towards centre in Fallaway and with L.F. point-
    ing towards the wall.                                                Q
6. Close R.F. to L.F., slightly back. in P.P. and body facing
    the wall.                                                            Q
   With L.F. continue into a Promenade, moving diag. to wall.

*Contrary Body Movement and Position.* C.B.M. on 2. The 2nd and
5th steps are placed in C.B.M.P.

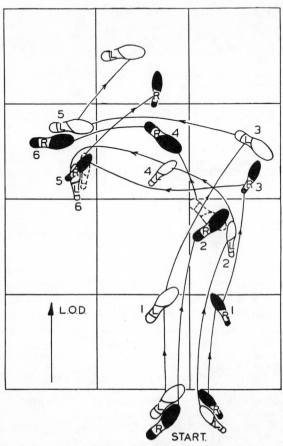

THE FALLAWAY PROMENADE
(Man and Lady)

*Amount of Turn.* Make a quarter to R. between 1 and 4 and an eighth to L. between 4 and 5, body completing the turn on 6.

*Footwork.* 1. H. 2. H. 3. B. H. 4. I.E. of B. H. 5. B. H. 6. B. H.

*General Notes.* Care must be taken to keep contact with lady on the 4th step by taking this in an "open" position, and on the 5th step by placing the L.F. back well under the body in C.B.M.P. It will be noted that, although the body is backing diagonally to centre on 4, the 5th step is placed with the L.F. pointing to the wall. Thus, when the R.F. closes on 6, the body will automatically turn to face the wall, which is the correct position to take the following Promenade diagonally to wall. The Natural Promenade Turn is a good figure to follow the Fallaway Promenade.

# THE FALLAWAY PROMENADE

## Lady

Commence in Promenade Position, moving along the L.O.D.

1. R.F. to side in P.P.     S
2. L.F. forward and across in P.P., pointing down the L.O.D. and turning slightly to R.     Q
3. R.F. forward in P.P., commencing to move down the L.O.D. but end facing almost diag. to wall.     Q
4. Still turning to the R. step back L.F., towards centre in Fallaway, L. shoulder leading. Body backing diag. to centre against the L.O.D.     S
5. R.F. back, towards centre in Fallaway.     Q
6. Turning slightly to the L., close L.F. to R.F., slightly back. End in P.P. with body facing the L.O.D.     Q

With R.F. continue into a Promenade figure, moving diag. to wall.

*Contrary Body Movement and Position.* Steps 2, 3, and 5 are placed in C.B.M.P. C.B.M. is used on 3 and 5.

*Amount of Turn.* A quarter to R. between 1 and 4. An eighth to L. between 5 and 6.

*Footwork.* 1. H. 2. H. 3. H. 4. I.E. of B. H. 5. B. H. 6. Whole foot.

*General Notes.* The turn on step 5 is made on the ball of R.F., with the foot flat. Note that the 3rd step commences to move in a direction down the L.O.D. but will end with the R.F. and the body facing almost diagonally to wall. This will result in the step ending in C.B.M.P.

## THE OUTSIDE SWIVEL and BRUSH TAP
### (From an Open Promenade)

### Man

The Outside Swivel and the Brush Tap are two separate figures and both have a variety of uses. They are, however, often used as a complete variation after an Open Promenade, when they are joined together by steps 2 and 3 of a Promenade Link. This amalgamation is described below and notes on further uses of the figures are given under General Notes. The Outside Swivel turning to the Left, a more difficult variation, is described overleaf.

Dance an Open Promenade along the L.O.D. End with the R.F. forward, outside partner, in a direction between the wall and diagonally to wall. Then—

**Outside Swivel and Link**

1. Take weight back to L.F. with the partner outside, and cross R.F. in front of L.F. without weight. End in P.P.   S
2. Move the R.F. forward and across the L.F. in P.P. in a direction diag. to wall.   Q
3. Turning body to face diag. to wall, place the L.F. to the side of R.F. without weight. At the same time turn the lady square.   Q

**Brush Tap**

1. L.F. forward, diag. to wall, in line with partner.   Q
2. Turning to L. step to side R.F., now facing L.O.D.   Q
3. Brush L.F. swiftly to R.F. without weight.   &
4. Place the L.F. to the side, a small step, without weight.   S
   The next step is a forward step with L.F. Note that steps 2 and 3 are danced to the time of one Q.

*Contrary Body Movement and Position.* Outside Swivel: Steps 1 and 2 are placed in C.B.M.P. C.B.M. is used on 1. Brush Tap: Step 1 is placed in C.B.M.P. and slight C.B.M. is used.

*Amount of Turn.* Outside Swivel: There is a slight turn to R. on step 1, and a slight turn to L. on step 2, the body completing the turn as the L.F. taps on step 3. Brush Tap: Slight turn to L. between steps 1 and 2.

*Footwork.* Outside Swivel: 1. B. H., with pressure on B. of R.F. 2. H. 3. I.E. of B. Brush Tap: 1. H. 2. B. H. 3. Foot slightly off the floor. 4. I.E. of B.

*General Notes.* When leading the Outside Swivel it is advisable to allow the R. side of the body to move back as the lady turns. This will avoid a cramped position on the Swivel. Some advanced dancers prefer to leave the R.F. forward and not cross it in front as the lady turns. Make sure that the R.F. is pointing diag. to wall on step 2. There must be no swivel on this foot as the lady turns square.

An advanced method of dancing the Outside Swivel is for the man to turn to the L. When the weight is taken back to the L.F. on step 1, the L.F. will move under the body and step back in a direction *against* the L.O.D. and the R.F., instead of crossing in front, will move leftwards across the front of L.F. Step 2 will then move in a direction diag. to centre and at the end of the Link (step 3) man will be facing diag. to centre. Man will continue by stepping forward L.F. into a Reverse figure.

When turning the Outside Swivel to the L. after an Open Promenade it is advisable to end the Open Promenade facing diag. to wall.

## THE OUTSIDE SWIVEL and BRUSH TAP
### (From an Open Promenade)

### Lady

Although the Outside Swivel and the Brush Tap can be used as two separate figures they are described below as a complete variation, joined together by steps 2 and 3 of the Promenade Link.

Dance an Open Promenade along the L.O.D. End with the L.F. back, in a direction between the wall and diagonally to wall. Then—

**Outside Swivel and Link**

1. Take the weight forward to R.F., outside partner and swivel to R. on R.F. to face the L.O.D., allowing the L.F. to close near R.F. without weight. End in P.P.     S

2. L.F. forward in P.P., moving in a direction diag. to wall.   Q
3. Turning to L. to get square to man, place the R.F. to the
    side of L.F. without weight. Now backing diag. to wall.   Q

### Brush Tap

1. R.F. back, diag. to wall.   Q
2. Turning to L., step to side L.F. Backing L.O.D.   Q
3. Brush R.F. swiftly to L.F. without weight.   &
4. Place the R.F. to side. a small step, without weight.   S

    The next step is a backward step with R.F. Note that steps 2
and 3 are danced to the time of one Q.

    *Contrary Body Movement and Position.* Outside Swivel: Steps 1
and 2 are placed in C.B.M.P. and C.B.M. is also used.

    *Amount of Turn.* Outside Swivel. Turn just over a quarter
turn to R. on step 1 and three-eighths of a turn to L. between 2
and 3. Brush Tap: Slight turn to L. between steps 1 and 2.

    *Footwork.* Outside Swivel: 1. H.B. (Foot flat) and I.E. of B. of
L.F. 2. H.B. (Foot flat). 3. I.E. of B. Brush Tap: 1. B.H. 2. Whole
foot. 3. Foot slightly off the floor. 4. I.E. of B.

    *General Notes.* When dancing the Outside Swivel some advanced
dancers lift the L.F. from the floor as the swivel is made on R.F.
When this "flick" of the foot is used, the knees should be kept in
contact. The lady may turn her head to the R. at the end of the
Swivel and then back to normal position as the Link is danced.
When the "flick" of the L.F. is used it is smarter to keep the head
turned well to the L. throughout. Remember to keep in contact
with partner on the swivel and to keep the hips well forward.

## THE OUTSIDE SWIVEL: TURNING TO THE LEFT
### (Taken after 1, 2, of a Reverse Turn)

#### Man

This is a far more advanced method of dancing the
Outside Swivel but is most effective and enjoyable to
dance.

Commence facing diagonally to centre after a walk
on R.F. or after a Promenade Link ended diagonally to
centre.

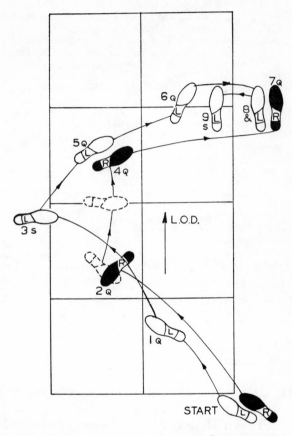

OUTSIDE SWIVEL TURNING TO LEFT AND LINK INTO THE
BRUSH TAP
(Man)

1. L.F. forward, across the body, turning to L.     Q
2. R.F. to side, backing diag. to wall.     Q
3. Turning to L. with a sharp swivel on the R.F., step back L.F., diag. to centre. with the partner outside. As the weight moves on to L.F., the R.F. will be kept forward and will move leftwards across the front of L.F. End in P.P. with body facing diag. to wall against the L.O.D. Keep weight on L.F.     S
4. R.F. forward in P.P., with R.F. pointing and moving towards wall.     Q
5. Turn lady square and place L.F. to side of R.F. without weight and turn the body to L. to face wall.     Q

With L.F., continue by stepping forward into a Four Step.

*Contrary Body Movement and Position.* Steps 1, 3, and 4 are placed in C.B.M.P. C.B.M. is used on 1.

*Amount of Turn.* Make a half turn to L. between 1 and 3 and a slight turn to L. on the Link, steps 4, 5.

*Footwork.* 1. H. 2. B.H. 3. B.H. with pressure on B. of R.F. 4. H. 5. I.E. of B.

*General Notes.* There must be a sharp and obvious swivel on the ball of R.F. as the L.F. swings back, well under the body for the Swivel. Note that the R.F. remains forward and does not cross tightly in front of L.F. at the end of step 3. The lady has very little swivel to make on step 3 and it is only necessary for the man to keep firm pressure on the lady's L. side to ensure that she ends in P.P.

The man could make even more turn to the L. on step 3 and take the L.F. back in a direction diag. to centre but with the L. Toe pointing to wall. This will result in him ending with his body facing wall. He will then take step 4 diag. to wall and follow with the Link and Brush Tap as described on the previous page. See diagram on page 283.

## THE OUTSIDE SWIVEL: TURNING TO THE LEFT
### (Taken after 1, 2, of a Reverse Turn)
### Lady

This effective method of dancing the Outside Swivel is more difficult.

Commence backing diagonally to the centre.

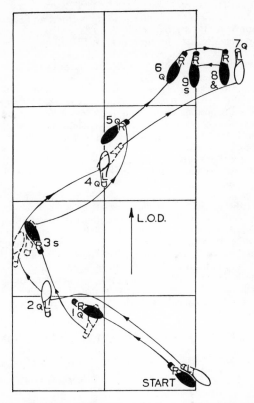

OUTSIDE SWIVEL TURNING TO LEFT AND LINK INTO THE
BRUSH TAP
(Lady)

1. R.F. back, across the body, turning to L.　　　　Q
2. L.F. to side and slightly forward with the L. toe pointing to L.O.D.　　　　Q
3. R.F. forward, diag. to centre, outside partner, and swivel slightly to R. on ball of R.F. to face diag. to wall, allowing the L.F. to close near R.F. without weight. End in P.P.　　　　S
4. L.F. forward, towards the wall in P.P., but with the L. toe pointing diag. to wall.　　　　Q
5. Turning to L. to get square to man place the R.F. to the side of L.F. without weight. Now backing wall.　　　　Q

With R.F. continue by stepping back into a Four Step.

*Contrary Body Movement and Position.* Steps 1, 3, and 4 are placed in C.B.M.P. and C.B.M. is used on these steps.

*Amount of Turn.* Make three-eighths of a turn to L. between 1 and 2 and a slight turn to L. as step 3 is taken. Make a quarter turn to R. on 3 to end in P.P. Make three-eights of a turn to L. between 4 and 5.

*Footwork.* 1. B.H. 2. Whole foot. 3. H.B. (Foot flat) and I.E. of B. of L.F. 4. H.B. (Foot flat). 5. I.E. of B.

*General Notes.* It will be noted that the L.F. is pointing down the L.O.D. on step 2 and the lady will then step across this alignment to take the 3rd step diag. to centre. Although there is a quarter turn to R. to the swivel (step 3) to end in P.P. it is better to underturn than overturn, as too much turn will make the Promenade Position too open and result in an ugly hip line. When the man overturns on his 3rd step to face the wall, the swivel of the lady will be negligible. Diagram on page 285.

## SUGGESTED TANGO AMALGAMATIONS

1. Walk R.F.—Progressive Side Step—Rock Turn—Walk L.F., R.F., turn to P.P.—Closed Promenade—Walk.

2. Walk R.F.—Progressive Side Step, turning slightly—Walk R.F. diagonally to centre—Open Reverse Turn ending with R.F. outside partner—Rock, turning slightly to R.—Second half of Closed Reverse Turn—Walk.

3. Walk R.F.—Progressive Side Step—Walk R.F

diagonally to centre—Progressive Side Step Reverse Turn—Walk L.F., R.F., turn to P.P.—Natural Twist Turn—Closed Promenade—Walk L.F., R.F.—Progressive Link—Open Promenade—Brush Tap.

4. Walk R.F.—Progressive Side Step—Walk R.F. diag. to centre—First 4 steps of the Progressive Side Step Reverse Turn ended with L.F. Rock, then R.F. Rock—Back Corté—Walk L.F.—Walk R.F.—Progressive Link—Natural Promenade Turn at a corner.

5. Progressive Link—Promenade Link—Four Step —Fallaway Promenade—Natural Promenade Turn ending with the Rock Turn.

6. Open Promenade—Outside Swivel turning to L. —2, 3 of a Promenade Link to end facing diag. centre— Open Reverse Turn.

7. Rock Turn—Four Step, turning slightly to L. to end in P.P. ready to move diag. to centre—Promenade Link, turning to L. to end facing diag. to centre (Lady square)—1, 2 of the Open Reverse into an Outside Swivel turning to L. to face wall in P.P.—2, 3 of a Promenade Link—Brush Tap.

## SECTION V

**FOR THE KEEN DANCER**

# AMATEUR MEDAL TESTS

In most sports and recreations it is possible to make a fairly accurate assessment of one's progress. Yet for many years devotees of ballroom dancing, unless they belonged to the comparative few who compete in public dance halls, possessed no yardstick against which to measure their prowess. To-day we have Amateur Medal Tests. There is no doubt that the general standard of ballroom dancing in this country has improved enormously since the leading professional associations and societies instituted these tests.

A few years ago the majority of pupils were content to reach a standard that would enable them to move round a ballroom without undue inconvenience to themselves or their partners; now the majority are only too glad to learn more thoroughly and to record their progress through the tests conducted by well-known professional examiners.

Since the adoption of these tests thousands of dancers have taken advantage of them. This is quite understandable, for ballroom dancing is such a delightful recreation, and the social atmosphere in most schools of dancing is so pleasant that to reach a reasonable standard is neither laborious nor expensive. Few other recreations provide such pleasure at such little cost. I strongly recommend Medal Tests to every amateur who finds pleasure in dancing. It is easier to improve when there is an incentive to work, and when that first medal has been won the dancer will derive confidence and pleasure, not only from the progress itself, but also from the knowledge that experts have acknowledged and set a seal to that progress.

Between Medal tests and competition dancing there is a large gulf. The "flare" and movement expected from the competition dancer is not expected in these tests, indeed, when used, it is liable to look out of place. The main points to concentrate on are—

1. Neat and correct footwork.

2. A good upright poise and a correct hold.

3. A *quiet* interpretation of the basic and standard figures and a soft movement.

In advanced tests consideration must be given to style and other technical details, but a careful study of the points enumerated above is sufficient for success in the Bronze and Silver grades.

Remember, it is not what you do, but how you do it. Although most societies issue a syllabus of recommended figures for each grade a certain amount of latitude is allowed. Marks are not lost through the omission of a figure in any dance, but they are lost when a candidate dances a figure badly.

Any qualified teacher can train and enter you for a Medal Test; or, if you prefer to enter direct, the entry form and syllabus can be obtained from the Headquarters of any Society of Teachers of Dancing.

## COMPETITION DANCING

Keen dancers who have reached Silver or Gold Medal Test standard will often turn their thoughts to competition dancing. Far more glamour and excitement prevail in a competition at a well-known ballroom than in a Medal Test where one's efforts are seen by none but the examiner.

Many medallists jump to the conclusion that if they have succeeded in passing the Gold or Gold Star test of one of the leading Societies they should have little difficulty in reaching one of the final places in a competition. Unfortunately this is far from true.

In Medal Tests the examiner looks for technical accuracy, good poise and movement, and style that does not offend, even if it does not attract. The candidate is not dancing *against* another couple but to a set standard, a standard which is unfortunately inclined to vary according to the examiner and the general standard of the dancing viewed by that examiner over a given period.

The dancer who passes the highest grade Medal Test can be sure that his dancing is technically sound and that he moves correctly and with good style. Such knowledge is a necessary basis for competition dancing, but is not enough to make a first-class competition dancer. The movement of the competition dancer must be free and flowing and effortless. A figure or group of figures which have been danced well enough to please an examiner must now be danced with the rhythmic expression to make them appear completely alive. The style of the dancer or the couple must be more than correct—it must *attract*. More difficult groups of figures must be learned and the man, who is responsible for leading them, must know how and when he may underturn or overturn them for effect—or to avoid another couple. Seventy-five per cent of competition success comes from experience and training. There is no short cut to success, but the following notes should help the young competition dancer to avoid some of the more obvious faults which have ruined the chances of so many young couples.

## The Hold

This is of vital importance. The general appearance of a couple will always strike the judge before he sees them actually dancing. Points to watch are—

The man's L. arm should be angled quite sharply and the forearm must not move outwards from the elbow. It is better for the angle at the elbow to be less than 90 degrees rather than more. The elbow should not be more forward than the shoulder. Watch the grouping of the fingers of the L. hand and make sure that the hand does not droop downwards from the wrist. The knuckles of the L. hand should be slightly higher than the wrist.

The R. elbow must not drop down when leading the lady, especially when leading her into Promenade figures. The R. forearm should slope downwards from the elbow to the R. hand. If the R. hand is held too high on the lady's back, there will be a tendency to drop the R. elbow. Many men keep the most pressure on the R. wrist when holding the lady, and when this is done, the R. hand, not being used, will dangle downwards from the wrist and will often move away from the partner's back. This fault ruins the appearance of the couple. Avoid this by keeping a little pressure on the lady's back with the index finger of the R. hand. Study the photographs in this book.

Ladies should watch the grouping of the fingers of the L. hand. They should not be completely straight and stiff but grouped naturally, with the fingers slightly bent.

## Dress

The appearance of a couple will obviously be enhanced if the lady has an attractive dress. It can just as obviously be ruined if the man is badly dressed. A really good evening dress suit is very difficult to make and the competition dancer would be advised to seek the advice of an expert before ordering a suit for dancing. Here are some points to watch.

When the arms are raised the coat should not lift from the shoulders. A good shoulder line is essential and it should be possible to see at least half an inch of the white collar even when the arms are raised. A coat that lifts and covers the white collar gives an appearance of raised shoulders. It is equally important that at least an inch of white cuff should be seen. The sleeves of the coat should be narrow to give a smart arm line, and a narrow sleeve will grip the white cuff of the shirt and keep it in the same position at all times. The coat "tails" should reach to the top of the calf. Tails that are too short look rather silly; when too long they look untidy, and spoil the line.

One of the worst faults is to wear the trousers too short or too narrow. When standing normally the trouser leg should reach to the heel of the shoe. It is inevitable that when dancing some figures it may tend to touch the floor, but that is far better than having a short trouser leg that rises almost to the ankles when a long step is taken. The normal width for the trouser leg is about 17 inches. If they are worn too narrow they give a man the appearance of dancing with bent knees. If worn too wide they look clumsy.

Dress fashions for ladies alter so much that it would be unwise to make too many comments. At the moment, net in pastel shades is the favourite material and it certainly flows better than most other materials. Twenty to forty yards are used by the majority of ladies to make a dance dress that will move and flow nicely. Ladies with narrow or round shoulders should wear a dress that covers the shoulders. It will give them a better and broader line. Ladies with a long neck are advised to wear the hair long; those with a short neck should have it dressed high.

## General

Presentation is a word very frequently used in connection with demonstration dancing by professionals, but presentation also plays its part in competition dancing. For example, the manner in which the lady uses her head in promenade figures can make a big difference to the picture presented by a couple in such variations as the Whisk and the Wing. Some ladies prefer to turn their heads to the right when in promenade, others keep the head turned to the left.

Both are correct. The lady should use the method that looks most attractive, but the most annoying fault is that of affectation. Very often a lady who does not turn the head into the promenade position will turn it more to the left and at the same time raise the left shoulder with a rather coy expression. This type of affectation is annoying to watch and should be avoided. The ladies whose dancing is the most pleasing to watch are those who can use their heads naturally, and make them appear as a part of the body—and the picture.

Facial expression should also be studied. It is absurd to grin like a Cheshire cat throughout the contest. It is equally absurd to wear a grim expression. By all means open the mouth when smiling, but do not keep it open all the time.

The man should keep his head still and not move it from side to side as he turns or sways. Only when he leads his partner into a very open Fallaway position and a few other advanced figures should he turn to look at her.

## Position

One of the most common faults in competition dancing is for the lady to dance too much on the man's right side. The popularity of outside figures tends to make her slip to the man's right side, and she often remains there. It is impossible to dance completely in front of the man but it will ruin the picture of a couple if the lady consistently dances on the man's right hip.

The habit of many ladies of leaning well back from the hips, so that contact with the man is felt only at the hips instead of from the hips upwards, is a bad one, and tends to restrict the man's movement. It also makes it very difficult for the man to step outside his partner without losing contact with her. Many points are lost in competitions through this fault.

Inadequate contact while executing outside steps is sometimes the fault of the man holding his weight too far back. The body must follow through with the foot. This will also help the man to avoid that "sitting down" effect so often seen on outside steps.

## Variations

The inexperienced competition dancer often thinks that if half a dozen really difficult and "flashy" variations are included in each dance the judge will be impressed. Perhaps the best advice that can be given is to assure him that whereas a variation, no matter how difficult, will very seldom gain a point for a couple, a variation badly danced will inevitably lose them several points. In a competition where the standard of the couples is nearly even, the judges find it far easier to notice something they dislike than to be impressed by something they do like. Do not take risks. Choose a few figures that can be danced well and without the risk of faulty contact and unattractive body lines, and repeat these several times rather than risk employing a figure of which some part might displease the judge. If you have what you consider is a beautiful variation which you feel you can dance well, make sure that it is used between some sound basic work. A jewel in a plain setting will look far more attractive than a jewel in an ornate setting that can only detract from its beauty.

The keen competition dancer should also read the following section on "Expression in Dancing."

# EXPRESSION IN DANCING

There are hundreds of dancers who have a good floor appearance, correct technique and reasonably good movement, and yet they do not achieve greatness. What do they lack? Perhaps the most important differences between the good dancer and the outstanding dancer are in Softness and Expression.

Most dancers know that the correct softening of the knee on a step such as the first step of any Waltz turn will give their dance a more pleasing appearance, and they strive to acquire it. Fewer competitors realize that to give their dancing better rhythmic expression means the difference between the ordinary and the great.

A few rather obvious examples will help to convey what is meant by expression.

Watch the manner in which some dancers place the third step behind in the Whisk. It can be placed there rather quickly, dead on the beat, in which case there will most possibly be a jolt as the weight moves on to the step—or it can be almost "caressed" into position, slowly, with firm control, perhaps arriving slightly late but with good rhythmic expression. The last three steps of the Natural Spin Turn in the Waltz can be danced with the strict timing of one beat for each step— or a little speeding of the movement on the fourth step can result in almost hanging on the fifth step with a rather late and light sixth step which completely alters the character of the movement. The Feather-step and Three-step in the Foxtrot can be given their correct technical timing; or a delayed timing of the previous step on the Left foot (last step of the Natural Turn) can be followed by a bold swing on the first step of the

Feather and a slightly delayed third step, which will completely alter the expression. There are dozens of other instances where playing with the timing, achieved through the movement of the body rather than the placing of the feet, can make the dancing fascinating to watch and intensely satisfying to the dancer.

How is it done? Can it be acquired? It is done by stealing time from one step to give a hovering effect to the next; by softening the knees, and by appreciating that if the lady is given the correct lead she will help to create the impetus to gain this effect without obvious effort. All this can be acquired by any skilled dancer who has a strong sense of rhythm, good balance and the patience to practise so that it appears as an integral part of the dance. The unrhythmic dancer will fail at first, but there is nothing to prevent the acquisition of such rhythmic interpretation by anyone who has shown sufficient ability to become an intelligent average dancer.

Possibly the best amalgamation to practise is the Natural Turn ending with the Impetus Turn in the Foxtrot. Here are some hints for the man.

Dance 1, 2, 3 of the Natural Turn and then continue into the Impetus Turn in the following way—

As the L.F. is taken back on the 4th step, give the lady a firm, but not too strong, lead with the R. hand so that she swings well forward against your R. side. Soften the knees and count this step "Q" (not the usual "S").

Dance the Heel Turn without worrying whether the feet are closed tightly together, and with the knees still soft. Keep the feet parallel even though they are not closed. Count this step "S." It will be noticed that the lady's forward movement will make you turn. Do not try. to turn yourself. The weight should be kept well back all the time you are turning, and about half a turn should be made on the Heel Turn.

Still keep the weight back as the body continues to turn slightly to the R. (not more than an eighth of a turn) and keep a firm hold of the lady to stop her swinging away from you. Do not try to rise. The speed of the lady's movement will cause you to rise without any effort on your part.

On the 4th beat move the L.F. to the side and rather more back than in standard technique. Make sure that it is actually placed on a *late* count of "Q," and placed lightly with the weight now forward, before stepping back on the R.F., diagonally to centre against the L.O.D. for the normal "S" count, to continue with the Feather Finish, diagonally to centre.

Thus the timing has been altered from SQQ S to Q SQ S. The effect will be to get early speed, then a Hover, and this expression will be found far more pleasing and attractive than the standard timing.

If, when practising the figure, it is noticed that the effort to quicken the movement between the first and second steps of the Impetus can be seen, you can be sure that it is bad and that you have not mastered the lead. The speed must be gained without obvious effort.

Another extraordinarily good amalgamation to practise is the Open Impetus Turn, followed by the Weave in the Waltz. The Weave from Promenade Position is described on pages 158–162 and is very much used by advanced dancers. Important points to watch are given below.

Dance 1, 2, 3 of the Natural Turn (Waltz) and then take the 4th step back, again giving the lady a firm lead with the R. hand to swing her forward against your R. side.

Instead of using the Heel Turn in the Open Impetus Turn, take the R.F. to the side and back, across the L.O.D. with the body facing diagonally to centre. Keep the L.F. flat. The R.F. is placed on the ball of foot, with the knees soft.

The lady's impetus will now compel you to continue to turn to the R. to face the L.O.D. and rise to the toes. Do not move the L.F., but allow the L. knee to veer inwards towards the R. knee. The lady, on the outside of the turn, will allow her R.F. to brush towards the L.F. Keep firm pressure on the lady's back to prevent her from overturning, and hover as long as possible before re-placing weight on to the L.F., moving diagonally to centre on a late count of "6." The body will now commence to turn to the L.

The attractive Weave ending should be danced as follows—

Step forward with the R.F., diagonally to centre in P.P., and as this step is taken, give the lady a *very firm lead* to swing her well across the front of you as you step forward on the L.F. (on ball of foot), moving almost to centre. On this step (2) the lady will take a long step to side with the R.F. on the ball of foot, having turned square to the man, but with her head still turned to the R.

The swing given to the lady on the first step will cause her to continue to turn on the ball of R.F. until facing the L.O.D., when her L.F. is placed to the side (3). This swing will also result in the man and lady rising from the ball of foot on the 2nd step, and the man will endeavour to hold this rise with a hover effect, before placing his 3rd step (R.F.) to side with the body backing the L.O.D.

The Weave is continued by the man stepping back with L.F. down the L.O.D. with the lady outside (4).

On the 5th step the man takes the R.F. back rather quickly, giving the lady a firm lead forward. Lady will step forward L.F. in line with man. Both man and lady use the ball of foot on 5.

With the body turning to the L. press upwards from the ball of foot (this will be assisted by the lady's forward swing) and get a slight hover effect before placing the L.F. to side, with the body facing wall on 6. Take this step slightly late, and lightly.

The next step will be taken outside lady with the R.F.; remember to lower the L. heel and release it again as the weight moves forward over the R.F. to continue into a Natural figure.

There are many other figures in which better expression can be gained by stealing time from one step and adding that time to the next. The Hover Telemark will look infinitely better if, instead of giving it the strict SQQS rhythm, the time is distributed to the approximate value of $1\frac{1}{2}$ beats, $1\frac{1}{2}$ beats, 1 beat, 2 beats.

The really first-class dancer will know whether an unusual rhythmic interpretation is justified on artistic grounds by the *feel* of it. The less experienced dancer should seek the advice of a professional who can tell at once whether an unusual interpretation is advisable.

**POPULAR DANCES**

# THE VIENNESE WALTZ

THE Viennese Waltz is one of the most attractive of the ballroom dances and has been a recognized competition dance on the Continent for many years.

Several societies in this country now include the Viennese Waltz in the Latin American section of their syllabuses for professional examinations and amateur tests. When danced in championships the Continental version of the dance is used. See page 307.

The music is inspiring and the dance is beautiful to watch. There is no doubt that it will now remain as one of the most popular additions to the four standard dances.

## General Notes

*Time.* 3/4. Three beats in a bar. The 1st beat is accented.

*Tempo.* Music should be played at about 56 bars a minute.

*The Hold.* The couple should stand slightly apart, with the normal dance hold except that the Left arm of the man is held slightly lower and wider than in the standard dances such as the Foxtrot and Slow Waltz.

*Basic Figures.* Natural Turn, Reverse Turn, Forward Hesitations on L.F. and R.F., Reverse Lilt.

*Variations.* Cross Swivel, Closed Wing, the Curtsey. The Off-beat Spin.

The following special notes should be studied as they apply to practically all figures throughout the dance.

*Rise and Fall.* The rise in Natural and Reverse Turns is a little more abrupt than in the Slow Waltz. The quicker music will make a full relaxation of the knee on the 1st step impracticable, and this alone will result in the rise being taken earlier. The normal rise is "Rise at the end of 1, up on 2 and 3, lower at the end of 3."

*Special Note.* Although the dance has been standardized in England with a Toe Pivot on the backward half of all turns, many Men dancers use a Heel Pivot on this part of the turns. The Toe Pivot often looks smarter and gives more rise, but there is no doubt that the Heel Pivot permits a more free and flowing movement.

*Footwork.* All leading forward steps are taken with a Heel lead, lowering immediately to the flat foot.

*Sway.* When the leading step of a turn is taken with the R.F., sway will be used to the Right on the following two steps. It should be noted, however, that the Sway will commence early—as the 1st step is taken, and this sway will be felt far more from the waist upwards than from any inclination of the body from the feet upwards. A similar sway to the Left will be used after a leading step with the L.F.

*Basic Amalgamation.* The basis of the dance is a series of Natural Turns, followed by a Forward Hesitation on the R.F., then a series of Reverse Turns, followed by a Forward Hesitation on the L.F. Advanced dancers will always time the changes so that they take place at the end of an eight bar phrase of the music, thus giving the dance a far better rhythmic interpretation.

# THE NATURAL TURN

## Man

Commence facing the L.O.D.

1. R.F. forward, turning to the R.
2. Small step to side L.F., still turning.
3. Close R.F. to L.F., now backing the L.O.D.
4. L.F. back, turning to the R.
5, 6. Close R.F. to L.F. without weight, making a Toe Pivot on L.F. to face the L.O.D.

*Notes.* The Natural Turn may commence diagonally to wall and end diagonally to centre, but a complete turn is the normal and most comfortable amount of turn.

*Contrary Body Movement.* C.B.M. on 1 and 4.

*Rise and Fall.* Rise at end of 1, up on 2 and 3. Lower at end of 3. Rise at end of 4, up on 5 and 6. Lower at end of 6.

*Sway.* Sway to R. on 2 and 3. Sway to L. on 5 and 6. (See note on Sway on the previous page.)

The steps for the lady are the normal opposite. Lady will commence backward with the L.F. and dance steps 4, 5, 6, and then steps 1, 2, 3.

# THE REVERSE TURN

## Man

Commence facing the L.O.D.

1. L.F. forward, turning to the L.
2. Small step to side and slightly back with R.F., still turning.
3. Cross L.F. in front of R.F., now backing the L.O.D.
4. R.F. back, turning to the L.
5, 6. Close L.F. to R.F. without weight, making a Toe Pivot on R.F. to face the L.O.D.

*Notes.* The Reverse Turn may commence facing diagonally to the centre and end facing diagonally to the wall, but a complete turn will be found most comfortable.

*Contrary Body Movement.* C.B.M. on 1 and 4.

*Rise and Fall.* Rise at end of 1, up on 2 and 3. Lower at end of 3. Rise at end of 4, up on 5 and 6. Lower at end of 6.

*Sway.* Sway to L. on 2 and 3. Sway to R. on 5 and 6.

The steps for the lady are the normal opposite. Lady will commence backward with the R.F. and dance steps 4, 5, 6, and then steps 1, 2, 3.

## FORWARD HESITATION ON RIGHT FOOT

### Man

Used after a complete Natural Turn. Commence facing the L.O.D. or diagonally to the centre. Follow with the Reverse Turn.

1. R.F. forward.
2. L.F. closes towards R.F.
3. L.F. closes to R.F. without weight.
    *Contrary Body Movement.* Slight C.B.M. on 1.
    *Rise and Fall.* Rise at end of 1, up on 2 and 3. Lower at end of 3. Note that the rise should be less abrupt than in a Natural Turn.
    *Sway.* There is no sway, although some advanced dancers use a very slight sway on this figure.
    *Notes.* It is important to remembei that the L.F. should close towards R.F. quite slowly and with firm pressure of the L. toe on the floor. This will help control the balance after making a series of turns. It will also result in a slightly later rise.

The steps for the lady are the normal opposite. Lady will commence backward with the L.F. and close R.F. slowly towards L.F. for 2, 3.

The Forward Hesitation may be danced by the man commencing with the L.F. after a Reverse Turn. This Hesitation may commence down the L.O.D. or diagonally to the wall. Follow with the Natural Turn.

## HESITATION TURNS TO RIGHT AND LEFT

### Man

Commence facing diagonally to the wall after a Forward Hesitation on the L.F. or facing L.O.D. after a complete Natural Turn.

This group of figures is similar to the Quarter Turns of the Quickstep. As a complete figure it is useful in a crowded room or as a change from the constant turning of the Natural and Reverse Turns. Although useful, it undoubtedly detracts from the rhythmic flow of the dance and should be used sparingly.

1, 2, 3. Dance the first 3 steps of the Natural Turn, underturning to end backing diag. to centre.

4, 5, 6. L.F. back into a Backward Hesitation on L.F.

7, 8, 9. R.F. back, diag. to centre into 4, 5, 6 of a Reverse Turn, making only a quarter turn to end facing diag. to wall.

10, 11, 12. L.F. forward into a Forward Hesitation on L.F.

*Contrary Body Movement.* C.B.M. on 1 and 7. Slight C.B.M. on 4 and 10.

*Rise and Fall.* Normal rise and fall for the Turns and Hesitations.

*Sway.* Sway to R. on 2, 3. No sway or slight sway to L. on 5, 6. Sway to R. on 8, 9. No sway or slight sway to L. on 11, 12.

The steps for the lady are the normal opposite.

## THE REVERSE LILT

### Man

This attractive Reverse figure is used to retain the lilt and rhythm of the dance without progression. It is most useful in a crowded room. It is usually danced after a Reverse Turn and followed by a Reverse Turn.

1. L.F. forward.
2. Move R.F. towards L.F.
3. Cross R.F. behind L.F. without weight.
4. R.F. back.
5. L.F. closes towards R.F.
6. L.F. closes to R.F. without weight.

*Contrary Body Movement.* C.B.M. on 1 and 4.

*Rise and Fall.* The rise and fall is the more gradual rise used in the Forward Hesitation.

*Sway.* The extent of the sway will be governed by any turn made on the figure.

*Amount of Turn.* The Reverse Lilt may be danced without turn, but usually about an eighth of a turn to L. is made on each three steps. In advanced variations it is often danced with as much as a half turn to the L. on each part.

The steps for the lady are the normal opposite. Lady will commence backward with the R.F. and dance steps 4, 5, 6, and then steps 1, 2, 3.

# THE CROSS SWIVEL AND THE CLOSED WING

## Man

Although the Cross Swivel may be used as a link between the Reverse and Natural Turns, especially at a corner, it is most attractive when combined with the Closed Wing, thus making a variation which retains the character of the dance. It is commenced following a Reverse Turn which has been ended diagonally to the wall.

1. L.F. forward, diag. to wall, turning to the L.
2. Close R.F. towards L.F. still turning.
3. Close R.F. to L.F. without weight. Now facing diag. to centre. Continue with the Closed Wing as follows—
4. R.F. forward, outside lady, diag. to centre.
5. Close L.F. towards R.F.
6. Close L.F. to R.F. without weight, still facing diag. to centre.

The next step is taken with the L.F. outside the lady on her L. side. The best ending is to follow immediately with a Reverse Lilt, making three-eighths of a turn to the L. on it, and then take the R.F. back, down the L.O.D. with the lady in line into 4, 5, 6 of the Reverse Turn.

*Contrary Body Movement.* C.B.M. on 1. Slight C.B.M. on 4.

*Rise and Fall.* Rise at end of 1, up on 2 and 3. Lower at end of 3. There is a rise in the body on steps 5 and 6, but the R.F. is kept flat.

*Sway.* Sway to L. on 2, 3. A slight sway to R. may be used on 5, 6.

## Lady

Commence backing diagonally to wall after a Reverse Turn.

1. R.F. back diag. to wall, turning to the L.
2. Close L.F. towards R.F., still turning.
3. Close L.F. to R.F. without weight. Now backing diag. to centre. Continue with the Closed Wing as follows—
4. L.F. back, diag. to centre, partner outside.
5. Small step to side with R.F., moving across the front of partner.
6. Small step forward L.F., outside partner on his L. side.

The next step is a step back with the R.F. diag. to centre, with the man outside on the L. side of lady. Follow immediately with the Reverse Lilt or a Reverse Turn.

*Contrary Body Movement.* C.B.M. on 1 and slight C.B.M. on 4.

*Rise and Fall.* Rise at end of 1, up on 2 and 3. Lower at end of 3. Rise at end of 4, up on 5 and 6. Lower at end of 6.

*Sway.* Sway to the R. on 2, 3. Sway to L. on 5, 6.

## THE CURTSEY

### Man

A very attractive variation for competition dancing. It is danced after a complete Natural Turn, ended facing the L.O.D.

1, 2, 3. Dance a Forward Hesitation on R.F. with no turn, but commence to turn the lady to the R.
4, 5, 6. Hesitate with feet together, leading lady to Curtsey on step 4, and to rise on 5, 6. Keep feet flat, with weight on R.F. and let knees relax very slightly as lady dances the Curtsey.

Step forward L.F. down the L.O.D. having turned lady square and follow with a Reverse Turn.

*Notes.* The normal hold is retained but the arms will move lower and to the R. to assist the lady with her Curtsey Head and body will turn slightly to R. on 4, regaining normal position on 5, 6.

## Lady

1, 2, 3. L.F. back, swivelling to the R. and moving R.F. back slowly.

4. Move R.F. back, well behind L.F. and Curtsey, keeping weight on L.F. and turning head and body well to the R. Body facing almost diag. to centre.

5, 6. Rise and swivel on L.F. to L. to get square to man, keeping the R.F. slightly behind the L.F.

Step back R.F. down the L.O.D. into a Reverse Turn.

The Curtsey may be danced after a complete Reverse Turn. Man steps forward L.F. and hesitates, while lady does a Curtsey, turning to the L., with her L.F. behind R.F. The man will loosen the hold with his R. hand so that the lady may turn well to the L. Regain normal position on 5, 6, and follow with a Natural Turn.

## THE OFF-BEAT SPIN

### Man

This variation is popular but should not be used too frequently as it tends to destroy the character of the dance. It is taken after a complete Natural Turn.

1. R.F. forward, turning strongly to the R.
2. Continue turning on R.F. to back the L.O.D.
3. L.F. to side and back, continuing to turn to R. on L.F., leaving R.F. forward between lady's feet.

These 3 steps could be repeated, or followed by a Natural Turn. A better ending is: R.F. forward down the L.O.D. and dance a Natural Lilt making a half turn to R. and follow with steps 4, 5, 6 of the Natural Turn.

Normal Rise and Fall is used on the Spin.

### Lady

Commence after a complete Natural Turn.

1. L.F. back, turning strongly to the R.
2. Continue turning on L.F. keeping R.F. forward between the partner's feet.

3. R.F. forward, down the L.O.D. between partner's feet and continue to turn to R. to end backing the L.O.D. with L.F. held behind R.F.

To continue step back L.F., to repeat the Spin or to follow with a Natural Turn or Natural Lilt.

# THE CONTINENTAL VIENNESE WALTZ

In May, 1953, the International Council resolved that the Continental version of the Viennese Waltz must be used in all championships. Only five figures are accepted: The Natural and Reverse Turns, The Forward Changes, and the Natural and Reverse Fleckerls. The technique of these figures is given below in chart form. The abbreviations D.C., diagonally to centre, D.W., diagonally to wall, and NFR., no foot rise, are used.

## NATURAL TURN

| 1. R.F. forward. | Facing D.C. | Comm. to turn to R. | Comm. to rise e/o 1. |
|---|---|---|---|
| 2. L.F. to side (Long step) | Backing centre. | ¾ between 1 and 2. | Cont. to rise on 2 and 3. |
| 3. R.F. closes to L.F. | Backing D.C. | ⅛ between 2 and 3. | Lower e/o 3. |
| 4. L.F. back and slightly to side | Backing L.O.D. | ¼ between 3 and 4. | Comm. to rise e/o 4. NFR. |
| 5. R.F. to side. (Small step). | Pointing D.C. | ⅜ between 4 and 5. Body turns less. | Cont. to rise on 5 and 6. NFR. |
| 6. L.F. closes to R.F. | Facing D.C. | Body completes the turn. | Lower c/o 6. |

*Footwork.* 1. H. T. 2. T. 3. T. H. 4. T. H. 5. T. 6. Foot flat.

*Body Sway.* S.R.R. S.L.L. *Note.* Although this is the normal sway most advanced dancers use a slight sway to L. on 1. gradually changing to a R. sway on 3, and a slight sway to R on 4, gradually changing to a L. sway on 6. It will be found that a greater fluency of movement can be achieved when this sway is used.

*Notes.* The Lady's steps are the normal opposite. She will commence with steps 4, 5, 6, and use a slight foot rise on 5, 6.

Note that the Natural Turn always commences diagonally to centre.

## REVERSE TURN

| | | | |
|---|---|---|---|
| 1. L.F forward. | Facing L.O.D. | Comm. to turn to L. | Comm. to rise e/o 1. |
| 2. R.F. to side. (Long step). | Backing wall. | ⅛ between 1 and 2. | Cont. to rise on 2 and 3. |
| 3. L.F. crosses in front of R.F. | Backing L.O.D | ⅛ between 2 and 3. | Lower e/o 3. |
| 4. R.F. back and slightly to side. | Backing D.C. | ⅛ between 3 and 4. | Comm. to rise e/o 4 NFR. |
| 5. L.F. to side (Small step). | Pointing between D.W. and L.O.D. | Nearly ⅛ between 4 and 5. Body Turns less. | Cont. to rise on 5 and 6 NFR. |
| 6. R.F. closes on L.F. | Facing L.O.D. | Body and feet complete ⅜ turn. | Lower e/o 6. |

*Footwork.* 1. H. T. 2. T. 3. T. H. 4. T. H. 5. T. 6. Foot flat.
*Body Sway.* S.L.L. S.R.R.
*Notes.* The Lady's steps are the normal opposite. She will commence with steps 4, 5, 6, and use a slight foot rise on 5, 6.

## FORWARD CHANGES

The Forward Change from Reverse to Natural is given below. The Change from Natural to Reverse will commence facing diagonally to centre and end facing the L.O.D.

| | | | |
|---|---|---|---|
| 1. L.F. forward. | Facing L.O.D. | Comm. to turn to L. | Comm. to rise e/o 1. |
| 2. R.F. diag. forward. | Facing D.C. | ⅛ between 1 and 2. | Cont. to rise on 2 and 3. |
| 3. L.F. closes to R.F. | Facing D.C. | — | Lower e/o 3. |

*Footwork.* 1. H. T. 2. T. 3. T. H.
*Body Sway.* S.L.L.
*Notes.* The Lady's steps are the normal opposite. She will have no foot rise on 1 of each Change. Changes are never danced backwards by the Man.

These three figures form the basis of the dance and they will look far more attractive if attention is paid to the phrasing. Always try to change from one turn to another at the end of an 8 or 16 bar phrase. To change in the middle of a musical phrase tends to destroy the flowing character of the dance.

The Fleckerl figures, described overleaf, are quite difficult to master. They should be used sparingly.

## REVERSE FLECKERL
### (Taken after a complete Reverse Turn ended facing the L.O.D.)

*Description*

1. Turn on L.Heel a quarter turn to L.

2. Swing R.F. round Lady. End with R.F. to side, facing against the L.O.D.

3. Continue turning to L. and Cross L.F. loosely in front of R.F. making a half turn to face L.O.D.

4. R.F. to side and slightly back, making an eighth turn to L. (Note that R.F. may travel more round Lady when moving fast.)

5. Cross L.F. well behind R.F. making three-eighth turn. Keep weight on R.F.

6. Turn on R.F. for a half turn to L. to face the L.O.D., letting feet uncross.

&. Transfer weight from R.F. to L.F. to repeat.

*Footwork.* 1. H. T. 2. T. 3. T. H. 4. T. H. T. 5. T. 6. T. H. "&". H.

*Notes.* No sway is used. The Fleckerl is a fast turn on one spot. Hold the Lady very firmly and close. Advanced dancers often turn more than a complete turn on each three steps. Follow with a normal Reverse Turn or a Natural Fleckerl.

The Lady's steps are the normal opposite. She will commence with steps 4, 5, 6. Technically there is no rise, but some dancers use a slight rise and it can look attractive.

## NATURAL FLECKERL
### Taken after a complete Natural Turn which should be overturned to end facing the L.O.D.

*Description*

1. Small step diag. forward with R.F. facing D.W.

2. L.F. to side, making three-eighth turn to R. to back the L.O.D. Weight divided between the two feet.

3. Turn on R.F. making a half turn to face the L.O.D.

4. L.F. to side, making an eighth turn to R.

5. Cross R.F. well behind L.F. making a half turn to R. with weight still kept over the L.F.

6. Continue turning another half turn to R. on L.F. allowing the feet to uncross.

*Footwork.* 1. H. T. 2. T. 3. T. H. 4. H. T. 5. T. 6. T. H.
*Notes.* No sway is used. Hold firmly and close as in the Reverse Fleckerl. Follow with a normal Natural Turn.

# RHYTHM DANCING

Rhythm Dancing is the name given to the type of dancing that is used in crowded ballrooms. It has, of course, existed for many years, and was frequently referred to as "Crush Dancing." There is nothing new in the figures used in this type of dancing, and they were, in the first place, only standardized as a guide to candidates in Amateur Tests.

It will be noted that many of the figures resemble those described in the Quickstep section of this book, but no attempt should be made to adhere to the strict rules of alignment that are so necessary in these dances. Very often the figures have to be danced with the absolute minimum of movement and with practically no progression; consequently, it is advisable to practise such figures as the Natural Pivot Turn and Chassé Reverse Turn in the form of a square, making no progress along the room at all.

The manner of expressing *rhythm* in these figures is most important since the execution of a set of basic figures with a complete absence of movement and body swing will tend to be very boring. The experienced dancer, with an inborn sense of rhythm, will interpret them with various types of rhythm, but easily the most popular, and possibly the easiest for the beginner to master, is the Charleston, and an appreciation of this subtle rhythm is essential if the dancer is to obtain the full enjoyment from Rhythm Dancing. The Charleston rhythm can be learned quite quickly if the following exercise is practised—

Commence with the feet together, and with the knees slightly relaxed.

|  | Beats |
|---|---|
| 1. Take a small step to the side with the L.F.—knees straight. | 1 |
| 2. Relax knees slightly. | 2 |
| 3. Close R.F. to L.F. without weight—knees straight. | 3 |
| 4. Relax knees slightly. | 4 |
| 5. Take a small step to the side with the R.F.—knees straight. | 1 |
| 6. Relax knees slightly. | 2 |
| 7. Close L.F. to R.F. without weight. | 3 |
| 8. Relax knees slightly. | 4 |
| Then step to side with the L.F. to repeat. | |

In practising this movement the dancer should give a slightly longer time value to the 1st and 3rd beats in each bar. Thus the step to the side and the closing will be held rather firmly, and the subsequent relaxing of the knees taken rather sharply. Unless this is done there will be a strong tendency to bend at once as the step to the side is made.

When the rhythm of the Charleston has been mastered, this action should be softened considerably, as it is not good form to use an obvious or staccato Charleston action in Rhythm Dancing. When using the Charleston as a progressive figure, the R.F. should be taken forward and the L.F. to the side alternately.

*Rise and Fall.* Rises are not used in Rhythm Dancing, the rhythmic relaxing and straightening of the knees being used instead.

The standardized figures in both Quick and Slow Rhythm Dancing are given, together with a few notes on their uses.

## QUICK TEMPO

*Tempo.* The following figures can be danced to any 4/4 music that is faster than 40 bars a minute.

### Standardized Figures

1. Walk.
2. Quarter Turns.
3. Chassé Reverse Turn.
4. Natural Pivot Turn.
5. Reverse Pivot Turn.
6. Back Corté.
7. Change of Direction.
8. Side Step.

### 1. The Walk

The steps must be short, and a lilting movement should be used. The action of the Charleston may be introduced in the Walk. Forward steps may be taken as in the Quickstep Walk, with the ball of the foot and then the heel skimming the floor, or the foot may be kept practically flat throughout. In the backward Walk, the ball of the foot meets the floor first, the heel lowering as the moving foot passes. Each Walk takes 2 beats of music.

## 2. Quarter Turns

The design of the Quarter Turns is the same as in the Quickstep. Chassé movements are very small, and it is immaterial whether the feet are closed right together, or an Open Chassé, in which the closing foot moves only half-way towards the side step, is used.

## 3. The Chassé Reverse Turn

The description of this figure is the same as in the Quickstep. It can be taken following the Quarter Turns or the Change of Direction. Very little turn should be made on the 1st and 4th steps, and side steps should be short. Repeat the figure two or three times to make a complete turn.

## 4. Natural Pivot Turn

The description of this figure is the same as in the Quickstep. Keep all steps very short, and repeat two or three times to make a complete turn. The 4th step should tend to be more sideways than back, and the turn continued on the ball of the L.F. The lady's 4th step will be forward, between the man's feet.

## 5. Reverse Pivot Turn

This figure is best taken after the 7th step of the Quarter Turns. It can be used once at a corner to change the dancer's direction to the new L.O.D., or it can be danced three or four times to make a complete turn in one position.

1 L.F. forward, pivoting very slightly to the L. and
  keeping the R.F. behind in C.B.M.P.                    S
2. Balance back on to the R.F., still turning slightly.   S

3, 4. Very small step to side L.F., then close R.F. to L.F.     QQ
L.F. forward, to repeat.

*Note.* The lady does a small Chassé on 3 and 4.

## 6. Back Corté

In this figure the man progresses backwards, or diagonally backwards down the L.O.D. It can be taken after the first four steps of the Quarter Turns.

1. R.F. back, turning very slightly to L.                          S
2, 3. Bring the L.F. back to the side of R.F., keeping the
    weight on the R.F. The L.F. should be kept slightly
    in advance of the R.F., and a slight turn to the L,
    made on the R. heel.                                  QQ
4. L.F. back.                                                      S

*Note.* The lady does a small chassé on the 2nd and 3rd steps. The man can use a slight body turn to the R. on the 4th step.

## 7. Change of Direction

The description of this figure is the same as in the Quickstep, counting SSSS. It is best taken after the Quarter Turns, and used as a lead into the Chassé Reverse Turn. In Rhythm Dancing the step "diagonally forward" on the R.F. tends to be placed more sideways, and less turn is made.

## 8. Side Step

Perhaps the most useful figure to use in a crowded room. It is taken sideways along the L.O.D., the man facing towards the wall.

1. Short step to side with L.F.                                    Q
2. Close R.F. half-way towards L.F.                                Q
3. L.F. to side.                                                   S
4. Close R.F. to L.F.                                              S

This figure can be repeated several times. It can be ended by stepping forward with the L.F. into the Walk, or by the man turning slightly to the R. as the L.F. is taken to the side on the 3rd step, and then stepping back with the R.F., diagonally to the centre, into the Back Corté, or the last half of the Quarter Turns.

## SLOW TEMPO

*Tempo.* The following figures can be danced to any 4/4 music that is slower than 40 bars a minute.

### Standardized Figures

1. Walk.
2. Side Chassé on the R.F.
3. Quarter Turns.
4. Natural Pivot Turn.
5. Chassé Reverse Turn.
6. Back Corté.
7. Side Step.

It will be observed that the standardized figures for the slow tempo are similar to those in the quick tempo, with the exception of the Side Chassé on the R.F., and the Side Step.

The whole dance should appear "lazy," and the relaxing of the knees should be much softer than in the quick tempo.

### The Side Step

In Slow Rhythm Dancing a different type of Side Step is used and this is described below. It is danced moving sideways along the L.O.D. with the man facing between wall and diagonally to wall, and with the lady held slightly in Promenade Position.

1. Small step to side L.F., along the L.O.D.             Q
2. Close R.F. half-way towards L.F.             Q
3. Small step to side L.F., along the L.O.D., and let R.F. move half-way towards it without weight.             S
4. Move R.F. sideways against the L.O.D. (to its position on step 2), and let L.F. close half-way towards it without weight.             S

Repeat two or three times. There are several other ways of dancing this figure.

(1) When more rhythmic or staccato music is played, a better interpretation of the music will be achieved by dancing the first 3 steps counting QQQ, then close R.F. to L.F. without weight, counting Q. Move the R.F. sideways against the L.O.D. counting Q, and then count another Q as L.F. closes to R.F. without weight.

(2) On step 4, instead of moving R.F. sideways against the L.O.D. step *forward* with R.F., along the L.O.D. in Promenade. The lady will step forward L.F. along the L.O.D. in Promenade on the 4th step. This variation of the Side Step is often referred to as "Conversation Piece." It can be repeated, and ended by the man turning the lady slightly to her L. to bring her square as he dances the Chassé (steps 1, 2) and then stepping forward L.F. into a Walk. Alternatively the man could turn slightly to R. on steps 1, 2, 3 to get square to lady and continue with step 5 of the Quarter Turns.

The additional figure is given below.

### Side Chassé on the R.F.

This is taken after a step forward on the L.F.

1. R.F. to side, short step.             Q
2. Close L.F. to R.F.             Q
3. R.F. to side, and brush L.F. up to it.             S
   L.F. forward to repeat.

In both slow and quick tempo, such figures as the Outside Spin, Natural Spin Turn, Cross Chassé, etc., can be introduced, but they should be attempted only by experienced dancers as it requires a certain amount of skill to use them without inconvenience to other dancers.

## SECTION VII

## BALLROOM NOVELTY DANCES AND GAMES

At both public and private dances it is a good idea to introduce one or two novelty dances or games, especially when such dances result in an interchange of partners. Some of the most popular of these novelties are described below.

# PAUL JONES

This is one of the most popular novelty dances in England, and is frequently used at social dances to effect an interchange of partners and to create a jolly atmosphere.

### Description

The M.C. or leader of the band announces a "Paul Jones" and the band then plays a bright tune such as "Life on the Ocean Wave" or "Here we Come Gathering Nuts in May." The dancers then form two large circles, the men on the inside and facing outwards, the ladies on the outside and facing inwards, that is, towards the men.

With hands joined the two circles move to the right so that they are moving in opposite directions. When the music stops, the man claims the lady directly in front of him and dances. The band should pause for a few seconds to permit the men to take their partners and then play a Waltz, Quickstep, Foxtrot, etc., or occasionally an "Old Time" dance. After playing about one chorus of music the band stops, the circle

317

is formed as before, and continued as described above.

It is sometimes advisable for the band to commence by playing a Waltz or Quickstep and then when all the dancers are on the floor to announce a Paul Jones and immediately break into the Call tune. This ensures that all couples will take part.

## MILITARY  PAUL  JONES

This is a variation of the Paul Jones described above. The band plays a Quickstep or Waltz. At the end of the tune, one or more of the members of the band (usually a saxophone or trumpet player) marches round the room playing a lively air, and the dancers follow in couples, walking arm in arm. When the column of dancers is well spread out, he stops, and shouts the command of "Gentlemen, take 6 paces forward"; "Ladies, take 3 paces backward." The man then dances with the lady standing beside him. When the music stops the march is repeated.

## "EXCUSE  ME"  DANCE

Three or more men and ladies are given cards with "Excuse me" written on them. The band then plays a popular tune and all couples dance. Those persons with the cards stand in the centre of the floor. A man with an "Excuse me" card is permitted to present it to any other man and claim his partner, whilst a lady can present a card to any other lady.

When a partner has been taken from a person it is not permissible for him or her to reclaim that partner immediately. The card must be presented as soon as possible to one of another couple.

# THE PALAIS GLIDE

The Palais Glide can hardly be termed a dance; it is reminiscent of the Gallop which has been a feature of Hunt Balls for many years. It has the advantage of creating a very jolly and friendly atmosphere in the ballroom and its popularity has spread rapidly throughout the whole of the country.

It can be danced to any Foxtrot tune, although sometimes an old tune such as "John Brown's Body" is used, and it is played at a tempo of about 30 bars a minute.

Four, six, or even more dancers form a line, all facing the same direction (towards the L.O.D.) and with their arms linked behind them. All dancers do the same sequence of steps.

|  | Count |
|---|---|
| 1. L.F. forward, without the weight on it, and the heel only on the floor. | S |
| 2. Bring the L.F. back behind the R.F. and step back on to it. | Q |
| 3. Bring the R.F. back and place it slightly to the side of the L.F. | Q |
| 4. L.F. forward. | S |
| *Note.* A quarter turn to the R. is made throughout steps 1 to 4, turning from a direction diagonally to the centre to one diagonally to the wall. | |
| 5 to 8. Repeat, commencing with the R.F. and turning slightly to the L. | SQQS |
| 9 to 12. Repeat, commencing with the L.F. and turning slightly to the R. | SQQS |
| 13. R.F. forward, well across the front of the L.F. | S |
| 14. L.F. forward, well across the front of the R.F. | S |
| 15. R.F. forward, well across the front of the L.F. | S |
| 16. L.F. forward. | Q |
| 17. Swing the R.F. backwards, off the floor. | Q |
| 18. Swing the R.F. forward, off the floor. | S |
| 19. Run forward on to the R.F. | Q |

20. Run forward on to the L.F.            Q
21. Run forward on to the R.F. and at the same time
    bend the body well forward and extend the
    L.F. backwards, off the floor.            S
    Repeat with the L.F. from the beginning.

# THE LAMBETH WALK

The Lambeth Walk is a novelty dance which has retained its popularity. It is based on the "Cockney" walk—a swaggering type of movement peculiar to Cockneys. This is the character of the whole dance. Music played between 38 and 44 bars a minute.

Man and lady stand about 3 feet apart, both facing the L.O.D. Man commences with L.F. Lady with R.F.

                                          Bars

Take 8 walks forward. On the 8th step the man turns
    slightly to R. to face lady.               4
Man and lady now link L. arms and strut round in a
    circle, again taking 8 walks. On the 8th step the
    man unlinks the arms and offers his R. arm to the
    lady, who links her L. arm into his R. Finish both
    facing the L.O.D.                     4
Man commences with L.F. and lady R.F. and continue—
    Take 3 walks forward counting 1, 2, 3.
    Transfer weight back to rear foot. Count "and."
    Transfer weight forward to front foot. Count 4.
    Repeat the 3 walks and the Rock, the man commencing
    with R.F. and the lady L.F. 1, 2. 3, and 4.     4
Unlink arms and continue—
    Man walks 2 steps towards the centre. Lady walks 2
    steps towards the wall. Count 1, 2.
    Both man and lady turn to face each other and close
    the feet together. Count 3.
    Slap both hands on the legs, just above the knees and
    at the same time bend slightly forward. Count 4.     4
Both man and lady walk two steps towards each other.
    Count 1, 2.
    Close feet together, facing partner and about 3 feet
    apart. Count 3.

Raise the R. hands about level with the head and give
the Cockney salute, shouting "Oi."                              4
Turn to face the L.O.D. and repeat from the start.

# THE ST. BERNARD'S WALTZ

The St. Bernard's Waltz is a sequence dance which
has become very popular in London and the Provinces
during the past few years.

It can be danced to any Old Time Waltz which has
even strains of 16 or 32 bars, played at a tempo of
between 40 and 46 bars a minute.

The couple commence facing each other and with
the man facing the outside wall. They hold slightly
apart, as in the Old Waltz.

## Man

|  |  | Count |
|---|---|---|
| 1. | Glide the L.F. to the side. | 1, 2 |
| 2. | Close the R.F. to the L.F. | 3 |
| 3, 4. | Repeat 1, 2. | 1 bar |
| 5. | Glide the L.F. to the side. | 1, 2 |
| 6. | Close the R.F. to the L.F. with a slight stamp. | 3 |
| 7. | Stamp the L.F. in place. | 1, 2, 3 |
| 8. | Moving in the opposite direction (against the L.O.D.) and still facing partner, glide the R.F. to the side. | 1, 2 |
| 9. | Close the L.F. to the R.F. | 3 |
| 10. | Glide the R.F. to the side. | 1, 2 |
| 11. | Close the L.F. to the R.F. without putting the weight on to it. | 3 |
| 12. | L.F. back, towards centre, lady in line. | 1, 2, 3 |
| 13. | R.F. back, towards centre, leaving the L.F. forward. | 1, 2, 3 |
| 14. | Step forward on to the L.F., towards the wall. | 1, 2, 3 |
| 15. | R.F. forward, towards the wall. | 1, 2, 3 |
|  | *Note.* The next few steps vary in different districts. In some places the man just closes the L.F. and waits whilst the lady circles round in place for 2 bars. | |
|  | The more correct version is as follows— | |
| 16. | Glide the L.F. to the side—along the L.O.D. | 1, 2, 3 |

17. Glide the R.F. along the L.O.D.                    1, 2, 3
     (See note regarding hold in the lady's descrip-
    tion.)
   Adopt the Old Time Waltz hold and do 4 bars of
   Waltz.                                                4 bars
                                         —————
                                       16 bars
                                       —————

### Lady

The steps for the lady are similar for the first fifteen
steps, except that she commences with the R.F.

After the 15th step, whilst the man is doing the
Gliding figures to the side, the lady does a solo Waltz
with very small steps, commencing with her R.F.

When the lady does her solo Waltz the man releases
his hold with his R. hand and raises his L. Hand, still
holding the lady's R. hand, and the lady turns under
the arch that is formed by the raised hands.

# SPOT DANCE

This is a good way of distributing a few prizes to the
dancers at a social dance. The M.C. or committee of
the dance arrange for a few "spots," such as under
certain electric lights or near a column or post in the
ballroom. The band plays a popular dance and then
stops the music abruptly, and the couple standing nearest to the selected spot are given a prize. Another way
of doing this is for the M.C. to announce (when the
music stops) that the winners are the couple standing
nearest to Mr. or Mrs. —— (a prominent person who
is known to most dancers).

Where "spotlights" are available it is a good idea
for the spotlight to play on the dancers during the dance,
and then when the music stops, the couple standing

in the direct ray of the spotlight are adjudged the winners.

# ELIMINATION DANCE

There are several forms of this dance that can be recommended.

The band plays, and all couples dance. The music is then stopped abruptly and couples stand still. The M.C. then announces that all ladies (and their partners) must sit down if they are wearing white dresses. Then the band plays again. Other suggestions for eliminating couples are: all men wearing silk socks; all ladies who have had a permanent wave during the past week; all ladies wearing Court shoes; all men who are non-smokers (or smokers). The type of request would obviously depend upon the company present. The last one or two couples to remain on the floor receive a prize.

# THE FINNJENKA

The Finnjenka is a bright party dance which can be danced in couples or in a "Conga" line. Arranged by Veikko Niemela of Finland, it was awarded the first prize in an international Party Dance competition held during the World Dance Congress at Clacton-on-Sea in 1964.

It can be danced to any bright "beat" tune played at about 40 bars a minute. One of the best tunes is "The March of the Mods" by Joe Loss and his orchestra.

Danced as a couple dance, the Man and Lady stand facing the L.O.D. with their right hands and left hands joined across the front of body. The left hands will be lower. The Lady will be on the Man's right side. Both commence with the L.F. and dance the same steps throughout. Variations of the dance are given following the description below.

1. Hop lightly on ball of R.F. and place the L.F. digonally forward with the heel only touching the floor.    1
2. Hop lightly on ball of R.F. and touch the L. toe near the R. toe with the L. knee well bent.    2
3. Repeat step 1.    3
4. Repeat the hop on R.F. but close the L.F. parallel to R.F., placing the weight on L.F.    4
5 to 8. Repeat steps 1 to 4 but hop on the L.F. and place the R.F. diagonally forward on step 5 and place the R. toe near the L. on step 6. End with the feet parallel on step 8.    1, 2, 3, 4
9. With the feet together jump a few inches forward on both feet.    1
10. Pause.    2
11. With feet together jump a few inches backward on both feet.    3
12. Pause.    4
13 to 16. Run four small steps forward, Left, Right, Left, Right.    1, 2, 3, 4

Repeat from the beginning.

*Notes.* Variations of the dance are:

1. On steps 13 to 16 the couple may wheel round on the spot, turning in a small circle to the left.
2. On steps 13 to 16 the Lady may move across the front of Man to end on his left side. At the end of the next sequence she will move across the front of Man to end on his right side again.
3. The Conga Line. All dancers form a single line, one behind the other, with hands placed on the waist of the person in front. Dance the steps as described and the leader will guide the line in any direction.